The True Lives of My Chemical Romance

———

Tom Bryant is a music journalist who has
written for *Kerrang!*, Q and *MOJO* magazines and
the *Guardian*, during the course of which he has had
an absinthe-fuelled sleepover at Marilyn Manson's house,
been attacked by the Red Hot Chili Peppers' bass player
and accused of starting a riot with The Prodigy.
He lives in Sussex and this is his first book.

Tom Bryant

———

THE TRUE LIVES OF
MY CHEMICAL ROMANCE

The Definitive Biography

SIDGWICK & JACKSON

First published 2014 by Sidgwick & Jackson
an imprint of Pan Macmillan, a division of Macmillan Publishers Limited
Pan Macmillan, 20 New Wharf Road, London N1 9RR
Basingstoke and Oxford
Associated companies throughout the world
www.panmacmillan.com

ISBN 978-1-4472-5357-0

1 3 5 7 9 8 6 4 2

A CIP catalogue record for this book is available from the British Library.

Typeset by Ellipsis Digital Limited, Glasgow
Printed and bound by CPI Group (UK) Ltd, Croydon, CR0 4YY

Visit **www.panmacmillan.com** to read more about all our books
and to buy them. You will also find features, author interviews and
news of any author events, and you can sign up for e-newsletters
so that you're always first to hear about our new releases.

FOR ASHLEY MAILE,

A GREAT ROCK 'N' ROLL PHOTOGRAPHER

Contents

═══

Foreword: Thank You for the Venom

=====

The first time I met My Chemical Romance, we were in New York. It was August 2004, a few months after their second album *Three Cheers for Sweet Revenge* had been released. Though the record had been out a little while, it had yet to make them famous. That would arrive in the coming months, but back then they were poised and on the brink.

The city was hot and muggy, and our photo shoot was on the shoreline of the Hudson River. The New Jersey where they grew up was outlined behind them, the bustle and energy of New York stood before them, almost like a metaphor for the way their career would take off from that point.

Gerard Way, chain-smoking, was fascinated with what the photographer Tony Wooliscroft was looking for. The singer was wearing the cheap black suit and striped black and white tie that was his uniform back then. It was the same suit he had worn all across the Warped Tour that summer, the same suit he had performed, drunk and flown across the world in for months. It did not smell good. But it looked fantastic. Alongside his band, in jeans and T-shirts next to him, he pulled pose after pose. He looked, I remember thinking at the time, like a star.

Mikey Way, Gerard's brother, was quiet that day. He fooled around with drummer Bob Bryar, who had been a member of the band for only a matter of days at that point. Ray Toro and Frank Iero were both polite and friendly. Frank was relaxed and cracked sharp jokes, but later in the interview he was intense and passionate. Ray was happier to take a back seat, but when he did speak it was obvious that everyone else listened and deferred to him. He seemed like the band's quiet mastermind, while Gerard seemed its visionary. That would make Frank, I remember noting down, the beating heart.

As the photo shoot finished, a great clap of thunder rolled luxuriously through the sky. A torrential summer downpour burst across the city. Caught out in it, we got soaked. We ran for cabs and I ended up sitting next to Gerard as we drove to my hotel for the interview. That was a mistake. New York became humid in the rain, and the taxi heated up quickly. Gerard's jacket began to steam: it reeked of sweat, of booze, of backstages and cigarettes; it smelled of the dirt of touring, the stench of truck stops and the rottenness of the road.

He turned to me apologetically. 'You know it's bad,' he said with something approaching embarrassment, 'when you disgust even yourself.'

There was something joyous and innocent about the band then. When we got to the hotel I asked them, half jokingly, what their plans were if *Three Cheers for Sweet Revenge* went on to sell over a million copies. Back then, the possibility seemed a long way off.

'We'll all go out and buy jets and space stations,' said Mikey, grinning happily. 'As long as we get our own action figures, we'll be happy.'

'I'd probably buy Dungeons & Dragons books,' said Gerard while Ray added, 'I'd buy a Pac-Man arcade machine, then take care of my family. I'd erase all debt from my friends.'

Would they all move out to LA like successful bands tend to do?

'No fucking way,' said Frank.

'I'll never move to LA,' reckoned Mikey.

'These guys are very Jersey,' said Gerard. 'I could see myself moving. Anywhere, though, not necessarily LA. I like California.'

But within years, Gerard, Mikey and Ray would all live in Los Angeles. Only Frank stayed behind in New Jersey.

They were happy, contented and enjoying each other's company that day. They started to describe each other and themselves, smiling as they did so.

'I'm the sensitive one,' said Gerard, grinning. 'I'm the girl of the band!'

'I'm the annoying father that everyone hates,' said Ray resignedly, to laughter all round.

'He's like, "Boysss" – that's the way he says it, "Boysss, we got ten minutes,"' said Gerard, mocking his guitarist good-naturedly. 'You'll be asleep and he'll be like, "Time to get up boyssss, we've got to make a video." Frank is the loose cannon – if he believes something, he'll stick to his guns no matter how much we push him. Mikey is the kid, we have to take care of him because he's always getting mugged and beaten up.'

'I'm the unlucky one,' Mikey confessed.

'Unlucky!' spluttered Frank. 'Dude – you took an electric heater into the shower once, that's not unlucky!'

'Well, sometimes I don't think straight,' confessed Mikey.

'He's kind of like Mr Bean,' said Gerard, laughing out loud until he looked at his brother's face. 'Well, a little bit.'

But then they got more serious. They talked about the future, about their hopes for their album and what it might do for them as a band. I asked them what their realistic expectations were for *Three Cheers for Sweet Revenge*.

'They are that we have a shot,' said Gerard. 'We have a chance to hold ourselves up against huge bands, to bring some new ideas and dislodge some of those bigger bands by pushing the envelope.'

'Because of the kind of record we made, we questioned ourselves,' said Frank. 'We worried no one would get the album – and then they did understand it. That made us realize we had a really big shot. We feel like we can be something amazing.'

In the next nine years before they split up, they became something extraordinary. They followed the visceral, buoyant punk of *Three Cheers for Sweet Revenge* with the gloriously grand, multi-platinum brilliance of *The Black Parade* and became the most iconic, stylized, and bombastic rock band in a generation. With *Danger Days: The*

True Lives of the Fabulous Killjoys, their creativity and visual panache exploded into technicolour. Yet throughout, they maintained something personal in their music and in their ferociously strong relationship with their fans.

I've lost count of the number of times I interviewed them. We met in glamorous photo studios, in plush hotels and in a handful of different countries. But we also met in dirty backstages and seedy bars. No matter where, though, I found them all to be that rarest of things in the music industry: genuine. Unfailingly friendly, loyal to a fault and immensely humble, they were always far more generous with their time than I deserved.

They were funny too – often eye-wateringly so. There are plenty of times they come across as dark and intense characters in this book – but they could also make you laugh in a split second. 'Dude, I always thought we were fucking hilarious,' Mikey told me once. 'But then I know us . . .'

Mostly, though, they were unfailingly honest. The second time I interviewed Gerard, he said, 'Oh good – it's you. We have good conversations, I can trust you,' while one of the last times I met them, Mikey let me know that 'we've always got time to talk to you, we'll always tell you the truth.' And in the intervening years, they told me their hopes and dreams, they confessed to me their addictions and failures, and they played down their successes. They allowed me a privileged insight into their lives. That's the story I hope to tell here.

I'd like to thank the band for their generosity from the first time I met them to throughout the writing of this book. Though this is not an authorized biography, Frank was good enough to subject himself to two extremely long interviews. Meanwhile, the band allowed me to speak to a number of their close friends, associates, producers, engineers and peers. The rest of the book is based on my library of interviews with them over the years, many of which have not been published before.

I sought My Chemical Romance's blessing before writing this book and they were kind enough to give it to me. Gerard wrote me a long email telling me to go for it and saying that he felt I was one of the few who could pull it off. It was a wonderful compliment and something I hope to live up to here.

My Chemical Romance's break-up caused grief to fans around the world. But their history is something that deserves to be celebrated. This is that history.

Tom Bryant
Sussex, January 2014

1: GIVE 'EM HELL, KID

A scene from Belleville, New Jersey, sometime in the mid-eighties. A wrestling show is blaring its pantomime brawls from a TV turned up to near the max. In front of it, the two Way brothers are re-enacting every move, leaping on top of each other, yanking at each other's limbs, pulling each other's bodies around. It was as close as Gerard and younger brother Mikey would ever get to fighting.

Their early lives were lived in tandem, the two of them always together as kids – in part because the world outside their door was not for them. Out there, on the streets, was a place that Gerard would describe as 'way too tough for me'. The stories of car-jackings, robberies and even mafia-related crimes (this was, after all, the area *The Sopranos* made famous) were rare and sensational, but enough to make responsible parents wary about what went on. So Gerard and Mikey got closer and closer inside, as outside got further and further away.

'Our parents were kind of scared to let us out of the house because where we lived was pretty dangerous,' Mikey said years later. 'We didn't have anyone else to hang out with. We had friends from the neighbourhood but it was mostly me and Gerard.'

New Jersey in the early eighties was not so different from what it is now. The blue-collar state, so fabled in Bruce Springsteen's songs, was working class and as some parts boomed while the economy took flight other parts were left behind. The town of Belleville was part of the latter group – and while it wasn't proud of that, it wasn't ashamed of it either. It was a place of working men and working mothers, of nine-to-five all week, then Friday-night fun and Saturday-night hook-ups. It was the sort of place that kept its arms around you until, before you knew it, you'd been there half your life and didn't stand much chance of leaving. You could get by, live a life, and die a death without ever escaping its confines.

It was into this world that Gerard Arthur Way was born on 9 April 1977 in Summit, New Jersey – just down the road from Belleville. His brother Michael James followed three years later on 10 September 1980 after the family had moved. Mikey, as he would become known, idolized his big brother and would follow him wherever he went, even attempting to literally run before he could walk when he saw what his older sibling could do. The bond between them was formed strong and early.

Their parents were Donald and Donna, their dad a service manager at a car dealership and their mother a local hairdresser. Donald embodied the blue-collar feel of the area: a hard-working man with hard-working morals who understood that it was his responsibility to keep the family afloat. He would instil these ethics into his boys.

'My dad shaped me morally,' said Gerard. 'I have such a respect for women and I got that from my dad. He really drummed that into me. My dad's a real man – he's not a womanizer, he's not a tough guy, he's not a show-off; he's a working-class guy who really worked hard to support his family. He never strayed and he worked hard for every single penny.

'He didn't do anything shady. He was never a big shot and there were a lot of those in my area because it was Jersey and full of Italian-American mafia kind of people. My dad was the opposite of all of them and I think he got crap for not being flashy. He wasn't one of these guys in sharp suits. What he didn't realize was that he was a real man. But I knew that.'

Yet Donald, though proud of his life, would tell his sons they didn't have to become embedded into the New Jersey landscape like so many others before them, not if they didn't want to. Instead, they could spread their wings and take flight. 'From when I was a kid, my dad said to me, "You can be whatever you want,"' Gerard said. 'And he was dead serious. He kept saying it until I was in my teens.' But what he meant was that his kids should go to college and get a good job, not trade it all in for the risk of a band. They didn't listen to that last bit.

Donna, their mother, brought different influences. She had always had an interest in horror and fantasy, and when Gerard and Mikey were older, she would rent horror films for the family. She collected dolls, too, much to her kids' despair.

'She had hundreds of creepy dolls that she'd collected and there was a room in my house filled with nothing but creepy fucking dolls,' said Gerard. 'I would have to walk through this room to get to my room and at night I'd hold my breath and run through it because I was so terrified.'

But it was this that sparked both Gerard and Mikey's early imaginations, and the pair would be inseparable as they played together. 'We brought each other up creatively and emotionally,' said Gerard. 'We were very solitary together, if you see what I mean. We would entertain each other or talk nonsense for hours.'

So the two of them explored life in a Belleville duplex (a house divided into two separate homes). They turned to each other for friendship, for ideas and for fun. The interests they developed sparked from each other, the outside world rarely creeping in except from the TV. Gerard, from an early age, would invent scenarios and daydream.

'What I had to do – and my brother had to do – was really create our own space in our heads,' said Gerard. 'I drew pictures, I made stories up, I lied a lot – I lived inside my own head.'

Not that he knew it then, but it would be the birth of a creative process that would take him far away from the closed front door, far away from Belleville and far away from New Jersey. Those stories he made up would spiral into wild comic book ideas and fantastic musical schemes. They would unfurl in grand concept albums and detailed plot arcs on records that he and his brother would go on to make. Back then, though, it was simply for escape.

Music began, slowly, to become important to them. By the age of nine, Gerard would hear the Top 40 songs his parents played on the radio. But he had a more important musical influence – his maternal grandmother, Elena Lee Rush, who lived upstairs in the Ways' duplex. Elena was a talented artist who had converted their garage into a ceramics studio. She would encourage the boys to follow their own imaginative paths when she looked after them, whether it was drawing or creating pottery with her.

Elena liked to play her upright piano and the music would drift down to the apartment below. Gerard or Mikey would wander up and she would stop, shy. But they would ask her questions, ask her to continue and she would – pleased they were taking an interest. And then, ever so slowly, she would urge them towards taking part in talent shows and school plays, always pleased to nurture their creativity.

'She was so instrumental in my life,' said Gerard. 'I guess I just found music because, when I was growing up, she just let me find stuff. She let me find what I was good at and then she would sit with me and encourage me.'

Elena noticed Gerard might have talent of his own and bought him a cheap Silvertone acoustic guitar for his ninth birthday. Also among his presents was a Slave I Star Wars model spacecraft. If Gerard was honest, he preferred the spacecraft. It was partly because the guitar meant he had to start taking lessons, something he didn't particularly enjoy. 'That was a big mistake, I probably shouldn't have started, because then I immediately became disinterested,' he later admitted. But it was the beginning of something, and he would return to that guitar again and again as he gradually learned to make it do what he wanted, rather than what his lessons demanded.

Gerard was a sensitive child and overweight too, something that kept him divided from his peers at his first elementary school. He struggled there, never quite fitting in, and later moved schools.

'I used to be fat,' he admitted. 'That's the ultimate outsider – the fat kid. Girls aren't interested in you, you don't fit in and you're always easy to make fun of.'

He suffered from terrible dreams, often waking up in a panic. 'I was terrified of death,' he said. 'I used to wake up in the middle of the night having nightmares about my family. It took me a good five years to get over that. I was afraid to go to school because I thought I'd lose somebody.'

He changed schools before the fourth grade and, determined not to be the awkward kid, got more involved in all the new school had to offer. Which is why he ended up, aged nine, auditioning for a part in the school play. 'I just opened my mouth and I was able to sing,' he said. 'And then my grandma was really excited about it. I wasn't so excited about it – I guess I just wanted to prove to myself that I could do it. Then, after I got the part, I was stuck into doing it.'

His grandmother happily made him a costume and encouraged him all the way. But he was less sure. Perhaps, he reasoned, it wasn't wise to mark his arrival at a new school by stealing the lead part in the play and then singing onstage while wearing tights. 'Of course, it's a great fucking idea to play Peter Pan in your first year in a new school . . .' he later admitted, sarcastically.

But it proved one thing to him: he could sing. And it would not be quite so damaging to his reputation as he thought. Slowly but surely, Gerard made friends and settled in – never quite part of the mainstream, but no longer the outsider. Then, when he went to Middle School, aged eleven, that changed again. Cliques and groups formed and once again he retreated back into fantasy worlds, playing the Dungeons & Dragons board game he had become obsessed with and spiralling away from reality once more.

At home, his grandmother still encouraged his artistic urges, particularly drawing. However, she was dismayed that he was increasingly finding darker inspirations – in part because of his interest in horror, in part because of the imagery of the fantasy games he enjoyed. And if Gerard was into it, then so was his brother Mikey.

The pair had begun to discover new music too. Like the fantastical worlds they were enthralled by, this music contained elements of horror, darkness and showmanship. Iron Maiden's *Live after Death*, the album culled from the influential metal legend's mammoth 1984–5 tour, was the first record to grab both Mikey and Gerard. Beginning with a roaring crowd, and opening with the iconic 'We

Shall Fight on the Beaches' speech from the British wartime prime minister Winston Churchill, it has long been heralded as one of heavy metal's great live albums. A bombastic, rollicking, spitting and wildly entertaining romp, it is stuffed with their biggest songs: 'Aces High', '2 Minutes to Midnight', 'The Trooper', 'Number of the Beast', 'Run to the Hills'. It thrilled the Way brothers – so much so that Mikey immediately decided that music was what he wanted to do with his life.

Mikey would grab Gerard's Silvertone acoustic and strap it around his shoulders on a piece of string as *Live after Death* played. Still not ten years old, he would leap on the sofa, banging at the cheap, out-of-tune guitar, pretending to be a part of a band. It would be how the pair lived out their rock fantasies, envisioning them-selves in front of glorious crowds from the mundanity of their shared bedroom.

They explored more and more music, from the theatrics of Queen, to the horror-punk of local legends Misfits – both bands with a strong visual element and, like Maiden, a commitment to performance as well as music. The grand imagery of the Misfits' music played into the Ways' growing love of horror films, which ranged from the relatively tame *Lost Boys* to the vampire film *Fright Night*. They splattered their room with pictures and posters from horror movies – 'Anything that would bum my parents out, basi-cally,' admitted Gerard – as they increasingly explored a darker world. They would hide away albums like Slayer's *South of Heaven* because of the skull on its cover, and had to convince their maternal grandfather to buy them the Misfits' classic 1982 horror-punk album *Walk Among Us* after their mother refused when she saw it included a song called 'Devil's Whorehouse'. It would go on to be an album that deeply inspired the pair of them.

Gerard would lead the musical explorations, frequently discover-ing new music that his brother would pick up on – often from watching MTV's influential *Headbangers Ball*. 'He would consistently play something that would blow my mind,' said Mikey. Gerard began to expand his tastes beyond metal and the brothers switched allegiance from *Headbangers Ball* to the alternative rock of *120 Minutes*. As Nirvana exploded onto the scene in the wake of 1991's *Nevermind*, so the grunge movement began to appeal – as did its forebears in the shape of the Pixies. Punk and metal lost favour and the likes of Smashing Pumpkins took over.

Gerard also began to listen to the Britpop that was filtering over from the UK as he discovered Blur, Oasis and Pulp and then went back further to hear those bands' influences in the shape of The Smiths and The Cure. One moment still resonates with him. The family were on a long car journey to the Busch Gardens theme park in Virginia in 1992. Gerard, fifteen, sulked on the back seat of the car with his Walkman. He hadn't wanted to go on the trip and would have preferred to stay at home, alone with his comics. Instead, he plugged in one earpiece, shared the other with his equally bored brother and they listened to a tape of The Smiths compilation, *Best . . . 1*. It opened up a new world for him.

'I liked punk rock, but after that cassette I didn't take it as seriously any more. There was a split between me and punk rock at that point,' he said. 'Those Smiths tapes saved our life on that drive. Mikey and I would sit there in the back of the car, with one Walkman earpiece each, sharing The Smiths. That's something I remember to this day.'

It was an important journey. Inspired by the rich, dense music and the poetry and bitterness in Morrissey's lyrics, Gerard's thoughts turned to making music. In middle school, still fifteen, he joined his first band – Dracora – who were an instrumental act solely because they didn't have a singer. Mikey says they sounded like Led Zeppelin during the periods in which they drew influence from *Lord of the Rings*, though he is perhaps blinded by brotherly loyalty. Gerard says they sucked. He was kicked out when Dracora attempted to add 'Sweet Home Alabama' to their set. Gerard, it turned out, was a lousy guitar player and couldn't come close to playing the Lynyrd Skynyrd staple.

Crushed and a little resentful at being fired, he decided to abandon playing music entirely. But he was still desperate to find a place and a role in life – he decided it would be art, and particularly comics. So as he put down his guitar, he picked up his pen, starting off by tracing strips – largely those made by Marvel – before beginning to draw his own.

He was talented too. He would lock himself into his grandmother's tiny office – wedged in among her books and without much room to sit, let alone create – and he simply drew and drew. He found a job in a comic book store in Bloomfield, the next town from Belleville. He felt at home flicking through the racks, away from school and lost in the elaborate worlds on offer inside the magazines.

'That was really my solace,' he said. 'The guys at the comic store were my closest friends. They were older than me, in their thirties. I think that's why I grew up fast because I knew a lot of older dudes. They were grown men, with a bit of a childish side to them – otherwise they wouldn't hang out in a comic book store with someone like me.'

Working late one night, he and the two other store clerks were watching the anime film *Record of Lodoss Wars*. Suddenly, two men in hoods burst in and pulled what Gerard later described as 'a giant gun' on him. The robbers were after limited edition comic books, which they assumed would be more valuable than they were. They forced Gerard onto the floor on his knees and put a gun in the back of his head. He later recalled the incident and said he was a little disappointed that his life didn't flash before his eyes. Instead, he was more worried that, if he was shot, he might not be able to finish the Daredevil comic book he was reading. '*Man Without Fear* was out at the time. I was thinking, Oh man, I'm never going to get to finish *Man Without Fear*. I swear to God, that's what I was thinking!'

The other clerks cleared out the register and handed the robbers what they wanted and then, almost as soon as the thieves had run back out of the shop, the shocked staff burst out laughing – almost uncontrollably. 'It was the craziest thing, it was stress laughter because they had scared the shit out of us,' Gerard said.

Rather than traumatize him unduly, the experience taught him that life was not something to be wasted. He was determined to break out of New Jersey – out of 'that rut of drinking, fucking and working a shit job. The whole mundaneness of it all,' he once told me. He redoubled his efforts to draw, certain that this was his way out. He approached the maverick comic book publisher Hart D. Fisher, whose Boneyard Press had recently published a controversial comic book on the serial killer Jeffrey Dahmer, with an idea of his called 'On Raven's Wings'. Fisher agreed to publish the relatively graphic horror story, which lasted two editions – though Gerard's name was oddly changed and the author credit went to 'Garry Way'. Although the comic didn't last long, being published told Gerard he had talent and that he could do something with art.

'I'd set the benchmark very high for myself because, at fifteen, I wrote my first comic that got published. I'd already accomplished something when I was fifteen and I felt that I needed to live up to that.'

But though comics were a passion, music was still a big force. Despite putting down his guitar following his firing from Dracora, he was still listening to music avidly. Two weeks after the robbery, the comic book store closed and Gerard began to work part-time at the local A&P Supermarket chain. With his earnings, Gerard saved up to buy a Mexican Fender Stratocaster – the cheapest Strat you could buy, but a beautiful thing for a teenager to own. He decided it didn't matter if he wasn't a great guitarist – but what did matter was that he should be a great songwriter. He compared technically brilliant guitar players like Steve Vai to the simple punk of a band like Green Day and had an epiphany. 'Steve Vai is a really great guitar player,' he reasoned. 'But I can't hum any of his songs, yet I know all these Green Day songs.' Gerard began to write songs for himself. And instead of trying to dazzle with technical brilliance, he wanted to write songs that would lodge themselves in people's brains. It was a smart move.

At school he noticed a change. He had graduated to high school and discovered that the musical landscape had moved on in the wake of Nirvana's *Nevermind* album, and now, for a brief period,

alternative rock was the mainstream. The kids who had been listening to it before it broke – once bullied and derided for their taste
– were now respected. Gerard was one of those kids.

'Suddenly, any kid that was outside smoking cigarettes and listening to those bands was cool,' said Gerard. 'Everybody who was a
little weird or a little punk became very cool. All those jocks and
cheerleaders would look to people like me for advice on what to
listen to. That was very strange. I doubt it was ever like that again in
school.'

Soon after starting high school he found a group of people into
similar music as him, and though he would find the experience there
reasonably lonely, it was largely through his own choosing as he was
not short of friends. Mikey goes so far as to say Gerard had a 'Ferris
Bueller thing going on'; he had the mystique and cool of the hero
of the classic eighties high-school film.

'One of my first days in high school I sat all alone at lunch time,'
Gerard said. 'It was the classic story – the weird kid in an army
jacket, a horror-movie T-shirt, long black hair. This group of metal
heads – who were the only outcast group at the school at the time,
who all listened to Agnostic Front and stuff – turned to me and said,
"Hey, why don't you sit with us?" That was cool, we could all sit
together and nobody would fuck with us. Not that I hung out with
them after school.

'I didn't really get bullied. Lots of people bullied me more emotionally and called me a loser but I never got beaten up or anything.
It was never the popular kids that did it either, it was the other weird
outcasts, the kids who were going to be criminals and everyone
knew it. People were never really mean to me though, they mostly
just left me alone. I think I wanted to be alone too.'

He would get through his day then head straight home to the
sanctuary of his room. There he would lose himself in drawings and
in music, happy to be on his own and happy to have no one to
please but himself. 'Having the group was a bit of a turning point I
guess and, oddly enough, not having the peer pressure to do drugs
and that sort of stuff,' he said. 'But I was more interested in music

and being creative. I had no real desire to hang out; I was writing stories and drawing comics. I'd been doing that for years.'

He wanted to be a comic book artist. He was a fan of writers like Grant Morrison, Richard Case and Todd McFarlane, particularly enjoying Morrison's Batman run. For him the appeal was that Batman was just an ordinary person doing something extraordinary – rather than a hero with supernatural powers. It suggested to him that he too could do something extraordinary with his life.

By 1995, Gerard was chasing the dream hard. He had slimmed down, graduated from high school and enrolled in a four-year fine arts degree at the respected School of Visual Arts in Manhattan. Gerard was particularly interested in the cartooning and animation courses on offer – but also in the freedom afforded by being in the city. Outside of New Jersey, in an environment where creativity and individuality were encouraged, he began to expand his horizons by going to goth clubs and meeting like-minded artists. The problem was that he still lived at home with his parents. Some of his friends shared a house and he envied their independence as he commuted back and forth from Belleville. Yet as much as he found his new sur-roundings invigorating, he says he still felt like an outsider.

'Even when I had friends and even when I was in art school, which is a school of outcasts, I still felt like an outcast,' he said. 'That's one of the things that doesn't work about art school – you have hundreds of outcasts together and so nobody talks to each other. They all sit there, in black! You get hippies, kids in black and graffiti kids – that's an art school.'

With Gerard off in Manhattan, Mikey was left alone at high school and he didn't fit in. Mikey, like his brother, had once been over-weight but in the summer between tenth and eleventh grade, he dieted hard. Over five months, he lost seventy pounds. The change was so pronounced that the school's counsellors approached him and asked if he was on drugs.

'They thought I was on heroin, or something,' said Mikey, 'so all the cool kids came up to ask me what I was on. They'd be like, "What have you got?" I was like, "Nothing, dude." So they'd ask how I lost so much weight and I'd go, "Erm, exercise?"'

He was heavily into music, obsessive about The Smashing Pumpkins. He would follow them up and down the East Coast whenever they would tour, spending the money he earned from working in Belleville's Comic World or the local supermarket on train tickets and bus rides to out-of-the-way venues. He says his look – skinny and young – meant he would get followed by strange men with dark intent in train stations late at night. Still, his passion for the band meant he gladly braved the dangers.

Mikey would occasionally pick up Gerard's Fender guitar – though he was intimidated by how much it had cost. He watched videos of bands like Radiohead and Smashing Pumpkins playing, looking at their fingers on the fretboards and trying to figure out how they played. He worked out the Pumpkins' 'Disarm' first, constantly rewinding the video and trying it out for himself.

He convinced Gerard to come and see the Pumpkins play at Madison Square Garden in 1996 while his brother was at art school. Gerard was reluctant, prone to spending his time alone and not always willing to put down his art projects. Mikey was insistent.

'I dunno if I can go, I've got homework,' Gerard said.

'Dude, you've got to come,' Mikey said. 'This is the most inspirational thing I've ever seen, you've got to come.'

Eventually Gerard was persuaded. It was a show that would change both of their lives.

As the brothers were sat watching the band, Gerard turned to Mikey and said, 'This is what we've got to do.'

'I know,' Mikey replied. 'This is exactly what we've got to do.'

They never forgot the moment and it planted a seed that would come to fruition later in their lives, while Madison Square Garden continued to shine like a shrine. To play there would be everything.

They began to seriously consider playing music properly. Gerard had written songs on his Fender Strat and was anxious to see if they worked. He started a band called Ray Gun Jones with local friends.

Influenced by the likes of The Get Up Kids, it was loosely a post-hardcore band but it would not last long. The band's bass player was originally Gerard's then girlfriend but she soon quit. However, when she left, she also left her bass behind and Mikey would play about on it until she demanded it back. Still, it put him briefly in the band. Mikey says they sounded like 'a cross between the Pumpkins and Weezer' but it wasn't to be. Shortly afterwards, their drummer left and that was the end of things. It was next to impossible to find a new one, given that drums are the least appealing and most unwieldy instrument to play and transport, and so Ray Gun Jones came to an abrupt end.

It wouldn't be long before Gerard would start another punk band called Nancy Drew. He posted adverts on notice boards as he looked for members. But the response was not encouraging. He either struggled to convince those who replied that his was a viable project, or was put off by the fact that some of them were utterly unsuitable. Only one person who got back to him showed much promise – a guitarist called Ray Toro. They played together for a little while, until the band fizzled out.

Still inspired by The Smashing Pumpkins' performance at Madison Square Garden, Gerard wanted desperately for music to be an outlet for him – but he began to concentrate on art, since that was offering him more of a future. As it turned out, he was wrong.

2: EARLY SUNSETS OVER MONROEVILLE

In the late nineties, New Jersey was the centre of a musical scene that would come to shape the underground of alternative rock at the turn of the century. While Gerard was commuting back and forth to Manhattan and the School of Visual Arts, his local area was beginning to teem with new bands. The likes of Thursday, Saves The Day, Midtown, Poison The Well and others were taking the early-nineties sound of post-hardcore and giving it a more emotional edge. Both enraptured by the rage of Black Flag's punk and the sensitivity of the late-seventies post-punk band Joy Division, they began to create sounds that were angry and emotive. It was a scene that was then fiercely independent with bands playing basement shows, in basic Veterans of Foreign Wars Halls (known universally as VFW Halls) or in rooms without stages, but it would be vastly influential. And it was all springing up from Thursday's New Brunswick base – a mere thirty miles from Belleville.

Formed in 1997, Thursday and its singer Geoff Rickly would become, inadvertently, the figureheads of what became known as emo – though Rickly preferred to call it post-hardcore. The music he was making was inspired by the hardcore bands he would see in Manhattan, but shaped by the fact that he was unable to scream and shout as viciously as those acts. By a happy accident, it made his music into something new, accessible and very exciting.

'I listened to a lot of post-hardcore music and what became known as screamo,' Rickly said. 'That music was so super-charged, so passionate. They had the intensity and fury of hardcore bands, but the complexity and sensitivity of a band like Fugazi. That made me want to play music – that made me really want to play music. But it turned out my voice just didn't work the way I wanted it to. Everything came out sounding New Wave- and Cure-influenced! We sounded like Joy Division doing hardcore, which seemed very weird to people at the time.'

Though not to everyone – because Thursday quickly found an audience. Rickly was heavily involved in the underground scene, allowing his New Brunswick basement to become a makeshift local venue and putting up touring bands on his floor as they travelled around the country. It meant that not only did Thursday get plenty of support slots, as they were putting on a lot of the shows, but they also became extremely popular with touring musicians, who spread their name by word of mouth. Slowly, a scene was cropping up around them.

Alongside Thursday, a label grew out of Kearny – a town two miles from Belleville, just over the Passaic River. There, Alex Saavedra – a young, ebullient idealist – heard the new sounds of the bands around him and realized that there was nobody to put the music out. So he figured that he might as well do it himself and set up a label called Eyeball Records.

'I started the label in high school and then, due to a few unfortunate events, I ended up homeless for a while – so I was doing the label and living out of a car,' says Saavedra. 'Then, as I gained small successes, I always shared them – which meant there was always an open door policy to everyone at Eyeball. People would come through with a spark of an idea, then we were able to help people make that idea a reality. There was no caste system at Eyeball; there was nothing exclusive or arrogant going on – we didn't give a shit who you were. We didn't care if you couldn't pick up a guitar; we were all there to have fun.

'I was lucky to be surrounded by tons of great talent. Eyeball was in the midst of a really good community. Every band you could think of from around here came through at one point or another.

I think I was fortunate to have so many talented friends. We liked to have a good time and we were easy to approach, so I think that led to people wanting to come around and be a part of it. So we kept growing and growing.'

Eyeball would eventually become based at the house he rented, and he would frequently – and often entirely accidentally – throw massive parties there as the label's bands played shows for the local fans. Though based on Main Street in the residential area of the town, the neighbours mostly tolerated the parties, partly because a lot of the other houses were also used as businesses and were therefore empty at night.

'Some of those parties were insane,' says Saavedra. 'One New Year's party, we had to get sixty people to stand outside because you could feel the floor sagging! It was the strongest built house around. A ton of people would come round, and you'd see everybody there. There were no boundaries, scene-wise – there were people from bands, fans, writers, everyone. It was crazy. You'd have huge rock stars, huge artists, actors, porn stars even. It was pretty awesome and a very cool, supportive community. People would come there to get inspired.'

As Thursday's reputation spread, they came to the forefront of the New Jersey post-hardcore scene – a scene that was fast becoming the centre of the US post-hardcore movement too. It meant that everyone locally looked up to them, and everyone wanted to form a band because of them.

'Thursday opened a lot of doors for the community here,' says Saavedra. 'They may not have become one of those iconic bands, but they were definitely the band that everyone here used as a basis for comparison at that time.'

And it was towards this scene that the two Way brothers would slowly gravitate. Though still focused on comic books and in the final year of his art degree, Gerard would go out to watch Thursday. He spent the rest of his time in the basement of his parents' house.

'One of the seeds of playing music for me was when I went to see Thursday play in [local venue] the Loop Lounge,' said Gerard.

'I didn't go to a lot of shows at that point. If I was going to go to a show it would have to be to see a band like Morrissey or Pulp, normally a big British act coming over. It was rare for me to even do that – I once bought Pulp tickets and didn't go because I spent a lot of time holed up in my basement, depressed. I found it hard to leave the house at times.'

Mikey, though, was far more involved with the live scene. After high school he had tried going to college, but largely only because he thought he might meet some people he could form a band with there. He drifted away from it, and ended up interning at Eyeball Records – not that he or Saavedra remember exactly how it happened. More outgoing and sociable than his brother, he quickly became a notorious part of the furniture there and, eventually, Saavedra thinks he must have just decided to put him to good use by getting him to mail out records.

'Mikey was out all the time,' says Saavedra. 'He more or less lived with us at the Eyeball house – by which I mean that he would drink all our beer and vodka and then never leave. Then again, that's a description that would apply to a lot of people back then, so I can't just put the finger on him. You'd always have to make sure Mikey was around and included. He's a very smart kid and super analytical, often a little quiet too – but when you got him out of his head, he was a total blast. He's a genuinely funny dude, and a genuinely good person.'

Rickly remembers how much fun they would all have with Mikey – though agrees too that he was always someone they had to keep half an eye on.

'Mikey was always the more sociable one who'd come out to the Eyeball Records parties that we threw,' he says. 'Mikey could be really crazy. He'd stay over at our house and we'd often find ourselves asking him, "Who the hell was that girl that ended up with you last night?" He'd say, "I've no idea." He was a little out of control.'

He became someone they would all watch out for and someone they would all affectionately mock.

'Mikey became our surrogate little brother,' says Saavedra. 'He was the little runt that you always had to look out for. We used to taunt Mikey too. His posture was so terrible that we'd go, "Dude, you have no confidence – what is wrong with you? You look like fucking Mr Burns! Stand up straight." We put him in "man school" to build his confidence. He was such a little nerd in the early days, but you could see his confidence grow. To see him play music in front of thousands of people makes me laugh now. When I think back to calling him Mr Burns and "man school" – then I see him jumping around onstage, it's very funny.'

While Mikey was embedding himself into the local scene, the late nineties found Gerard retreating from anything that wasn't drawing-related. He graduated from the School of Visual Arts with a degree in cartooning in 1999 and was set upon making it as a penciller, the first step in the artistic process of creating comics. He wasn't having much luck.

'I had been hitting the pavement with my portfolio – taking it round to every major comic company, showing them my work and trying to get *anything* out of them,' said Gerard. 'Nothing was working.'

He helped out some of the Eyeball bands with T-shirt designs – including Thursday, who had become nationally recognized following the release of their debut *Waiting* that year.

'The Eyeball house was a road-stop for a lot of touring bands, and a good meeting point for the local community,' recalls Saavedra. 'And that's how Gerard got involved in designing things for bands – he did the best Thursday design they've ever had.'

But largely, Gerard was focused on getting a foothold in the comic book industry. Over the next two years, he interned every-where he could – including at the legendary DC Comics. To his dismay, he found that his art was often overlooked. Instead, he was largely the photocopy boy. Despite his inner comic book nerd's satisfaction at seeing all the latest releases long before they were in the shops, Gerard was creatively unfulfilled.

'I'd been to art school and got out and realized there were no jobs for me,' he said. 'It was the basic story of having lots of dreams in school and, once I got out, I realized I couldn't get a break at all.'

At DC Comics he interned for a young inker called Joe Boyle, who recognized that there was something a bit different about Gerard. Though Boyle admits Gerard was frequently shy, he also says there was a confidence within him about his own talent.

'He was a character,' he says. 'He definitely wanted to make his presence known. He would photocopy comic book covers, but he would replace the character on it with his face. Then he'd leave that up on the door, with a sign saying something like "The awesome Gerard is in today." I told him, "Listen, you're only going to be here for a short time – so you need to go and meet people and make some connections." But he was already on top of that.

'Gerard was kind of confident back then but he also kind of wasn't. He was shy, but in the right circumstances he would get more ballsy. For the most part, he was unsure of himself – except when he was drawing. Then, though, he knew what was good.'

Boyle left DC Comics and began to work in animation in 2001 at Curious Pictures, who made shows for the Cartoon Network. He asked Gerard to intern for him again, which is when the pair began to collaborate on ideas together. They quickly went from co-workers to friends. Gerard would pencil out the artwork for Boyle to ink, the pair constantly discussing ideas for comic books and TV shows they might make.

Gerard worked ostensibly on the Cartoon Network show *Sheep in the Big City* – though admitted it was basically 'just another photocopy gig'. But alongside Boyle, he had begun to work on his own project *The Breakfast Monkey* – an often surreal cartoon about a monkey obsessed with breakfast.

Breakfast Monkey had been a minor character in another comic book idea the pair had worked on with a friend called Stu. It hadn't worked out but Boyle wanted to develop something with the monkey, seeing potential in him. He and Gerard took the idea and ran with it. 'We would just throw stuff out there and nobody could tell us no because it was ours,' says Boyle. 'So whatever made us laugh, we just did it. It was a lot of fun.'

It was good enough to earn the pair a meeting with Curious Pictures executives – something which created problems for Gerard.

'All of a sudden, people started to take notice of my work,' said Gerard. 'But I was the photocopy boy, so it was kind of weird for a few of those people – to be the photocopy boy and get a break like that made it a little weird in the office for a while.'

Boyle and Gerard found Curious Pictures receptive to their idea – but they wanted Breakfast Monkey to go through extensive remodelling. Gradually, the pair began to feel as though their creation was being morphed into something else, something they were uncomfortable with.

'You always hear these stories of people coming in with scripts and everyone having a little tweak until ultimately it is nothing like it was in the first place,' says Boyle. 'That's kind of what happened. They were really nice about it and encouraging, but they wanted to make it something that it wasn't. At one point they wanted to make it an educational show where people would learn how to make a new breakfast each day and we could do breakfast recipes from around the world. We were like, "That's not what we're doing! That would be nonsense! We're not teaching kids to make waffles!"'

Gerard was equally disillusioned with how their ideas were being interpreted.

'I discovered I was dealing with a committee about something that I had created,' he said. 'People were talking about merchandise, toys and fucking stuffed animals and they were missing the point. That wasn't why I got into it at all.'

The company told them they had a show that was already similar to *Breakfast Monkey* – *Aqua Teen Hunger Force* – so the changes were necessary. Gerard and Boyle would not budge, and so inevitably *Breakfast Monkey* withered on the vine.

It was yet another knockback for Gerard, who was beginning to feel that the commercial art of cartooning might not be for him. He was twenty-four now and though he had interned at some top companies, had a page published in DC Comics' *Big Book of the Weird Wild West* and more work in Image Comics' *Footsoldiers*, he felt cynical about the business. While his brother Mikey was running riot at the Eyeball house, Gerard would hole up in his parents' basement, downbeat and disinterested.

'We'd always joke with Mikey,' says Geoff Rickly. 'We'd say, "Is your brother still at home in his underwear, eating cereal and drawing comic books?" We always joked that Gerard was a shut-in.'

When Gerard did come out, though, Alex Saavedra remembers he was fun to be around.

'He wasn't the dark, depressive character that's often been portrayed. He was actually really, really funny. But he was a quiet dude. When you got him to go out, he was a ball; it would just take a lot of work to actually get him out. It was normally pretty hard to get him away from his drawing table, mostly because he was getting closer and closer to becoming the artist he always dreamed of being. That kid could have done any comic he wanted – he was really on the verge of breaking through and he worked really hard on it.'

That's not how Gerard felt. In that basement, he would draw and write, occasionally picking up a guitar but mostly slumping into a kind of despair. He was seeing a therapist in order to attempt to make sense of his life, and taking anti-depressants. He would fill book after book with his ideas, short stories and angry thoughts.

'I went through a lot of negative stuff in the early days. I'd sit there beating myself up about not accomplishing anything,' he said. 'I'd worry, think too much and get myself depressed but the positive side was that I ended up with notebooks and notebooks full of ideas. I didn't necessarily know what any of these ideas were for, but I ended up writing a short story called 'I Brought You My Bullets, You Brought Me Your Love'. It was about gangland murders in Chicago – nobody's ever read it and I think it's probably lost now. But, the point was, I had all these ideas. It meant that I was already shaping an aesthetic for a band – I just didn't have a band yet. I wanted it to be a new kind of thing, to have a new kind of vibe that wasn't out there.'

That would come later though. At the time, he had no idea that what he was doing might lead to a musical project, and was convinced that graphic art was the future for him. But then something happened that would change everything.

In the late summer of 2001, Gerard appeared to have made the advance he was looking for. He was designing action figures full-time at Fun House in Hoboken, New Jersey, who would take on work for comic book companies including powerhouses such as Marvel. It was a dream job – 'probably the best job that I'd ever had,' he admitted – but he still wasn't happy.

Then an intervention of the most dramatic kind would force Gerard to re-evaluate his life. On 11 September 2001 he was in Hoboken on the day of the terrorist attacks on the Twin Towers. He stood aghast on the edge of the river as he watched the atrocity unfold.

'There were four hundred people and me, and I was at the railing. Right in front of us, it just went down,' he said. 'It was the biggest fucking neutron bomb of mental anguish you've ever felt. I knew I didn't have anybody in that building but these were all co-workers and stuff and they were just freaking the fuck out. Crying, screaming and cursing and yelling about the devil.'

It shook him dramatically – and, at first, deeply negatively. Gerard has always claimed to have deep and occasionally intrusive sympathy for others – 'I have a high level of empathy and that makes me ill. It's a gift and curse. I have a level of empathy where I can feel emotion so strongly that it can make me sick,' he once said – and this kicked into overdrive following the attack on the Twin Towers. '9/11 fucked his head up for a while,' remembers Saavedra. 'Along with a lot of people.'

As with the hold-up in the comic book store, the tragedy forced Gerard to take stock of his own life. 'When 9/11 happened, that just made the decision for me,' he said. 'I almost used it as a catalyst – I decided to take it, to say fuck off to the rest of my life and start a band. I just knew that's what I wanted to do right away.

'From then on, I was in my parents' basement with a very small practice amp, and my Fender guitar. That's when I wrote "Skylines and Turnstiles" and some of the earlier material. I actually wrote "Fashion Statement" too at that time, though we didn't use it until [second album *Three Cheers For Sweet*] *Revenge*. I wrote those songs sitting in my pyjamas or underwear with a tiny amp.'

He went through all his notebooks, looking at all the stories he had written and the ideas he had come up with while depressed. In them, he found anguish and imagination in equal measure. He began to pour everything out into songs.

'It was me going, "All this stuff has been inside me for years and I want to get it out,"' he said. 'I was just trying to make sense of all the notes, thoughts and dreams I had written down in the last two years. I wasn't depressed exactly but I was certainly a hermit. I looked at every single short story, wondering if there was a song in it or wondering if it could be the title of a song or a record.'

He worked as if in a frenzy – very quickly and very intensely. He approached a drummer he half knew called Matt 'Otter' Pelissier in the Loop Lounge, the Passaic rock bar that was central to the Jersey post-hardcore scene. Pelissier was then working as a mechanic but had also played locally in a band called The Rodneys with Ray Toro, who had played with Gerard in the short-lived Nancy Drew.

'[The music was] more or less entirely written – I just needed the drums under it,' said Gerard. 'I rented a room for an hour, I plugged in my Fender and played him the songs and sang them while he played. It was just the two of us. It came out OK but I realized I couldn't sing the way I wanted and play guitar. I just couldn't do both of them well enough, so the first person who came to mind was Ray.'

Raymond Toro was a quiet kid, another who had grown up more inside than out. He was from down the road in Kearny, a small working-class town across the Passaic river from Belleville. Born on 15 July 1977, Ray grew up in a small apartment with two brothers and parents of Puerto Rican and Portuguese heritage. His parents, like the Ways, were concerned about crime in New Jersey and so he too learned to keep himself entertained inside. 'There was definitely a funny collection of people who would hang around my block,' Ray said. 'There was this guy named Bertine who was this drug addict who, every couple of months, would OD outside my house. I would see an ambulance come and take him away.'

He shared a room with his two older brothers in a cramped apartment. The oldest brother was the first to really get into music – the classic rock of Jimi Hendrix, Pink Floyd, Led Zeppelin and Black Sabbath, and then the more metallic leanings of Iron Maiden, Metallica and Ozzy Osbourne's solo work. His brother would always be idly picking at his guitar – often until late into the night in the shared bedroom, working out riffs from books of guitar tabs and keeping Ray awake. Aged thirteen, Ray began to pick at the guitar too.

'I thought it was great that he was always playing and always practising. That's how I got into it – because I always looked up to him and wanted to be like him. When I started listening to metal and punk, he could already play those songs on the guitar. That really impressed me. I just got swept up by it all.'

It was Ozzy Osbourne's guitarist Randy Rhoads who particularly struck Ray. He was impressed by the way he appeared to blend classical music into his metal licks and so Ray tried to emulate his playing. He took lessons, and even enrolled in a typing course in order to improve his dexterity on the guitar, but he became a technically excellent musician mostly by dint of endless practice.

'I didn't have much of a social life, I didn't go out very much,' he said. 'I had friends but we'd hang out in school, not afterwards. The only thing that was always there for me was the guitar when I came home.'

Ray was not someone who stood out at school. He says he was

'one of the invisible masses', someone who neither excelled nor failed, someone who simply existed.

'I felt kind of invisible because nothing about me set me apart from anybody else. My friends were kind of similar though they were kind of misfits. There was a lot of separation at my school between kids who were into rap, kids into pop and then the small group of kids who liked punk and metal. I fitted into the last group.'

His guitar playing did get him noticed though. He had already played briefly with Matt Pelissier in The Rodneys, who released a 1997 album called *Soccertown USA* – Kearny's local nickname. But despite small-scale local success, Ray's heart was not really into being in a band. After graduating from high school, he joined a film-editing course at William Paterson University in Wayne, New Jersey, and more or less put his guitar down.

'I went to college to study film. I wanted to be an editor. I thought that's all I really wanted to do. I got really into movies, into dissecting them and analysing them. I was really interested in learning how they were made, how they were put together – that was my focus. The whole time I was in college learning that, I stopped playing in bands. I played drums in one band for about a year, that was about it.'

That band was called Dead Go West, but it was far from serious and Ray was happy to just beat out the rhythm at the back.

'It was me and my friend George and we were a couple of friends who had nothing to do on the weekend and we would just play,' he said. 'I hadn't really played guitar in a band for a couple of years before Gerard called me.'

'He's so talented,' said Gerard. 'He was the best guitar player in Jersey, yet he was playing drums because he just wanted to play. That really says a lot about him. He's never been in it for the glory, he's just in it for the joy.'

Gerard told him about the music he was writing and asked if he wanted to stop by at Pelissier's house to hear it. He didn't even know if Ray wanted to be in a proper band, but figured he had little to lose by asking. 'I wasn't sure what he was doing at that point and I thought he wanted to make films,' said Gerard. 'I asked him to come and play, no pressure – just to check out what I was doing.'

Ray figured it would be fun, and was used to playing in Pelissier's attic since it was where The Rodneys had previously rehearsed.

'[Pelissier] had a really annoying staircase that leads up to the attic – it's really steep and winding, so brilliant for carrying a guitar and amp,' said Ray. 'The attic was destroyed because all his friends would go up there and smoke weed and drink, so there was shit everywhere. That's the place we used to practise. [Gerard and Pelissier] played me 'Skylines and Turnstiles' because that was the only song they had. I heard it once and worked out what they were doing and it kind of went from there.'

Gerard was instantly impressed. 'Ray's the kind of guy who can pick up anything immediately and we played "Turnstiles" once for him and then he improved it tenfold instantly.'

Ray was an immediate fit and, with a guitarist and a drummer in place, Gerard doubled the intensity.

'It just snowballed,' said Ray. 'I remember Gerard talking about wanting to do it "for real". Most of the bands we'd ever been in had been about getting together and having fun. There was something immediate about the music in this case, though. We knew we wanted to bring it to other people, we knew we wanted to play shows and we knew we wanted to get into a van and tour.'

Ray began to write too, showing his songs to Gerard for him to put words to. Quickly, they began to build up a repertoire of their own material.

'We met once a week for the next four weeks to practise,' said Gerard. 'It seemed that anything was possible at that point. Ray wrote "Our Lady of Sorrows" – which was the second complete song we had. It fitted because it didn't really fit. That was something we always wanted to do – to put songs together that shouldn't work together but do. This song was really aggro and metal – there were bits we cribbed off Helloween in it. There were a lot of bizarre references around that time.

'The genesis of the sound came from sitting in Ray's room in his

Mom and Dad's apartment that he shared with his brothers and sitting at his computer with two guitars and just talking about the sound a lot. We were completely on the same page about it, 100 per cent.'

'It's funny,' said Ray, 'There was something about this that was so right that we had to keep going.'

They quickly began to work on a demo, recording it up in Pelissier's attic on a cheap 16-track board and beaten-up microphones. It was a rudimentary set-up, with drums and guitars on the top floor and Gerard in a bathroom downstairs howling. They recorded 'Skylines and Turnstiles', 'Cubicles' and 'Our Lady of Sorrows' – then called 'Bring More Knives' – and there was something in the roughness of the demo that simply shone. They called it *Dreams of Stabbing and/or Being Stabbed*, but referred to it simply as *The Attic Demo*. Certainly Eyeball Records' Alex Saavedra was impressed when he heard it.

'We were like, "Holy shit! Gerard can sing! Where has this been?"' he said. 'He just discovered this talent that he'd always had.'

Saavedra knew Gerard well by now, but hadn't seen Ray around much. But when he heard him play, he was blown away.

'Ray was definitely the most talented of them,' he said. 'He was a nerdy metalhead kid. I didn't really know much about him. He had this weird little afro and big glasses – I'd think to myself, "That kid is so strange looking." I couldn't figure him out; he was a mystery to me. Then I heard him play guitar and I was like "Holy shit!" No wonder he didn't come out much, he was probably just shredding on his guitar on his own at his house the whole time. He was just great from the start. He was like a professional guitar player – he killed it. It would have been a real shame if no one had ever heard him play guitar.

'He was very quiet. He was a super-nerd too; he used to walk around with a Spider-Man figure in his pocket. I didn't know much about him other than the fact he had an awesome name. Ray Toro – it sounds like a fake porn name or something. Ray Toro! You don't forget a name like that, but he was just a quiet dude from Kearny.'

Saavedra started to take more of an interest, always keen to urge his friends forward in their artistic pursuits. When he pointed out that they didn't have a bass player, the nascent band even considered asking him to play for them.

'I was just going to help out for a bit, but in a very casual way,' Saavedra said. 'That's just the way it was back then – asking someone to fill in in your band was treated the same as asking someone to, say, help you move house. So I was like, "I guess, if you need somebody – or you could teach your brother." In the end it made more sense to teach Mikey.'

Mikey was not much of a bassist and had recently failed an audition to play in another Eyeball band, Pencey Prep, who featured a guitarist called Frank Iero. There were no hard feelings and the two bands would go on to become firm friends, Pencey Prep helping out My Chem with a clutch of early shows. But despite Mikey's failure to land a role in Pencey Prep, Gerard liked the idea of including his little brother in his own band.

'Mikey was like, "Fuck, man, I want to be part of this. This sounds incredible. This band sounds like everything I always wanted to be a part of,"' said Gerard. 'So he learned his stuff. I'd never seen a band learn its stuff and get itself off the ground so quick.'

Mikey had something important up his sleeve too. He was failing his college course and working in the US chain bookstore Barnes & Noble. One night he was stacking shelves and came across a pile of novels by Irvine Welsh (the author of *Trainspotting*). One of them, a collection of three novellas, was called *Ecstasy: Three Tales of Chemical Romance*. Mikey wrote the title down on a piece of paper, slipped it into his pocket and went home at the end of the night. The name My Chemical Romance was born.

With the band personnel in place, and a name selected, My Chemical Romance were ready to go. Everything was done in a mad rush because Gerard was riding a wave of inspiration and, as tended to be his way, could focus on nothing else until he had seen it through.

'There was an urgency to it at this point. We had to play in front of people, we had to get it out there,' said Gerard. 'There was a magic to it that felt so unusual. I'd never felt anything like it in anything I'd done before in my life – be it in art, other bands I'd started, other projects that these guys had been involved in. When you're creating a new sound and it's great, then it's one of the highest feelings in the world to you. It felt really unique and, most importantly, it was all ours. It felt right immediately.'

They talked themselves up to everyone they knew. Gerard, for so long the shy shut-in, could barely stop talking about his new band when he bumped into Geoff Rickly at a party.

'Me and my brother are going to start a band,' he said enthusiastically.

'OK, whatever,' said Rickly, his scepticism clear.

'No, I'm serious,' Gerard insisted. 'We're going to be called My Chemical Romance.'

Rickly laughed. 'Well, at least you've got a great name. I'm sure you're gonna be huge . . .'

Undeterred, Gerard picked up a guitar and tried to play Rickly some songs.

'I didn't really want to listen because we were at a party,' Rickly confessed.

But a few weeks later, Alex Saavedra phoned him excitedly and said Rickly should come and see them rehearse. He did, but didn't think much of them as they were struggling to gel. He went off on tour with Thursday without giving My Chemical Romance much more thought. Which is when Saavedra phoned him again.

'Dude, I've got to tell you about My Chemical Romance,' said Saavedra in high spirits. 'They've got this one song that they've recorded and it's really good.'

'OK, whatever,' said Rickly again, unconvinced. But Saavedra sent him a CD of a song called 'Vampires Will Never Hurt You' and it blew Rickly's mind.

'I called them right away and said, "This is really cool. I've never heard anything quite like it." You could hear their influences, I heard some Thursday, some AFI and some other things in there but it was unique enough – and especially for a band only a month old. I was really impressed.'

It was clear something was happening with My Chemical Romance. With the demo under their belts, and a buzz beginning to form, the band knew there was only one more major step. They needed to play live.

3: THIS IS THE BEST DAY EVER

October 2001, Ewing, New Jersey. All four of My Chemical Romance were sat in a beaten-up, bright yellow school bus belonging to Pencey Prep. They were parked outside a VFW Hall, paralysed with fear. Inside, a small crowd was forming for the three-band bill. First on were My Chemical Romance. Second, Pencey Prep and headlining were Frank Iero's cousin Patrick's punk band. It was My Chemical Romance's first show – one they got solely because Frank had swung it for them.

'My cousin Patrick put that show together,' said Frank, who met My Chemical Romance through Eyeball. 'He asked if Pencey could play and I said, "Yeah, is there an extra spot though? My friends are starting a band."'

Little did he know that he and his bassist, John 'Hambone' McGuire, would have to talk My Chemical Romance onto the stage. Little did he know how drunk they would get.

The Way brothers were particularly nervous. They reached for beer after beer, chugging them down like water, barely noticing the taste.

'I drank seven beers in five minutes,' said Mikey. 'I was petrified and everyone was giving me a pep talk to get me onstage. I had never played a show before. I was very nervous; I had to drink to the point of intoxication. I had about ten beers because I was so nervous.'

'They were drunk,' agreed Frank. 'Really drunk.'

Ray and Pelissier were in better condition, though still apprehensive.

'I was nervous too but I had played in front of people before in a couple of other bands,' said the guitarist. 'It felt different in this band though: we were making music that I had never heard before.'

There were thirty or forty kids waiting for the band inside the hall – a little room that was, ironically given the state of the Ways, occasionally used for Alcoholics Anonymous meetings. They were pressed in tight, looking at a stageless space with a couple of microphones, no monitors, a ramshackle PA and a drum-kit. At some point My Chemical Romance were going to have to get over their nerves. At some point the Way brothers were going to have walk into that space and face the crowd eye to eye.

In the bus, all four of the band took a breath then headed into the hall and up to their instruments. They were as ready as they would ever be. 'So we just plugged our shit in and looked at each other,' said Gerard. 'Then we said, "Let's go!"'

They opened with the only recently written 'Skylines and Turnstiles'. At first nothing happened. People stood and stared, jerking awkwardly to its rhythms. No one knew what to make of My Chemical Romance. No one was sure what this weird new sound was. But then, as the song came clattering to a close – jagged, impassioned and eloquent – something happened. Something amazing.

'As soon as the song finished, the room blew up,' said Gerard. 'It was the first time some of the people there had heard that sound and I really wish I could meet some of the people that were there that day. It was the best first gig I think we could possibly have had. We played the rest of the songs on this wave, we felt totally on fire. We ploughed through the songs and each one got that same response. It was a fucking big deal for us.'

'I stood up on a chair, and they powered through their set: it was like a hurricane,' said Frank, watching from the back of the room before Pencey were due to follow them. 'No one knew what to expect as it was the band's first show, so they stood back for a bit. Then it went crazy. Ray and G were kicking each other, it was awesome. You just knew something important was happening. The band was just too good for something not to happen. From that day,

I went to every single one of their shows: from the first note they played, they were my favourite band.'

Everyone in the band felt it, everyone in the room too. Even Ray – polite and reserved, technical in his playing – lost control.

'It felt like we were doing something new and that was exciting,' said the guitarist. 'There was this kinetic energy. I don't know what it was but, as soon as the music hit, all of those pent-up emotions came out. I'm a quiet dude and I keep to myself, but that music made me want to open up and let everything out.

'As soon as we started playing, it was on. Something about that music – it took over everybody in the band, it took over everybody watching – it was just something to see. I had never moved around onstage when I had played in bands before, I had always just stood there. This time though, the music made me move, headbang and thrash around. I was wild onstage and I had never experienced that before. From that very first show, we knew there was something special about the band.

'I remember not thinking at all. That's how it was for those first shows. If you're not thinking up there, then you're in the moment. It's almost like it wasn't me up there.'

Even then, at the very first show, Gerard knew how to work the crowd. There was some instinct in him, some showman that had long been buried. Instead of repeating the band's name over and over to get it known, he knew there was greater mystique in not saying it at all. Hambone was stood at the back of the room yelling: 'Say the band name! Say the band name!' But Gerard refused.

'Back then we didn't ever say our band name – we made it a point not to, in fact,' he said. 'We made it a point not to sell anything either; if someone wanted something, they got it for free. We were very anti-self-promotion because people who were like that really turned us off. I hate meeting people who are all about networking. We wanted to keep this as bullshit-free as possible. Honesty and sincerity was important to us. We didn't want to ask kids to pay $5 for our demo, in fact I think we lost a lot of money on those demos because we were just giving them away.

'We didn't talk much at all, I don't think. It meant that people couldn't figure us out – they didn't know if we were political, if we were straight, gay or whatever. That was cool.'

The band staggered outside afterwards, full of fire and energy, feedback ringing in their ears. 'We were like a gang, we felt unbeatable,' said Gerard. 'Afterwards, I felt like I had been in a car accident – but a really great one. It was really magical.'

'It was a crazy feeling – it was like a drug you had never tried before that triggered new emotions in your brain,' said Mikey.

They grinned wildly at each other as more and more people came up to compliment them, slapping them on the back. Then all four of My Chemical Romance shared another look. Mikey still remembers it: 'It felt so good. It felt like we were part of something. I was thinking, "Something's going to happen here, I can feel it". It felt like a spark on a pile of woodchips.'

Word of mouth spread, as did the band's demo. Frank said the songs on it were badly recorded and out of tune, 'but it had something'. Pencey Prep would listen to it on their way to shows, using it to psych themselves up.

People began to talk about the band on a local message board called NJ Scene. The reaction to My Chemical Romance there was split neatly in two.

'It was about the only place you could gauge what anyone thought of you,' said Gerard. 'There was a pretty mixed view of us on there. Some of them thought it was the best thing they'd ever seen, and others didn't get it at all – they thought we were shit. There was nobody in the middle, though, nobody said, "Yeah, they're all right." But there was word of mouth, which was exactly what we wanted to happen.'

They wanted to play as many shows as they could and, at first, the only people rooting for them were Pencey Prep. Whenever Frank's band got a gig, he would try to get My Chemical Romance on the bill too.

They would travel together in Pencey Prep's old school bus, a death-trap that would only barely get them to the show and back. 'That van was hell on wheels,' says Hambone. 'It drove us all nuts. It would break down everywhere. We were driving back from Wisconsin once and leaking gas, oil, transmission fluid, anti-freeze fluid and praying to God that we would make it.'

A friendly rivalry sprang up between the two bands; each would try to blow the other offstage. Frequently, and jokingly, they would resort to underhand tactics.

'I remember seeing Frank perform and I think we messed with him during one of the songs,' recalled Gerard. 'There was a line in one of his songs and we yelled at him in response to that and he just started laughing while he was singing. You could see that he was a born performer even then. He was the frontman of that band and he was a great and very unique guitar player.'

'That competition bred a certain degree of excellence, I think,' says Hambone. 'We would egg each other on constantly to try and better ourselves, then we'd take the piss out of each other afterwards.'

Hambone remembers that though the band were nerdish but friendly offstage, they were wild when they were on it.

'They were really good people, they were honest and the sort of people you just wanted to hang out with,' he says. 'They were also a bunch of dorks. But that's who they were, they were just being themselves. What you saw was what you got. Then they'd get onstage and it was like, "Fuck!" When they got onstage all hell broke loose. Nothing was planned but, from the first note to the last note, it was pure energy, pure feeling.

'There was a sense of us against the world back then. We all wanted to make music that would reach people. We all just wanted to make records that would last. Their music has done that tenfold.'

Something happened to My Chemical Romance when they hit the stage. There didn't even have to be much of a crowd – and frequently there wasn't – but they were overcome by the music and performed as if to a vast audience. For Frank, My Chemical Romance was the greatest band in the world.

'We couldn't play the songs without getting intense: we'd soundcheck and injure ourselves,' said Gerard. 'We soundchecked at the Loop Lounge once and me and Ray hurt each other somehow during it – that was when Frank came up to us and told us for the first time that we were his favourite band. The thing was, whether it was a soundcheck or not, we were playing the song – and the songs were so intense that we meant them every time we played them. Back then we couldn't play a soundcheck without destroying something.'

With such a show, their reputation began to spread – locally only, but just enough so that crowds were beginning to kick off just as much as they were.

'I remember one show of theirs in Jersey,' says Gerard's old *Breakfast Monkey* co-creator Joe Boyle. 'The kids went nuts. I mean they just went fucking bananas. I was like, "Wow." It was me and some co-workers who came to the show and none of us expected that. We were like, "These kids know what they're doing."'

Though My Chemical Romance's early performances were visceral and instinctive, behind the scenes they were working hard on their sound. Rather than simply relying on the carnage of their live shows, they knew they needed to learn how to play together and to write songs. Gerard was at the forefront of it, pushing them hard.

'There was a focus to him. He really wanted this to happen, he really wanted this to work,' said Ray. 'Pencey Prep were amazing to us too, they let us rehearse in their practice studio and really helped us. Watching that band was great for us. They had a real work ethic – they practised every day for hours and hours. We learned how a real band operates from watching Pencey. Most of the bands we had been in practised once on the weekend and that was it. Frank calls those bands "the case of beer bands" – bands who show up with a case of beers, get wasted and never really play. Pencey had such a work ethic though and that really rubbed off on us. Frank was so supportive, as were the rest of those guys back then, and that was new to me – bands had never looked after us before.'

Eyeball's Alex Saavedra began to champion them locally. He knew a good sound when he heard it, and he heard something impressive in My Chemical Romance. He, Frank and Geoff Rickly would frequently just watch them rehearse – something the band did with a rare intensity.

'Me and Geoff would go down to sit in, and they would play like they were playing to a thousand people,' says Saavedra. 'I wish there was a better story to their build-up but the reality of it was that they were just fucking brilliant from the start.

'We were surprised that Gerard was running around like a maniac. Then, secondly, we were surprised that he could sing like that. We had always known him as a storyteller, because his imagination has always been there. But now his lyrics were reading like comics, in that he was telling stories.'

Frank too was thrilled at what he saw. He would be there for all of their practices, and would tell anyone who cared about their demo.

'I just loved the band,' he said. 'I was just a big fan. I was a friend but I was a huge fan of what they were doing.'

He did not realize it then, but by May 2002 he would be their guitarist.

Frank Anthony Iero had music in the blood. Born on 31 October 1981, he was surrounded by sound from an early age.

'My dad's a drummer, my grandfather was a drummer – basically, everybody in my family was a musician and everybody in my family was named Frank,' he said. 'If you weren't Frank and you didn't play drums, your name was Anthony and you played piano. They started me out on drums – I remember being three years old and playing a Smurfs kit. But, eventually I wanted to write songs. I was the black sheep.'

His family was from South Jersey and it was a big one. His

mother had three sisters, his father had a sister and he was always surrounded by aunts and cousins. All the while, his dad was working as a drummer, eventually moving the family up to Kearny when he got a job at the Record Plant recording studios in Manhattan. Frank was a musical kid too, playing drums, then piano, then saxophone for a while.

Eventually, though, he discovered the guitar and realized it was a much better fit for him. 'My dad got me into the blues, like T-Bone Walker, Muddy Waters and Buddy Guy and then a lot of Big Band. That was the grassroots music that he listened to.'

He was not a healthy kid and would be in and out of hospital, needing treatment for a variety of problems.

'A few days after I was born, I got bronchitis so I had to go back in the hospital and they put me in an oxygen tent for a while,' he said. 'Growing up, I had bad earaches, had my tonsils out, had tubes in my ears, had my adenoids out, all that stuff. I was a kid who always had something going on and I'd get really high fevers because of my ears. I vividly remember waking up one day and saying to my mom, "Remember that time we were at the store and I fell," and this look of terror came on her face. She didn't know what I was talking about because I was really hot and hallucinating. I didn't understand why she was so scared. But there were a few instances of that sort of thing.'

His parents split up when he was three and divorced when he was seven. His father moved to Trenton in South Jersey and his mother stayed where she was. He would spend the weekdays with his mother and the weekends with his dad. Close as he was to his mom, it was the weekends that were exciting.

'If I wasn't watching my dad play on the weekends, or if he was playing in a club that wasn't suitable for a child, then I'd go to my grandfather's,' said Frank. 'He played at this old speakeasy every weekend. Every Saturday night, he'd be playing Dixieland or Big Band jazz and I'd hang out there until 1.30 a.m. or 2 a.m. If you stayed up late enough, you got to go with the band to the diner. And that was fucking huge! I got to hang out at a diner at 3 a.m. with musicians after listening to jazz at the bar all night. It was pretty cool.'

Frank's father and grandfather were not rock stars or millionaires but jobbing, working musicians who joined pick-up bands whenever there was a show. They played for whoever paid in bars and studios, chasing gigs for whatever scratch group would have them. They did OK out of it too. Frank loved the lifestyle. As a boy, he would watch them pull out these great diaries stuffed with contacts, flyers and half-remembered notes as they shifted things around, trying to squeeze shows in here, a studio session in there.

'That was so fucking rad to me, to have this huge date book of gigs,' said Frank. 'Every story started with, "It was the night we were playing such and such a bar." They would remember the night the kids were born by where they were playing that night. That was the legacy – you played, you gigged and that was just what you did. It was very romantic. In my head, as a kid, this date book, with its huge rubber band around it and all the slips of paper inside it, was like a bible.

'My dad had this old, brown leather briefcase. Who knows what else was in it, but it always had his date book in it. When he would drive, he would have the briefcase on the passenger seat and he would put a towel over it and he would play drums on it in traffic. So it was this beat-up briefcase covered in pockmarks from his drumming and he finally decided to get a new one. I went and fished it out of the trash and kept it. The lock code was the address from my childhood house – this thing just meant something to me. When My Chem got together, we had this idea of doing something cool with the merch with something we could pop open at every show. G and I went to a fabric store, and we lined that old briefcase and it became our merch set-up.'

Frank got by in school. He wasn't one of the cool kids, but he wasn't one of the outcasts either. He survived.

'School was weird,' he said. 'I remember being young at grammar school and coming to a realization that I didn't really fit in. It was a small school, so you were either like this one set of twenty-five kids or you weren't. And if you weren't, then you got beaten up. I wasn't like those twenty-five kids, but I was smart enough to know that I wasn't going to get beat up every day. So I would pretend that I was into what they were into. I got through it.'

There, though, he began to get ill again. Frank, in later years, would be plagued by stomach conditions when he toured with My Chemical Romance. They began at school.

'In grammar school, I started getting weird stomach issues,' he said. 'There was a period for a year and a half where I would get really sick every weekend and vomit uncontrollably. It was every fucking weekend. I've always had really bad intestinal, digestive issues. I always basically feel nauseous. I have a standing appointment with a gastroentorologist but we basically just hang out and she gives me pills. She goes, "Ah, I think you're just sick basically."'

It was when Frank hit high school that his life changed. He discovered punk rock and with it weed, rebellion, skateboarding and a new world. He had grown up listening to his father's blues and Rolling Stones records, but Frank discovered Nirvana and the other bands on their Sub Pop label. Aged thirteen, he met John 'Hambone' McGuire – a few years older than him – and Hambone began a musical education that would blow his mind. He introduced him to hardcore punk and to Jawbreaker, The Bouncing Souls, Misfits and Black Flag.

'I began to realize there were bands who weren't much older than me, who were from Jersey, and who were doing it,' said Frank. 'Then I found bands my age, from my town doing it. I realized you didn't have to be a rock star to go out and do it.'

He was playing in a punk-rock band with Hambone and even got a show at the Junior Dance. When high school was over, Frank and Hambone threw themselves into the local scene – the one driven by Eyeball Records – and fell in love with it. They formed Pencey Prep together and soon became part of the Jersey hardcore landscape. Alongside drummer Tim Hagevik, guitarist Neil Sabatino and keyboardist Shaun Simon (who would go on to work with

Gerard on comic books in years to come), Pencey began to generate a small but loyal following. It was a good time in their lives.

'When I found out there were punk-rock shows near me, I was like, "Fuck, are you kidding me? Young kids are renting out rooms and putting on shows? This is all I'm gonna do now." I just took off,' said Frank. 'I started putting on shows – there was a VFW in Lynd-hurst [the next town from Belleville] that my friend and I would rent out and put on shows there. If you figured out how to pay for a band you really liked, you could put them on and you could play with them. The biggest thing was finding someone cool at Staples, because then you could steal flyers.'

'There were so many shows to go to back then – the local scene was just wonderful,' says Hambone. 'There was always somewhere to go, always a band to see, it was wonderful. If I could go back to any time, I'd go back to then. No one cared about anything, you had money in your pocket to go to shows. We'd practise all day – for nine hours a day. Then we'd go to a show, then come back and practise some more. Back then it was Frank, Shaun, Neil, Tim and myself. We were pretty much inseparable.'

They recorded a demo and then pestered Eyeball's Alex Saavedra to sign them and release their album. 'Frank was a really confident kid with a lot of passion,' says Saavedra. 'Hambone was very tal-ented and such a genuinely good person that you would want to hang out with him. Frankie was very confident but I don't think he knew what the hell he wanted. He knew he wanted to do music but I don't think he knew how, or what kind of sound he wanted.'

Nevertheless Saavedra agreed to put out a Pencey Prep record, and so they set about recording *Heartbreak in Stereo* – in part at Nada Studios, where My Chemical Romance would later record. An album of vicious but unfocused hardcore, it featured Frank in full berserker mode: screaming, howling and raging into the microphone. It would be how he performed live too – venting and blood-letting on the stage.

'I tried not to hold anything back,' said Frank. 'That's the way I feel about music and performing. I have to come offstage with nothing left or it feels like I didn't do it properly. I think the reason why I play the way I do is probably because I never feel good. I'm always trying to spite myself. It's not an emotional thing, it's a physical thing – I always feel tired and run down, my immune system is destroyed because I have the Epstein Barr virus. I have a weird stomach problem that constantly makes me feel queasy to the point where I think I'm going to throw up. The only time I really feel good is when I just get offstage because I think I must have sweated everything out. It's the one time I don't feel sick any more.'

For all the energy of Pencey Prep's music, and despite the fact he agreed to release it, Saavedra says *Heartbreak in Stereo* wasn't much good. But then Eyeball's policy was never to solely concentrate on quality – instead, they believed that if you were part of the family, then you would get your shot.

'Clearly I didn't care if your band was good or not – I mean I put the Pencey Prep record out, didn't I?' says Saavedra. 'I actually disliked the record, but I liked the kids because they had a lot of heart.'

'I don't believe for one second that he really liked our band,' said Frank. 'By no means were we a fantastic band but we loved playing and we wanted it. We were nice dudes too, and that's how it worked. I think he saw the passion behind it and thought, "I guess I've got to give these guys a little bit of a shot – they need something."'

Heartbreak in Stereo was released in November 2001, two months after Gerard's epiphany while witnessing the tragedy of 9/11 and a month after My Chemical Romance's first gig. Pencey Prep went on a short tour to support it but their future was never entirely solid. Sabatino left the band, then their drummer Hagevik decided he wanted to go too and Pencey began to unravel. By now Frank had begun to hang out with My Chemical Romance – within a matter of months, Gerard, Mikey, Ray and Matt would change the course of his life.

★

At the start of 2002, My Chemical Romance were still working at speed. They felt they were nearly ready to start recording an album – just three and a half months after they formed. They were riding a wave of momentum.

'The whole history of the band has felt very go, go, go,' said Ray. 'It feels like we've never had a moment to breathe. I think that's the way we like it – we've always just gone for it.'

It was more or less understood that Saavedra's label, Eyeball, would release the music they were working on – though, this time, because Saavedra believed in them, and not because he was helping out friends.

'We were like, "All right, so when do you want to do a record?"' he says. 'The plan was to do two records on Eyeball and then hopefully somebody would come along and they could go to a bigger label if they wanted, or they could stay on an indie. But it didn't even get to that point – we got one record out and everybody went crazy. There were pissing wars all over the place.'

Long before that, Saavedra told My Chemical Romance they were ready. He wanted them to record a demo of what he considered their best song – 'Vampires Will Never Hurt You'. After that, they could think about an album. The next stop was Nada Studios.

4: I BROUGHT YOU MY BULLETS, YOU BROUGHT ME YOUR LOVE

———

The skies over New Windsor in upstate New York were bruised and heavy. A storm was brewing, and the clouds swirled inkily above. It wouldn't be long before torrential rain would come pouring down.

Below, in John Naclerio's Nada Studios – in reality the basement of a small and anonymous house belonging to his parents – Gerard Way was being a pain in the ass. It was March 2002 and My Chemical Romance were in the middle of their first ever proper recording session, laying down an early demo before they would start work on the rest of their debut album a month or so later.

An abscess in Gerard's tooth had been causing him pain for weeks. He had been bitching and moaning, complaining at one point that he might have a brain tumour. Finally, mid-session, he went and got the emergency dental work he needed.

He returned woozy and slurring, his mind numbed by painkillers and his mouth full of blood. Time was tight, as was money, and there was no wriggle room in the schedule to allow for Gerard to take more time out. Meanwhile his painkiller-induced fogginess was hardly helping. And so his pills had been hidden, which hadn't done much for his state of mind.

Angry and in pain, he was stomping around the small studio in no mood to sing. He was due to be laying down vocals to what would become one of My Chemical Romance's most important early songs, 'Vampires Will Never Hurt You', but very little was happening. And so Alex Saavedra, who was producing the session, took matters into his own hands.

He walked towards the singer and gave him a reassuring hug. Next, he took a step back and punched him hard in the mouth. Then he said, simply: 'Now go sing.'

Gerard was furious. Incandescent with rage and shocked by what Saavedra had done, he went into the live room. And then he unleashed everything into the mic. 'I was fucking riled,' he admitted. 'I went up to the mic and nailed it first time.'

He delivered all the pain he was feeling into that performance. Pissed off at being punched, fuming about his hidden painkillers, and incensed about his teeth, he went crazy – a performance building to a frenzy as he screamed, whispered and yelled the brutal poetry of his lyrics.

'Then John [Naclerio], the engineer, goes, "Fuck, that was amazing . . . Could you do it again? I was just setting the levels,"' said Gerard. 'I was like, "Fuck!"'

But do it again he did. Immediately he summoned up those reserves once more, ripping himself apart in the studio. 'It sounded like venom. It sounded like a really pissed-off kid wanting to tear himself apart and it was great,' said Geoff Rickly, who would produce the rest of the album.

The finished recording is far from flawless – and, given that it was intended as a demo, it didn't need to be – but it had something powerful: a vicious, violent beauty that had more spirit and emotion than any more polished track might contain.

'Nothing beats that recording of "Vampires". Even the stuff that we've spent a lot of money on,' Gerard said years later. 'We were worried "Vampires" wouldn't work. But it was the greatest thing we'd ever fucking heard. We piled into the van and drove home afterwards and we couldn't stop listening to it. It was just the loudest, gnarliest, darkest most melodic song I'd ever heard. It was fucking amazing.'

And it all started with a fist to the mouth.

'Hey,' says Saavedra, 'sometimes everyone just needs a good punch in the face.'

My Chemical Romance's first experience in a proper recording studio was an important one. They had travelled to Nada simply to work on the 'Vampires Will Never Hurt You' demo. The idea was to get the track down, and then return later in the month with Rickly, who would produce a full album. But two key moments occurred while they were there.

The first was that punch. Inspired by the stories and comic book ideas he had been writing while in his parents' basement, Gerard was playing with different characters and plot arcs in his lyrics and accessing them in the studio as a means to act out his vocals. A punch in the face made it all the easier to get into the part.

'The punch was definitely like method acting in a weird way,' said Gerard. 'The song is about something pretty dark. I guess, looking back, it's about the early signs of my alcoholism and how I felt I was wasting my life. It was about feeling generally like a scumbag.'

Its recording was so passionate that, despite being intended as a demo, My Chemical Romance decided that they should use it on the album. It would go on to become the central cog of the record they were about to make, *I Brought You My Bullets, You Brought Me Your Love*. It would be the album that launched their career.

The second key moment at Nada arrived as Ray attempted to weave in the various different guitar parts he had dreamed up for 'Vampires Will Never Hurt You'. Saavedra and Rickly had previously urged My Chemical Romance to add an extra guitarist. They felt that if Ray put all his ideas onto a record, he would struggle to recreate them live. Ray was resistant, saying to Rickly, 'I'll just choose between the important parts and the not so important parts.' However Rickly pointed out that 'if there were unimportant parts then they shouldn't be on the record in the first place.' Getting a new guitarist was a topic that came up again as Ray worked on his parts at Nada. It just so happened that the perfect man for the job was right under their noses.

Frank Iero, still the frontman for Pencey Prep, had come along to the session to hang out. He had done some screaming on the track, but mostly he had sat on the studio sofa and smoked weed. When the subject of adding a new guitarist came up, Frank was so stoned that he immediately became paranoid they might ask him to try out and knew he was in no fit state to do so.

'The song was sounding great in the studio,' Frank said. 'Ray had laid down about fourteen different guitar parts – most of them at the same time – and somebody said, "Have you guys thought about adding another guitar player, so you can do this stuff live?" I can't remember who answered, but they said, "The only guy we've ever considered is currently too high to get off the couch."

'I just lay there and pretended I hadn't heard because it made me so goddamned nervous that they were going to ask me to play some guitar on the track. I was so fucked up I couldn't even think about doing that. But that was the first time I thought it might be possible for me to play in my favourite band – and it scared the shit out of me.'

After finishing 'Vampires Will Never Hurt You', My Chemical Romance began to think more seriously about asking Frank to join the band. They suspected that Pencey Prep were not going to last long, and they also knew that Frank would fit in well. But, according to Saavedra, Ray was initially resistant.

'It took a lot of talking to Ray to convince him that Frank would be good for the band,' says Saavedra. 'We did really have to work on him to get him to open up to the idea. I think Ray really liked being the only guitar player and the guy that wrote the songs and I can understand that.'

Rickly, too, thought Frank would be a good fit and had already spoken to him about it. 'I loved Frank and thought he was very talented but I didn't think Pencey Prep was a very good band,' says Rickly. 'I told him that he should join My Chem because they needed another guitar and he could sing the back-ups that Gerard couldn't do. The best thing, I thought, was that he wouldn't have to be in Pencey Prep any more.'

Though Ray remained unsure whether My Chemical Romance needed another guitarist – 'I was a bit nervous,' he admitted – Gerard took less convincing. He knew how electric Frank's live performances could be and how visceral his playing was. Though Frank may not have had Ray's technique, he had power and energy to add to the My Chemical Romance sound.

'I felt that we were missing something and, when we watched Pencey Prep onstage, it was obvious what it was,' said Gerard. 'We already had some dynamite but we needed more: Frank was the extra dynamite.'

Eventually they made up their minds. Late one night, a week before recording was due to start on the rest of *I Brought You My Bullets, You Brought Me Your Love*, My Chemical Romance went to Frank's house and asked if he wanted to go for a stroll. They explained that they were going to be recording an album in a few days' time, and told him how much they liked him. And then they asked if he wanted to join their band.

'That was the best leap of faith we ever took,' said Gerard. 'We just kind of knew it would work. We try to work on instinct.'

'I was like, "Fuck yeah!"' said Frank. 'And from that point, it was a fucking whirlwind.'

As with so much of My Chemical Romance's beginnings, everything was done at speed. With Frank on board, and all still buzzing from the recording of 'Vampires Will Never Hurt You', they returned to Nada Studios in May 2002.

They had convinced Rickly to produce the record for them, despite the fact his band Thursday were in the middle of a demanding tour schedule following the release of their iconic 2001 album *Full Collapse*, a record which was fast making them post-hardcore's biggest stars.

'They asked me to produce their record,' he said. 'I said, "I'd love to but our touring schedule is so intense that I can't fit it in." They instantly replied, "That's OK, we checked your schedule and you're free this week." So between two three-month tours I had ten days and I had to go into the studio with them for seven of them.'

'We totally bullied Geoff into producing that album,' said Gerard. 'He had the smallest amount of time off and we made him work for almost all of it. It was amazing.'

Rickly had already heard 'Vampires', had watched My Chemical Romance rehearse and had previously offered them advice as to how their career should proceed, but now that he was producing them he took a closer listen to the material they had demoed in Pelissier's attic.

'I thought about half of their songs were great and the other half weren't,' he said. 'But they were young enough that you wanted to help them rather than crush their dreams. I didn't want to say, "This sucks and you shouldn't put it on the record." They'd only been playing for a few months when we went into the studio.'

Rickly was diplomatic and vowed to do the best he could. Had he told the band his concerns, it's unlikely they would have cared, such was their excitement at recording. Whether the songs were good enough or not, My Chemical Romance believed wholeheartedly in what they had written and simply wanted to get it down.

'We were enjoying ourselves so much,' said Ray. 'We weren't doing all this stuff because we were thinking about getting signed or anything like that; it was just because we wanted to play the music. We knew it deserved to be heard. None of it was done because we were thinking about anything else down the line.'

These days Nada Studios has moved from Naclerio's parents' basement. He still runs it, but it is now housed in a 2,000 square foot warehouse in New Windsor, where he engineers, masters, mixes and produces international bands while running a record label called Broken English. Back when My Chemical Romance rolled through his doors, things were very different.

'I would get bands from all over New Jersey in, and My Chemical Romance just happened to be one of them,' says Naclerio. 'My mom would be vacuuming upstairs, and I had a dog who would bark the whole time. We had to stop recording every time the dog barked. I actually don't know how my mother put up with it – for eight years bands would be trudging in and out of her basement and it's not a big house. Fortunately, the neighbours were just as crazy as I was so they didn't mind too much.

'As soon as you got in, there were a huge amount of amps. For some reason, I always had a lot of amplifiers in there. The studio itself was about ten feet by twenty, so it was small and it would get really hot. The control room was eight feet by eight, and the whole of My Chemical Romance would try to squeeze into this little room. It would get so hot that the condensation would drip down the control room window. I had a small air conditioner in there and it was the loudest air conditioner in the world, but we had to run it non-stop even though it never cooled the room once.'

For all its limits, what Nada did have was some very good equipment for its size. Naclerio had just invested in his first Pro-Tools rig and My Chemical Romance's debut would be one of the first he recorded with it. That wasn't the reason that Saavedra had chosen to put the band in there though.

'I was on the cheap side,' admits Naclerio. 'But I also knew Alex from a band he was in called Bomb Paris. He had played bass on a record and he had told me about his record label, and I was pretty impressed by it. I mentioned that he should bring some bands up to me, and he did. He brought Pencey Prep up, so I got to know Frank pretty well before he was in My Chemical Romance.'

Small, hot and crowded though Nada may have been, it was a palace to My Chemical Romance, who were simply thrilled to be laying down music at all.

'To get to the studio itself, you would have to walk into a basement through a washer/drier room,' remembers Ray. 'If you'd been there when we were recording, you would have seen a few of the guys hanging out on the couch playing Nintendo, then you would have walked into the control room where we played most of our parts. It was a lot of fun and it was all new to us. We really respected Geoff too. Because he had done it, he gave us the hope that we could too.'

For Ray, the chance to work in any kind of professional studio was heaven. He threw himself into it, keen to explore all the new possibilities that the technology offered him.

'Playing in the studio was my first introduction to multi-tracking and it was a lot of fun to experiment and try a bunch of things,' he said. 'I enjoyed mixing our shitty demos into something better. I just really enjoyed all of it and it felt like such a new experience that we were all having together. It was all because we felt that the music deserved it. Everybody was just working really, really hard. I loved it. I wished we had had more time but it was still awesome. It sounded better than any recording we had ever done. It was very cool.'

Rickly remembers that Ray was by far the most accomplished musician in the band and the producer would frequently look to him whenever musical decisions needed to be made. However, he says there were times that his more technical approach could be tricky.

'Ray was the sort of guy you'd find working in a guitar shop,' says Rickly. 'You know, he was one of those people who was a great guitar player but would never normally find a band. He looked like one of those Guitar Centre people who'd be too talented for a band and who was a little hard to deal with because he'd be such a good player that he'd turn around and criticize people who weren't as good as him. There were times he was a bit of pain in the ass.'

'Ray was definitely the leader of the band [musically],' believes Naclerio, but he disagrees with Rickly. 'He was really excited to be in the studio, but I never felt that he was a pain in the ass particularly.'

Ray did much of the guitar playing on the record and initially Frank felt that he should take a back seat. Having joined the band after they had written much of their material, he did not feel he could or should impose himself.

'I had never been in a band with people I didn't know well,' said Frank. 'And though they tried to make me feel a part of it, I hadn't been involved in the creative process so I still felt a little like a fan. I felt like the kid in the crowd who had been pulled up to play a song. I was just easing into the band and I didn't want to start throwing a lot of parts around.'

It was only as the sessions progressed that he was able to make his mark, and the partnership between him and Ray began to flourish. 'Recently I found the notes I had written on the songs,' Frank told me in 2011. 'Ninety per cent of the record was fleshed out when I joined, so I had to learn a lot of parts. At that point, Ray was already playing about three different guitar parts for each song at once. He was doing the rhythm, the lead and a harmony part too – so I came in to lighten his load and take some of the harmony parts off his hands.

'When we started recording songs like "Honey, this Mirror Isn't Big Enough for the Two of Us" and "Early Sunsets over Monroe-ville", there was more room for me to write. So I wrote parts to those and also some of "Headfirst for Halos". Those were the first songs that I really got involved in.'

'Most of those songs were pretty much just the two guitar parts because of how much time we had and how recently he had joined the band,' said Ray. 'There really wasn't much time for Frank to learn the songs let alone write much so I just tried to fill out what he was doing. I tried to write two parts that I could see us both playing. But the songs that stand out are the ones that both of us got to write on. He was taking demos of the songs into our van, then he'd write his part and run into the studio and track immediately. He brought a very different way of thinking and a different style of playing than I could.

'It was definitely a learning curve. Frank and I come from a different background and we hear music in different ways, so it was interesting. I think the first song that it really clicked on was "Honey, this Mirror Isn't Big Enough for the Two of Us" – the stuff Frank played on top of the opening riff just completely complemented it. That was when I knew it was going to work, and that his style would interweave with what I was doing.'

Ray and Frank had entirely different approaches to playing: Ray was the technical, expert player whose picking was precise and fluent. Frank was the punk kid: his playing was not a patch on Ray's in terms of technique but what he had was spirit and spit. He once said that comparing both of their styles was like comparing 'an egg salad sandwich to a Rolex'. But the combination worked very well.

'As far as our relationship, there was a certain amount of coming to terms,' Frank said. 'It was like, "All right, this is the new relationship for the band." Ray's always been a perfectionist in certain respects and I feel like I dirtied him down while he cleaned me up. Early on, I imagine it was hard for him.'

But any awkwardness didn't last long. Alex Saavedra remembers that Frank and Ray's relationship flourished in the studio. 'If it was uneasy, it wasn't something Ray spoke about,' he says. 'Really, it was just a bunch of dudes having fun.'

Footage of them recorded by Saavedra on a home movie camera shows them all really enjoying their time in the studio. Ray laughs constantly, while Gerard appears thrilled to be recording. At one point, everyone who was there – all the band, Saavedra, Rickly, Rickly's girlfriend and Naclerio, all join in on one big gang vocal – and there's a spirit of real kinship and togetherness as they record.

One song that really shone in particular was born out of that spirit of fun. It would go on to be the most accomplished on the album and point the way for My Chemical Romance's future direction, but at first it was not entirely serious. 'Headfirst for Halos' opens with a fanfare of the Queen-esque guitars that would emerge on the band's second album *Three Cheers for Sweet Revenge* and then explode on their third album *The Black Parade*. But it also incorporated the jagged bubblegum punk that would become the basis for their future sound while, for the first time, featuring a proper melody. It was the song that told them they had a future, that they could develop.

'There's a song on every record that allows us to push ourselves further,' said Gerard. 'On *Bullets* it was "Headfirst for Halos". It actually started out as a joke. Then we realized that, if we could pull it off, it would allow us to do so much more because it would prevent us from getting pigeonholed.

'We had a thrashy pop song in our laps and we thought, 'This doesn't sound like anything.'' Maybe it was a bit of a Beatles rip-off, maybe it was a bit Britpop but that was all I could think of. It was only after we finished writing it that we realized where it might take us.'

It was a song written with a spirit of fearlessness – though it may not have entirely fitted among the metal and hardcore riffs elsewhere, or the doomed, delicate guitars of the ballad 'Demolition Lovers', it shone. It suggests an attitude of adventure was at work in the studio.

Saavedra remembers that they had a blast recording the album. 'We were having a really good time,' he says. 'We were rushed, and we had no money, but we had a great time. We were all staying in the same hotel room, hanging out. We were like a family making a recording. We would record all day, go back to the hotel and goof off at night, talking and drinking.'

The actual recordings didn't go quite so smoothly, not that it interfered with the fun they were having. The first problem was that Mikey was not much of a bassist – he had, after all, only been playing for a few months.

'Could Mikey play? Hell no!' says Saavedra. 'He could pick the instrument up, obviously, but he couldn't play well. But that was all right because he wanted it so much that he made it happen. I'm not going to lie and say that none of us helped him and that he did it all out of nowhere. But he did progress very quickly. But, at the time, he couldn't play well at all.'

'Mikey had a great record collection but had no idea how to play bass,' says Rickly. 'He knew his brother was on to something so he found a way to be a part of it.'

Mikey almost admits as much: 'I was petrified. I didn't know what I was doing; I was just going on instinct and playing from the heart. It was all new to me – I had only really fiddled around with guitars and bass in my parents' basement and then here I was in a proper recording studio. It was a little scary.'

But while Mikey may not have been much of a musician, he did have a clear idea of what the band should sound like. 'We always said things like, "Wouldn't it be great if Glenn Danzig was in The Smiths or if Morrissey was in the Misfits?"' Perhaps more importantly, he also played a crucial role in keeping studio morale high.

'Mikey was definitely the saviour of that whole recording session,' Naclerio says. 'His musicianship maybe wasn't as good as everybody else's but it meant that we all got behind him. Everyone would all cheer after every song he completed, like, "Mikey's doing it again!" He was so likeable and everyone wanted things to work for him, so we all cheered him on. He was very light-hearted and easygoing all session long, so he definitely helped keep the mood up.'

There was a bigger problem, though. Matt 'Otter' Pelissier refused to use a click track, the metronomic device drummers often use in the studio to keep time. As a result, the songs would speed up and slow down as Pelissier played. At the time it was frustrating, though later Ray was diplomatic about it.

'You can hear the nervousness and excitement on that record,' he said in 2011, thinking back to that time. 'Every track would speed up because Otter wasn't playing to a click track. I think the songs have a lot of character as a result.'

Saavedra is more outspoken and critical of Pelissier not using the click track. 'Thank God for Ray. Ray saved the day on that record – he's the reason they were so tight because he followed Matt's beat. But the timing is so off on that record, it speeds up and slows down, the tempo is on and off.'

Rickly was equally unimpressed with the drummer, but says the band were determined to stick with him because he was a friend. 'I even told them that they should probably spend more time rehearsing before we went into the studio or consider the fact that they probably wouldn't go very far with that drummer,' he said. 'They said, "No, he's our buddy." And drummers are hard to find anyway, so they didn't want to give him up.'

Saavedra says he attempted to convince My Chemical Romance

that they should simply re-record Pelissier's parts without telling him, using Naclerio, who was an accomplished drummer. 'We were going to sneak back in at night and re-track everything but Ray wouldn't let us,' says Saavedra. 'We would have told [Pelissier] that we had cut it up in Pro-Tools, he would have had no idea. We totally could have bullshitted him: "Yeah, yeah, this is all you, man. We just cleaned it up a little." But Ray was really adamantly against it.'

Naclerio doesn't remember it that way. Though he says that Pelissier 'might have been the hardest member of the band to record because he was so headstrong', he adds that that's the case with most drummers. 'He was definitely combative,' he says, 'but to say he was a bad drummer is wrong. He was a great drummer. Some drummers can have a perfectly tuned kit but that doesn't make any difference if they can't play good in the first place. This guy could have had a drum-kit that wasn't tuned at all and he still would have made them sound good. I don't remember Alex asking me to play drums on the record, to be honest.'

Asked for his thoughts on this, Pelissier declined to comment, but it is clear he did not agree with the criticisms.

If Pelissier and Mikey's playing needed massaging, one person who shone in the studio was Gerard. His talent was to have an eye for the bigger picture. Though My Chemical Romance were a fledgling band, recording in a basement and signed to a small independent label, he saw them operating on a grand scale.

'I wanted it to be more than a band,' he said. 'It was supposed to be this really intense art project because I didn't have an outlet creatively. The band was all I had. So titles of short stories I had written ended up being album and song titles: 'I Brought You My Bullets', for example.

In the studio, he was developing a trick that would come to define his songwriting. Like an actor, he was learning to create characters to inhabit in his songs. Once inside them, he would write stylized lyrics as if from their point of view and then act them out when he was recording. It was a process that Saavedra's punch had accelerated when 'Vampires' convinced Gerard of how powerful the results could be.

So he poured his emotions into the stories and then into the recordings too – 'I was always singing cranked to eleven and never backed off.' Largely, he was writing explicitly about himself but he would mask this by incorporating characters into his lyrics, and later he claimed that the album was a concept record based on two Bonnie and Clyde-style lovers. Rickly encouraged Gerard's invention, realizing that the characters were essentially masks from behind which he could write about his true feelings.

'Early on, I told Gerard that he should think of his band like a comic book,' says Rickly. 'He was a great artist and was so imaginative that I thought he should draw himself a character and draw his band as a scene.'

Gerard did not need much encouragement. On 'Vampires Will Never Hurt You', he had already brought in gothic imagery and with the *Dawn Of The Dead*-inspired zombies of 'Early Sunsets over Monroeville' he added more dark, comic book ideas – themes which would come to define the band. '"Vampires Will Never Hurt You" gave us a real sense of identity,' Gerard said later. 'It brought in the entire gothic thing. It was those songs that made people think we were a vampire band.'

Elsewhere, with the doomed romance of 'Drowning Lessons' and the revenge drama of 'Our Lady of Sorrows', Gerard sought both to define and to find metaphors for the dark forces (dejection, nihilism and rejection) that had sent him into his parents' basement with his notebooks. On 'Honey, this Mirror Isn't Big Enough for the Two of Us', he writes about swallowing anti-depression pills and guzzling booze and lays into his own body image, but he layers the song in rich imagery.

'Gerard is so smart that he made each of his songs into a comic book and an allegory,' says Rickly. 'There's the superficial theme to it – whether that's vampires or whatever – and behind that, the song is actually about something more personal, like how he's afraid that his little brother might get AIDS or something like that. Everything had deeper meaning.'

Alex Saavedra had worked with a lot of bands before, including Rickly's Thursday. But he had never seen anything like Gerard in the studio. 'He really brings those characters in his songs to life. Every word he writes is so important to him – he puts so much into them and they take so much out of him. He has a knack for making things come alive.'

Rickly thinks it was Gerard's performance that made *I Brought You My Bullets, You Brought Me Your Love*. 'He never shied away from using his deepest fears,' he says. 'That's the one thing I think we really brought out of him on that first recording. They weren't the greatest songs, they didn't sound great and there are some parts that might be cheesy, but there's real emotional honesty there.

'Once I realized what Gerard had in front of a microphone, I thought, "Wow. Let's go." His melodies were very repetitive at first. He'd sing something, then I'd suggest something else to him. Instantly he'd rip into something completely new that was better than either of our first efforts. I'd sit back and go "Wow" again. There was a level of humanity in there that meant people would be able to relate to them more than anyone would ever be able to relate to our music [in Thursday]. I'd never seen that in a person before.'

The recording of 'Early Sunsets over Monroeville' was a case in point. As the song built from tender ballad to something darker and angrier, Rickly saw that Gerard had accessed something very personal. 'Just go with what's inside your head. Don't even listen to the music,' said the producer. Gerard took his advice and howls his way through the song in an emotionally charged performance.

'Afterwards, everybody just left and went outside to smoke cigarettes because they couldn't deal with looking at him after he had sung that,' says Rickly. 'He had just ripped himself open in front of everybody. He'd taken it so far that it was uncomfortable for anyone who was friends with him. They hadn't seen him as Gerard the singer, they still saw him as their buddy Gerard. It's a little scary to see someone do what he did.'

Naclerio believes that Rickly was just as important a cog in the machine as Gerard's passion and Ray's musicianship. 'He kept everyone grounded and focused and was especially good with Gerard,' he says. 'He was very hands-on with him because Gerard was absolutely going for it. He was doing whatever he thought was good, even if it wasn't sometimes, and Geoff was able to get him to take a step back and listen to what he was doing. Then they would work on it together to improve it.'

The combination was a powerful one and Rickly was quickly impressed with My Chemical Romance's potential, even if they didn't realize it themselves. He turned to Mikey at one point in the sessions and told him as much.

'If you stick with this, you're going to be the biggest band in the world,' he said.

Mikey laughed and blushed.

'Seriously, Thursday can never be as big as My Chem can be,' Rickly insisted.

Mikey told him he was being ridiculous, but Rickly was convinced. Saavedra knew too and, once he had stopped being delighted for his friends, he began to rib Rickly mercilessly that My Chemical Romance were going to far outstrip Thursday.

'Geoff and I had a conversation pretty soon afterwards,' says Saavedra. 'I remember teasing him, going, "My Chem are going to be headlining over you pretty soon. You're going to be opening for these guys. You just dug your own grave! You fucked up! You should have sunk that production. Thursday is doomed." He was like, "I know, man! They're going to destroy us!"

'But that's what we wanted – we wanted the people around us to be successful; we've always wanted that. I loved the fact Eyeball was a stepping stone for so many artists, it was really great.'

The only problem they had was a lack of time. 'It felt as if we abandoned it, rather than finished it,' says Naclerio. 'But then everybody has their budgets and time constraints so we did as much as we could. Having said that, I always thought we could have done something better if we had had more time – but I'm incredibly proud of what we did given the time we had. Could it have been better? Of course, but I have no regrets.'

Nor did the band. They were delighted with what they had done, playing it constantly to anyone who would listen.

'I thought it sounded fucking great, I was really proud of it,' said Ray. 'To think that we had actually written a record was pretty amazing to us. I was used to recording maybe three songs at most. A record was beyond our wildest dreams.'

For all the potential of *I Brought You My Bullets, You Brought Me Your Love*, it was an album that struggled for direction. Written in a whirl, recorded in a rush and played by a young band who were still gelling, this was hardly a surprise. Furthermore, My Chemical Romance were still not entirely sure who they wanted to be – hence there are elements of Britpop, the influence of The Smiths, and Ray's classic metal and the punk and hardcore of the New Jersey scene. The return is an album that lacks focus. Which is not to say it wasn't good.

Released on 23 July 2002, it went under the radar critically. In the US, the one magazine that might have been expected to fall upon it – *Alternative Press* – did not review it and a host of others did not include it either. But the notices were glowing in the rock magazines that did pick up on it. Rae Alexandra's *Kerrang!* review pointed out that 'Gerard Way is open in interviews about the fact he's got some problems. He'll admit freely that his band is therapy. But nothing prepares you for his contributions to *I Brought You My Bullets*. Way's vocals are one part vicious attack, one part desperate plea and one part nervous breakdown. Whiny emo this ain't – murder, vampires, ghosts, suicide, drug dependency – they're all here . . . almost everything here is done at breakneck speed; secondly "everything" really is everything. Razor-sharp metal riffs, bouncy punk melodies, hardcore breaks and post-hardcore intricacies cling to each other, tugging at heartstrings while avoiding cliché. My Chemical Romance are astonishing. And they are going to be huge.'

Oddly, given that many specialist music magazines failed to review it, the *Guardian* – a British broadsheet newspaper not normally given to reviewing the debuts of underground US punk bands – did pick up on it. Caroline Sullivan was scathing of the 'self absorbed "emo" angst' and somehow compared the band to the vastly dissimilar nu-metallers Korn ('the ensuing whinge-athon makes contemporaries such as Korn look the picture of emotional health'), yet she still realized the vitality and urgency of Gerard's vocals and the thrill of the music, even if she assumed the vitriol would be more at home in a keep-fit class. 'If Way is just acting, he's bloody convincing,' she wrote. 'The plus side is that the relentlessly frenetic pace, coupled with melodic melodies ("Vampires Will Never Hurt You" is the juiciest tune the Ramones never wrote), leaves you feeling like you've just had the most vigorous gym workout.'

In a lot of other magazines, though, the debut of an unknown punk band on a small-scale label simply went ignored. It would not be long, however, until those magazines would change their minds about My Chemical Romance.

5: HEADFIRST FOR HALOS

Alex Saavedra's strategy for breaking a new band was tried and tested. He would mount an extensive mailing campaign, sending off copies of the album to radio stations, DJs, journalists and promoters, and he began that process with *I Brought You My Bullets, You Brought Me Your Love*. He was acutely aware that for a band to have credibility within the snobbish Jersey scene, they had to have had success outside of it. However, he was surprised when My Chemical Romance bucked that trend.

'You had to break on the other side of the country before anyone gave a shit about you in your own back yard,' he says. 'My Chem, however, were the first and possibly only band to break locally here in Jersey before breaking on a countrywide or worldwide level.'

He gives a lot of the credit to the influential local DJ and scene stalwart the late Mario Comesanas. He used his *Under the Stars* slot on the South Orange, New Jersey college-radio station WSOU to air 'Vampires' for the first time.

Comesanas, who was also first to play Thursday on the radio, remembered the response was overwhelming. 'The reaction was ridiculous – I knew that there was something special here,' he said. 'When we counted the requests, there was so much more for them than there was for any other band at that time.'

Saavedra noticed the reaction too and decided to capitalize on it. 'College radio started picking up on it because we hired someone to run a campaign for us,' he says. 'We ended up hiring them to come and work for us full time. We needed it because, as My Chem grew, so did the label. But really, the thing that got My Chem to grow was when fans started picking up on them; then their friends would follow suit.'

That was a process that started happening when the band went out on the road. Saavedra was their de facto manager then, largely because he ran the label that had put out their record. His strategy to further raise My Chemical Romance's profile was not complicated: he shoved them out on tour as quickly and frequently as possible.

'It was the same with any band on the label – you'd just take any tour you could get, especially if it was an overseas tour, because those were really hard to come by,' he says. 'It grew pretty rapidly for My Chem. It went from being pretty sporadic, to a lot of shows that were just in the north-east area in garages, Masonic halls and the Loop Lounge. Six months later, they were playing around the world. It was pretty amazing.'

My Chemical Romance, for their part, were equally delighted to be on tour. 'It was about survival, basically,' said Gerard. 'We wanted to do enough that we could get gas and food to get to the next city and play another show. It was about not having to go home and work in that shitty job again. If you're good at something that you love to do, then that's your reward. If you get to put a roof over your head, even if it's a small roof, then you're doing OK.'

One key early show was in Pennsylvania at the Allentown Fairground. Frank would write a blog post about it nine years later calling it their 'big break moment'. A band they all idolized, Jimmy Eat World, were set to headline the show with the prog-punk of Coheed and Cambria as support. At the last minute, though, Coheed were forced to pull out and My Chemical Romance – who were then playing dive venues – got what Frank described as a 'magical' phone call to fill in and play to the biggest crowd they had ever faced.

'The night before, we had played a weird basement in Philly,' said Frank. 'There were three people there, one of who was a homeless guy with a tape recorder on a rope around his neck. He recorded our set and tried to sell it to us afterwards. Another of the people in that fucking room was a representative from a label [Mike Gitter,

A&R for Roadrunner Records]. Then the next day we played this huge show and there were thousands of people there.'

At first they were intimidated, but Frank said it was not long before they realized something was happening. 'Halfway through the first song, this weird pogo started and, by the end, we had won that crowd over,' he recalled. 'I will never forget that feeling. That was the first time any of us had ever played a show that big and it was the first time we ever got that connection with a crowd. Someone taped it and I lost my mind; I couldn't believe we had done that. It was a definite vote of confidence for us. But did I ever think it would get bigger than that? No. That was also the day I signed my first autograph and I felt really weird about it.'

Frank was in a good position to gauge My Chemical Romance's tentative first steps. Having released a record through Eyeball already with Pencey Prep, he had a point of comparison when *Bullets* came out.

'It definitely felt different than the Pencey album,' he said. 'Pencey recorded in about five days, we put together a record and it came out . . . kind of. You know, there wasn't a release party or anything like that. We basically just went on tour and tried to just sell copies. We only sold about a hundred copies but that was huge to us, it was awesome.

'So with My Chem, it was completely different. People were already psyched about hearing what we had put together; it felt like something had already started when we put the record out. Put it this way, we sold a hundred copies at the release party! So it was a lot different to Pencey – even just to the point we actually had a release party.

'And that's when the real touring started too. With Pencey, we'd pull up in a town and we'd try to meet some cool, punk-rock kid who might have a show, or might have known of a show, and we'd hopefully just be able to come along to the gig and play too. The aim was just to make gas money but we hardly ever did. With MCR we had a booking agent – so we knew there were actually shows at the end of the drive and that was such a relief to me.'

Matt Galle was that booking agent. He would go on to become an influential industry figure and work with the likes of Bruno Mars and Ke$ha, but then he was a Massachusetts promoter who ran a music festival and agency in Boston. He came across My Chemical Romance thanks to Geoff Rickly.

'I was very close with the group Thursday,' says Galle. 'I had put on a lot of their shows in the north-east in Massachusetts, Rhode Island and Connecticut. Thursday's singer handed me this demo and said he had just produced this new band from New Jersey. He thought they were great but said Thursday's agent didn't want to take on any new stuff right then. He wanted someone to book their shows.

'He gave me the demo, I really liked it and I wanted to see them live so I put them on my festival, Skatefest. It wasn't their first show but it was an early one. I still have the poster of that show because I thought they were so great. They were really energetic and, though the crowd hadn't heard them or even heard *of* them before, they got wholly engaged. Even at the time, Gerard was owning the audience. He had them eating out of the palm of his hand.

'They were really amazing that day and so I wanted to be involved. I called them a couple of days later and told them I wanted to do it. They talked it over, called me back and said they wanted me to be the guy.'

At first though, he struggled to find a place for My Chemical Romance – Frank recalls Galle telling them, 'You don't sound like anybody.' Their first tour was with a band called North Star but Galle would put them on any bill that had an opening – often irrespective of the style of music the headliners were playing.

'He tried everything – sometimes it worked, sometimes it didn't,' said Gerard. 'We played with Christian bands, metal bands, hardcore bands, indie bands, anyone.'

'It was trial and error at that point,' says Galle. 'We put them on with American Nightmare, who were a hardcore band, then [the metalcore band] Underoath or [the post-hardcore] Static Lullaby. They just wanted to work, they wanted to go out there and play. So we tried to keep them busy constantly. The goal was to keep them away from home and on the road because their live show was so good. They were winning everyone over too. We were like, "Let's see what crowds you work to, man. Let's see how far we can take this." It was fun too and they were down for it. They wanted to win over audiences.'

'The point was just to go out on the road as much as possible,' said Frank. 'We'd just be going round asking, "Do you have a show? Does anyone have a show? Put us on it, we'll open for any-fucking-body, any-fucking-where. We don't give a shit, just let us play." We would play anywhere because it was all we had.

'Thursday were one of the best live bands I have ever seen and I remember one show in particular at a VFW Hall before I joined My Chem and just before [2001's breakthrough album] *Full Collapse* came out. It was insane. Kids were just losing their minds. I wanted that so bad. I wanted that give and take from the crowd. That's all I ever wanted. I wanted to get in a van and go. I wanted to play shows in cities I had read about in books. I knew that if I could do that with my life, I would be completely fulfilled. I just wanted to be in a band that meant something. Stadiums? That never felt plausible. That was never on the radar.'

Most nights, they would be playing to a very small crowd – and one largely only there for the headliners or because My Chemical Romance were from the respected Jersey scene. It was far from easy: on the tour with Underoath, they would beg the headliners for T-shirts from their merch stall, simply because they didn't have enough clean clothes to wear. But they kept at it and, while the crowds may not have swelled exactly, they did grow. It was not glamorous, but then that was never the point.

'I remember some of those early tours,' said Frank years later. 'I remember staying in a [cheap motel chain] Knights Inn and the door wouldn't close. We had to push the dresser against the door and we were all sharing the same bed.'

'That's right,' laughed Mikey. 'We'd send one person in to get the room, then we'd all sneak in when no one was looking.'

'It would just be the five of us,' added Gerard. 'But occasionally we'd force a friend to suffer for us and act like a tour manager. His only job, really, was to call ahead and ask for chips, salsa and water.'

Galle remembers those early shows as ferocious. 'They would go off as hard as they could, they would break stuff and, every night, it became about how to one-up the show, how to make it grow as the tour and the venues grew,' he says.

Having the Eyeball stamp of approval was a boost, as was being backed by Rickly who was then probably the figurehead for the whole post-hardcore movement. While some bands may have struggled for attention in an area congested by so many good bands, My Chemical Romance began to break clear.

Their early small audiences saw something in them: kindred spirits whose songs made it clear that they were just as much of a mess as their audience. Part of the appeal of the band was that they were not only able to articulate the frustration of small-town US life but also to provide escape through their dark, vampiric imagery.

'The way it snowballed was this – we would play at these shows and we wouldn't fit in,' said Frank. 'There would be kids there who didn't fit in either and they latched onto us. They would tell their friends who didn't fit in and it would build and build from there. Suddenly a whole bunch of kids who didn't fit in would come to our show and they would find somewhere they could be themselves because we were just the same as them.'

He says the band began to feel as though they were a voice for disaffected loners, for the socially awkward, for anyone who was different.

'Yes, because we were the same,' said Frank. 'We were being spat on and had people making fun of us too. We dealt with it by not caring or by allowing it to fuel us. We felt that was important and we felt we were doing something important by saying it was OK not to fit in. That gave other kids who felt the same way a voice and that was fucking awesome. Those are the kids who are going to rule the world one day. If we can make people feel like they're worth something, then our job is done.'

Frank fell in love with the road immediately, and in an act of commitment to it and rebellion from ordinary life, got a tattoo of a scorpion as high up on his neck as he could so that he couldn't cover it up with a collar. In this way, he hoped to ensure that he would never be able to get a nine-to-five job, even if the band failed. 'My dad freaked out,' he admitted.

But it was slowly becoming clear that My Chemical Romance were not going to fail. Gerard saw that, when they played with other bands, they would have their own support group among the crowd – fans who were there for them alone.

'I began to notice a division in the crowd,' he said. 'We might only have had five or ten people there to see us, but they were five or ten people who liked us like no one else. They were ours. And none of them would hang out with each other. They'd all stand in separate corners.'

The more they played, the more they settled into their sound. The longer they were out on the road, the closer they bonded. It led to an us-against-them attitude. For Gerard, in particular, going on tour was like going to war. They had to go out and slay every night.

'The one thing I have to stress about the beginning of the band was that, to the people inside, it was a pretty magic thing,' he said. 'We felt like we were on fire, that nobody could touch us. Nobody could figure out what we sounded like, they just knew they liked it. We would just roll into a place and play and, by the end of the set, there was broken glass and things that had been destroyed everywhere.

'During one show at the Loop Lounge I flung myself against the air-conditioner; I was slamming my body and face into everything. I was very self-destructive back then but there was a charm to it. There was this energy surrounding us – we were like a gang. We were up against the whole nation, the whole world. It was us versus the world.

'I had watched a Ramones documentary and it was dead-on accurate as to how you feel when you start a band – you feel like a gang, you're totally stand-offish, you only hang out with each other, you all look the same and nobody can approach you because they're either afraid or they think you're assholes. That's how we were back then. We were a gang.'

There was an irony here, of course. One of the inspirations behind forming a band in the first place was because they felt as though they were outcasts, unwelcome in Jersey. They hoped that, after long drives through the night, they would find like-minded people in venues and might no longer feel so alienated. It didn't quite work like that. 'Not at all,' said Gerard. 'We were idealistic. Then we went out and realized there weren't many other people like us. So we went to war with them.'

Unusually for a touring rock band – though not so much, perhaps, for a post-hardcore band guided by punk ethics – they had little interest in girls on the road and were dismissive of those who were less abstemious.

'We disagreed with groupies, we disagreed with how some promoters were, and it all went into our band and allowed us to shape ourselves,' said Gerard. 'We'd love some bands we toured with and we'd hate some others. We'd hear bands complain about us, which would make us hate them even more.

'I'm not saying we didn't enjoy ourselves though. It was a chance to see more of the world too. Before that, we'd barely been out of Jersey, so it developed our perspective too. It was a learning experience and built our characters up too.'

It stimulated the outcast spirit that drove them in the early days and continued to do so for much of their career. 'That started to fuel the shows,' said Mikey. 'That adversity gave us an edge that nobody else had.'

'Whenever you put five guys on the road, it's them versus the world,' agreed Frank. 'Especially when you're playing in front of a crowd every night. You have to think of even your fans as the opposition. Your show is a game that you have to win. We went up onstage to kill everybody. No one stood in our way and the five of us were there to destroy every person in that room. That's the way we went onstage every night. To kill everyone.'

This attitude would come to define their touring. Even years later, they would liken being on the road to being at war, while that defiant approach was a mentality that remained with them until at least the end of the touring cycle for their third record *The Black Parade*.

But as they played those early shows, gradually more fans joined them. Those supporters adopted exactly the same way of thinking as the band, meaning My Chemical Romance's crowd may have been small but it was fiercely loyal. And those fans would tell their friends, who would tell their friends too, until the band had built up an incredibly supportive network.

'I watched a kid clock another kid right in the face one night in Atlanta because he'd been having a go at us,' said Gerard of that time. 'He just hit him, and the other kid shut the fuck up. It was kind of awesome.

'We were there to represent those people who didn't have a scene or who were sick of that bullshit. We were there for those kids who'd get shoved because they didn't have the right scene clothes, or the right Mohawk. They were safe for the half-hour that we were playing. And if they didn't feel safe, they would lash out at other kids.'

'It was great to see these outcasts finally finding a place,' said Frank. 'That was when we realized that there were people like us out there – it's just that they were in the crowd, rather than in some of the bands we looked up to. We didn't set out to be that, we didn't try to be marauding for the underdogs. We were never trying to be superheroes or role models. But to feel that we were looking out for kids that don't have anyone else to look out for them felt pretty good. I wish I'd had people like that when I grew up. Then again, it was a weird position to be in because we were kids, just like them, and we didn't have all the answers.'

As the intensity of support from their fans grew, it inspired the band. For the five of them, this was the first time they had achieved anything. Gerard was fresh from his rejection from the world of comic books, Mikey and Frank had dropped out of college, Ray was well aware that he was a long way off from being a film editor, while Matt Pelissier had little else going on but the band. For the first time, as crowds sang their lyrics back to them, they realized that there was something they excelled at.

'It felt good to prove people wrong,' said Frank. 'People would tell me I would never make it; they would say the band would never make it, three times a day. But you can't take it to heart. The people that tell you that are only saying it because they didn't succeed. They're working a shitty nine-to-five that they hate and they'll be doing it for the rest of their lives and they want everyone else to be unhappy too.'

Slowly, they did find bands that they shared a spirit with. They made firm friends with The Used – whose self-titled 2002 debut had put them on the brink of real mainstream success. It was The Used's tour manager Brian Schechter who first picked up on My Chemical Romance. Though young, he was an experienced hand on the circuit and was ambitious and forceful. He had been impressed by *Bullets*, and had seen My Chemical Romance firsthand when they had supported The Used in Chicago in November 2002. He suggested to The Used's singer Bert McCracken that they should take them on tour in February 2003. It would be the start of an important bond and The Used were quick to take My Chemical Romance under their wing – something that undeniably helped the smaller band's profile.

In fact, Gerard and Bert formed a fast friendship, the pair of them similarly charismatic, self-destructive and quick to reach for a drink. They would go on to have an intense, dangerous friendship. One minute they might wander out onstage together to duet, the next they might kiss for the cameras.

During that first tour with The Used, My Chemical Romance flourished. Although Eyeball didn't have the distribution of a big label – which meant *Bullets*' sales were modest as it wasn't always easy to find – Schechter was keeping an eye on both the crowd reaction and the amount of merch the support band were selling. He was impressed. 'They just slowly started winning new fans and selling more merch,' he said. 'That's really how you could put it in a barometer of seeing what was working. The more merch they sold, the bigger their band was.'

Impressed, Schechter offered to become their manager and My Chemical Romance accepted. If they thought they had toured hard until then, they would now find out what touring hard really meant. Schechter packed them out on the road in March 2003 – this time to Europe, again in support of The Used. It was hell.

'It was awful,' said Frank. 'Our first trip to the UK and Europe was fucking terrible. Part of us was thinking, "Oh my God, we're here!" The other part was thinking, "This is fucking terrible."'

They could not afford the UK tour, so their new manager funded the trip by sinking his life savings into it. It meant there was little extra cash for luxuries – not even a European road map to help them get around. They were crammed into one van, all the gear piled in with them. Alongside the band were their tour manager, Eddie, who was also their guitar tech, drum tech and everything else, and a friend, Sean, who was selling their merch.

Eyeball's Alex Saavedra had gone along with them too, partly because he could drive. 'That whole tour was funny because not only were we driving a stick shift for the first time, everything was on the wrong side,' he says. 'We almost crashed so many times. It was so surreal. And our reaction every time was to just laugh. We were driving on the wrong side of the road, people were coming head on at us, and we were just laughing like a bunch of fucking idiots. What were we thinking? Why did we think we could drive ourselves around the UK in a manual van?'

Their tour started in Wolverhampton at Wulfrun Hall on 2 March 2003 and the band would play London, Cologne, Amsterdam, Hamburg, Barcelona and Madrid in seven dates over the next fortnight. The first show itself was fine, with little to distinguish it other than the fact it was My Chemical Romance's first performance outside the US. What happened afterwards, though, would make it more memorable.

'I'll never forget the Wolverhampton show,' says Saavedra. 'It was right after George W Bush had got us involved in another war [the 2003 invasion of Iraq] and there was an anti-war rally going on next door to the gig. I went down to a cafe to get a drink and catch up on some work and the people in the rally thought that we were pro-war because we were American. So they set our bus on fire.

'But what they didn't realize was that we didn't have any money and we were driving a splitter van – we didn't have a bus. So, what they had actually done was set somebody else's bus on fire, somebody who was nothing to do with the show. We drove away in our splitter, going, "Wow – that was fucked up."'

A narrow escape. Yet, chaotic though the short European tour with The Used was, they noticed that the same thing was happening there as in the States: sections of the crowd were beginning to be there exclusively for them rather than the headliners. It was at the end of the tour in Spain, after more hair-raising driving, that they had something like an epiphany.

'We were in Spain, lost, and with one map, which was of the UK anyway,' said Frank. 'We were in a UK van with the steering wheel on the wrong side, but now we were in Europe so the wheel was even more on the wrong side. We also had our friend Sean selling merch with us. Halfway through the trip Sean lost his shoes and flipped out, so he was going mad. It was fucking terrible.

'But, from the get-go, the shows were awesome. That's the only reason I didn't phone my mom and go, "Come get me." Kids were singing along, pounding their fists. Our last show was in Spain and there were kids there from Portugal with homemade My Chemical Romance T-shirts. That was amazing. We felt like we were really doing something important and, from that point, there was no turning back . . . just as long as we could survive the fucking tour!'

They returned to the US scarred but jubilant; the experience of touring abroad had pumped them up. Immediately, they went out on the road with another band they would come to bond with – Taking

Back Sunday. All the time, they were learning their tradecraft from the headliners and, if they were honest, attempting to blow them off the stage each night.

'There was a healthy competition,' said Frank. 'If you tour with friends like Taking Back Sunday, you see how the fans react because they're such a good live band. Backstage it's all buddy-buddy but when we get onstage it's like, "Right, now it's our turn." I think that's the way they see it too. It makes you play better – we brought out the best in each other because we were pushing each other harder each day. It's all about giving everything you've got – seeing how much they kicked ass and how much better you're going to have to be to live up to that. We learned a lot from those tours.'

And part of what they learned was that they wanted to move on to the next level. My Chemical Romance knew they wanted to be big.

There was something else creeping into the lives of at least two of My Chemical Romance at that point. While the support of their growing legion of fans provided inspiration, and their defiant mind-set offered a little more, both Gerard and Mikey were increasingly leaning on alcohol while they toured.

It was beer that got them onstage for their first ever show, and it was still proving to be a crutch. Both brothers would drink to build themselves up. Then, when they left the stage, they would drink some more to help them come back down. And, when they found themselves with time to spare in a strange town, it offered an immediate end to their boredom.

'You would be amazed that, most of the time, it's easier to get beer than water on tour,' said Gerard. 'It's just easier to get warm-assed beer than anything else. So we would drink. It was a boredom killer and that's where things started getting serious. The only thing that was important to me was the half-hour we had onstage – that was the only thing that mattered to me, everything else was bullshit. We were still a gang and very antisocial so I would spend the rest of my day staring at a wall before we went on. I started drinking to kill that boredom.'

As well as offering an escape, alcohol helped him re-inhabit the characters in his songs, offering access onstage to the dark thoughts and strange moods that had informed his songwriting. Afterwards, it became a means to blocking them out again. 'The music was so intense; it was about a lot of dark, fucked-up things and I realized that I had to live through them again every time we played,' he said. 'That's why I was drinking. It never felt like I was partying; it felt like I was coping, killing time, then decompressing so I could pass out.'

It helped that drinking fed into Gerard's singer fantasy: there was undeniably a part of him that enjoyed playing the role of the doomed, debauched, self-destructive frontman. Drinking was something that helped form that character.

For Mikey, though, the drinking was just something he did. It was something he had always done, in fact, ever since the days he would hang around the Eyeball house. But on the early tours, it became part of his routine. 'I don't ever remember really enjoying it,' he said. 'It was just a means to an end. I was still so nervous to get onstage then so I would drink, and I missed being at home which didn't help. It was all new to us.'

Gerard believes that another thing to blame for his boozing was the fact that their early successes offered no guarantees. Though their record had been well received, and though their audience was growing, he still felt there was a good chance the band might not make it despite his wholehearted belief in it.

'There was the stress too,' he said. 'We didn't know whether this would work, we didn't know what we would be doing with our lives. We knew we wanted it, but we still weren't sure it was going to happen.'

Mikey puts it better: 'We felt like we were on a pirate ship with no destination. We were just going and going and going.'

Increasingly, though, they were getting somewhere. The more they played, the better the bands were that they played with –

touring with Alkaline Trio was a particular high for them, while Taking Back Sunday and bands like fellow New Jerseyites Senses Fail became regular road buddies. It not only helped My Chemical Romance develop but increasingly placed them in front of bigger, more important crowds. And with that, came buzz and hype.

From even the earliest days, there was something about My Chemical Romance. It's why they were able to record their debut so soon after they formed. That, and being part of the hot Jersey scene, meant that word soon spread. They had long been used to A&R men sniffing around. 'You couldn't walk down a street without having a major label A&R jump out from an alleyway,' remembered Frank. And those talent scouts had really got hold of their scent during the spring and summer of 2003.

'We were getting phone calls from labels way too early on,' said Frank. 'It didn't make us feel good, it made us feel kinda gross. We wanted to be a band for a while. It definitely felt uncool. We told most of them to back off but we kept in touch with some of the ones we liked – like Mike Gitter. There were some who were cool guys and got it, but there were some who wanted to take you out for drinks and tell you how rich they could make you. That was always strange to us.'

Alex Saavedra watched on with a mixture of pride and pain as the young band he had signed, nurtured and developed was romanced away from him by major labels.

'It wasn't the first time a band was poached from us. I hated it,' he says. 'It was all bullshit. It was completely insane. But on the other hand, I didn't want to hold them back. I would never do that to my friends. I wasn't the sort of person to say, "You've got to hang out with us because, if you're getting big, then we want to get big with you." No, we were cool where we were. We were happy and I was really proud of them. But if I were to tell you that process was awesome and stress-free, I would be a total liar.'

'Everybody was flying out to try and see their shows,' says Galle. 'Everyone was promising them things; they all had ideas for them. Honestly, I just said to them that they should go wherever they felt they fitted. I said they should meet with everybody and that they would just know who the right people were. In the meantime, I tried to keep them busy, to put them in front of audiences to build their fanbase.'

The band found themselves being taken out to dinner by A&Rs and promised the world, after which they would trundle back from the nice restaurants to their van, still dressed in their sweaty road clothes. The difference between the world they were being offered and the one they lived in was stark for all to see.

'Some of it was hilarious,' says Saavedra. 'I won't tell you the name of the A&R man, or where he worked, but this guy took us all out to dinner at this Chinese place in Philadelphia before a My Chem show. He was a nice guy, who had been in an indie band earlier in his life, and he was talking a great game. He kept saying, "I'm with you guys, we're all struggling, so drink as much as you want – we can burn the label card up tonight." All night, he was telling us that he was cool, that he was with us. It turned out he was staying in the Four Seasons! We were all sleeping on the floor of someone's one-bedroom apartment. He wasn't with us at all. I was the one who was there, I was sleeping on the goddamn floor with the band – he was sleeping in the Four Seasons.'

Craig Aaronson was one of the first A&R men to come and see them. A former drummer, he had signed the influential post-hardcore band At The Drive-In to Grand Royal before joining Warner Bros. Once there he carved out quite a niche, signing The Used, The Distillers, Glassjaw, and he would go on to sign Avenged Sevenfold, Taking Back Sunday and Against Me! among others. He clearly had good ears. He found out about My Chemical Romance through Bert McCracken and Brian Schechter and flew out to New York to see them play in a dive club to a tiny crowd. He was immediately blown away.

'I didn't care how many people were there, I just knew they were really, really good,' says Aaronson. 'Gerard just had this look in his eye – it probably only lasted for twenty seconds – but it made me realize that they were a band I absolutely had to work with. I saw that glimmer, and I realized he had so much to say. They were so real and visceral to me. I had signed At The Drive-In earlier and this band made me feel the same way. There was such a passionate energy – and it was something you could feel rather than something you had to think about. It gave me the chills. It was an easy decision from then on: I thought, "No matter what it takes, I've got to sign this band." It took me another year because they were very coy about signing to a major.'

Aaronson continued to chase them, but at a distance. He was aware that they were wary of major labels and that a heavy-handed approach would scare them off. But he was also determined that they would sign for him. His approach was to let them know how impressed he was by their vision and to say that Warners would allow that to flourish.

'They were definitely a band who wanted to make their own path,' he says. 'They didn't want a strong arm to push them into a direction they weren't comfortable with. If they were ever going to step into another label, they needed to feel they were in trustworthy hands and that people were going to allow them to see their vision through. I wanted to get behind that. They finally surrendered to my persistence. I really wasn't going to let go because I was so committed to working for them and to protecting them from the stuff that happens at major labels.'

It probably helped that he wasn't one of the A&R men to go around buying them expensive meals in fancy restaurants. Quite the opposite, in fact.

'I think Craig Aaronson only ever took us to I-Hop [the cheap and cheerful American diner chain],' said Frank. 'One day we were hanging out with him and he asked if we wanted dinner, so we went for pizza. His credit card got refused, so I had to pay for it! But that's how we wanted it – the most impressive thing [an A&R man] could do for us was to understand where we were coming from and to bring us some cool CDs.'

My Chemical Romance eventually spoke to three or four of the A&R men who had been in touch since the very early days and made a decision in August 2003. They would sign with Aaronson, on the Warner Bros offshoot Reprise, home also to Green Day and Deftones. 'We decided it was about the label as a whole and every-one that works there,' said Frank. 'So that's why we decided on Warners because we felt they had the team that got us the best. The people there cared about the art of it and there were people there on our team that really got us and loved the band almost as much as we did. It was what I had always wanted from any label.'

As a result of Saavedra's consideration they parted from Eyeball as friends, but still Gerard in particular was worried about what their fans might think. After all, the band that those fans had fallen in love with was underground, close-knit and readily available to talk to after shows. Those fans might be suspicious that, once they were signed to a major rather than an indie, that would change. So Gerard took matters into his own hands and wrote an open letter on the band's website. He did so in typically defiant style.

'Dear friends, let this be a declaration and a threat,' he wrote. 'This is how I wanted to write this, just having played a show, with everything on fire. My insides, my brain, and in the pit of my heart it burns. There are some things I need to say and there are some things you need to know.

'We started this band for ourselves, to bare our souls, purge our own personal demons, and reclaim our innocence. When you are told you are not good enough your entire life sometimes the only thing you can do is scream "fuck you" at the top of your lungs. This band was started and will end with three virtues: Honesty, Sincerity, and Loyalty. You will hear these three words in any interview we give because it is what we stand for. Right now we're in Detroit, the rock city, and I've put this off for too fucking long . . . something is happening.

'There is a change. Not in music but in ourselves and in you. There are bands that have more to say to you than selling T-shirts from their personal clothing company. So frequently, especially when a band signs to a major label, they say, "I want to change music. This is going to be the next 'Smells Like Teen Spirit'." This is bullshit.

'People cannot change music, it's music that changes people. It is bigger than you and me put together. It's a neutron bomb with the detonator set on "kill" waiting for you to push the button.

'This is an evolution and you can be part of the change or stuck eating your own shit on a quest for fire.

'About respect: We were never on an endless search for it, like some Holy Grail or Noah's fucking Ark. If I wanted respect I would be a father. I would have children and raise them to take care of me when I'm old and hooked up to machines that keep me alive. Music is a message. The message is more important than the messenger. People ask us what we have to say and my answer is to find out for yourself. This is not a cop-out. If you find out for yourself it means more to you.

'About elitism: if for one minute you think you're better than a sixteen-year-old girl in a Green Day T-shirt, you are sorely mistaken. Remember the first time you went to a show and saw your favourite band. You wore their shirt, and sang every word. You didn't know anything about scene politics, haircuts, or what was cool. All you knew was that this music made you feel different from anyone you shared a locker with. Someone finally understood you. This is what music is about.

'Things are about to change for us . . . for all of us. From the kids who supported us at the start to those that are here now. We will always be an Eyeball Records band. The support, dedication, and love from that label got us where we are right now – and we did it as a family.

'I wanted to be the first to tell you before the gossip and the hearsay, I want to shout it from the street-lamps to the coils, in every fucked-up slum, where every seedy club lives and breathes. We are coming to your town. We are taking back what's ours. We're all in this together . . . And by the way . . . we've signed to Reprise and we are fucking ready for the world to hear us scream.'

It was quite the statement, with the news about signing to a major label snuck into the very end. Aaronson believes that the band themselves actually had few concerns about joining Reprise but posted the message as 'an insurance policy' to reassure fans that they would not lose their integrity.

In the short term, it changed very little. My Chemical Romance were still out on the road, and they were still touring hard. But they had started writing in earnest and by November 2003 had sketched out a good number of the songs that would form much of their second album.

But then something happened that would come to overshadow and then define that follow-up. With a major label deal in place, songs nearly ready and the future bright, the Ways would be brought back down to earth quickly. The day after they finished touring *Bullets*, Gerard and Mikey's grandmother died. It hit them like a bomb.

Elena had been ill and had gone into hospital for a heart operation. As far as Gerard and Mikey knew from out on the road, the operation had been a success. What they didn't know was that it hadn't been a total success. They had planned to visit her as soon as they stopped touring but would never get the chance. Gerard was furious at himself.

'I got home from tour, went to bed, woke up the next day and she was dead. She died the night I got home,' he said. 'I was so fucking angry because I'd spent a year and a half on the road and I hadn't seen her.'

Her death hit him and his brother hard. For Gerard, there was first grief at losing the woman who had cultivated and encouraged his creativity. But there was also guilt that he had missed her last days.

'I had the utmost respect for my grandmother. She was so instrumental in my life, I don't think I'd be doing any of this if it wasn't for her. I truly believe that,' he said. 'She encouraged me to do all of this. I guess I found music because, when I was growing up, she just let me find stuff. She let me find what I was good at and then she would sit with me and encourage me.

'She was just this little old Italian lady but she was so hard-working. I still remember her hands. They were a lot like mine. They were veiny and skinny but really strong. I have her hands. She was always working with them, or playing the piano. She always had a pencil behind her ear so she could always be drawing something. Her hands were so strong for a woman who was so small. When I lost her, I thought I was screwed. I thought I was done. I felt like I had lost my mentor. That's why I took it so hard.'

Already prone to drinking and increasingly reliant on anti-anxiety medication, Gerard began to lean more heavily on both. He became determined that Elena's memory would be honoured. He began to piece together a song about his grandmother – 'Helena' – that was savagely remorseful.

'There's a lot of self-hate,' he said. '"Helena" is a really angry open-letter to myself. It's about why I wasn't around for this woman who was so special to me, why I wasn't around for the last year of her life. Self-hate is always a big part of the lyrics.'

Though songs were already written for the band's second album, 'Helena' would shape the direction My Chemical Romance would head off in. It was a song that came straight from the heart, but which would set the tone for what was to come. Within months, My Chemical Romance would be in a Los Angeles studio making their major-label debut, *Three Cheers for Sweet Revenge*. Elena's death and Gerard and Mikey's reaction would come to colour it entirely.

'The emotions I went through [when she died] and over the next six days were what completely fuelled *Revenge*,' said Gerard. 'All the fucking anger, the spite, the beef with God, the angst, aggression and the fucking venom all came from those six days. Every single emotion you go through when you're grieving is on *Revenge*. When you really break down the record, it's about two little boys losing their grandmother.'

6: THREE CHEERS FOR
SWEET REVENGE

Before My Chemical Romance could get into the studio to start recording their second album, they had a short, three-date headline tour of the UK to conclude. It would prove vital in building up anticipation before their major-label debut.

Starting on 13 January 2004, My Chemical Romance played Manchester's Night And Day, Birmingham's Academy and London's Barfly with the Sunderland art-rock band Yourcodenameis:milo in support. It was a tour that their manager Brian Schechter had to battle hard for with Warners. The record company weren't sure of the value of a UK trip, but eventually conceded. It was the right decision, ensuring that a buzz would build.

It was six months before *Three Cheers for Sweet Revenge* would be released, and several days before they would even start recording it, but they arrived in England to a sense of expectancy derived from *Bullets*.

Paul Travers, an experienced *Kerrang!* writer, saw them in Manchester and wrote, 'Some bands you have a feeling about, an inkling that they could, given the right breaks, go on to at least moderate success and make music people will like. And some bands you know – from the moment you first see them – are destined to leave a swathe of palpitating hearts and jaws on the floor. My Chemical Romance are one of those bands . . . you need this band in your life.'

The *NME* were similarly taken that night. 'All [Gerard] lacks is a cape and mask to stop him from transforming into a full-blown extremo superhero,' wrote Rick Martin. 'Tonight, My Chemical

Romance's star quality leaves the rest of the chasing pack choking on their dust.'

Johnny Phillips, their UK promoter at SJM Concerts, was the man who had set up those early UK shows. He also remembers them as special.

'I brought them over for that first headline tour with the agent and ended up driving them and their manager around in their van,' he says. 'They were mental. I first saw them live at Night And Day in Manchester and Gerard offered me something he called Rocket Fuel. It was ten parts vodka to one part Red Bull. I declined.

'He had ripped black jeans on, black boots and gaffer tape around his left knee. At the Night And Day, there's a screen that comes down in front of the stage that you project films onto. Before he went on, he was just staring at his shadow on the back of the screen and shouting at himself. I'd never seen anything like it. He was really winding himself up. I was trying to work out what he was saying – and then the screen went up, and it was just mental.

'When they kicked off, it was the most incredible show I've ever seen. It was really visceral, really aggressive. It was gobsmacking. I texted my boss and said, "This band is going to be absolutely fucking massive." I kept that text message for a long time too.

'They were the nicest, most down-to-earth people – but live, something came over them. That first show will live with me forever. They were incredible to be around. Then as soon as they came offstage, they'd be smiling bunnies again. You'd speak to Gerard and he'd be really quiet and humble – the same with Ray, Frank and Mikey.'

As had been the case when they last played the UK, there was trouble offstage.

'After that first show, we got into a fight outside,' says Phillips. 'Then we went on to Birmingham for the next night. After we played there, we got followed to our rooms in this really moody hotel by some really horrible characters. We thought, "Fuck this," jumped in the van and drove all the way through the night down to London.'

Phillips remembers a band who were thrilled to be over in the

UK, flushed full of confidence even before recording *Three Cheers* and delighted to be on the road.

'They were having the time of their lives back then. Mikey came up to me and said, "When are we playing Wembley?" That was Mikey Way from day one – he hardly said anything through the tour but the only thing he kept talking about was when they would play Wembley. He'd talk about that, he'd go hunting for The Smiths T-shirts and comic books and he'd constantly be buying umbrellas for some reason.'

He remembers too that there was a friendliness to the band as well as an intensity, and that they grinned their way through the short tour.

'They were really focused,' he says, 'but they'd always have smiles on their faces. They're the same people now as they were then. Whenever I would see them later in the States, or go into the studio, they'd ask my opinion, take it on board and then have a laugh about the old days. We've got some wicked stories – but I can't tell any of them without incriminating myself . . .

'They always appreciated honesty. And more than that, they appreciated commitment to them. The music industry is so fucking cut-throat that they appreciated loyalty. And it went both ways. When they landed in the UK the second time, they still remembered my name. There are bands I've been working with for five or six years who don't have a clue who I am. It's a big deal when someone remembers you and they were very loyal to the people around them.'

Another person who worked with them closely then was Susie Ember, their publicist in the UK. She says that there was a great deal of press interest in them when they arrived in London to play the Barfly. 'What was so incredible about them was their work ethic,' she says. 'They could do interviews all day and not get tired and you got the sense that they treated each one like it was something new, not as though they were tired of doing them. Then they would still put on an amazing show.'

She was struck with how quiet and polite the five of them were when not performing but when My Chemical Romance hit the stage there was something visceral, primal and incredible about the band. Gerard preached to the crowd – drunk, generally – and leant out over them to perform. Frank span and wriggled in the tight space the band were allowed – and at the Barfly, space is always tight. Meanwhile Ray held things together, thrashing his Afro on the side of the stage.

'When they went onstage they morphed into a completely different entity. Gerard assumed his stage persona,' says Ember. 'I was always watching Frankie wondering if he was going to hurtle into the others onstage. They could be quite chaotic onstage then – but it was a good chaos.

'It blew us all away. It was the first time that most of the people in that room had seen them and everyone's mouths were gaping open. It was so exciting and such a special evening – you really got the sense that day that they were a band who would be huge. The crowd went absolutely mental.'

There was one problem. Matt used to do his own thing. He was just aloof,' says Philips. 'It wasn't as though he wasn't a part of the group, he was just different to the other four. The other four had an intensity about them, but he was just going along with things.'

Despite the potent vodka-Red Bull cocktail Gerard offered Phillips on first meeting him at the Night And Day, the singer's drinking didn't worry him then.

'I don't know if Gerard's drinking was a tool for him to get onstage or not,' he says. 'He got drunk, but it was a little later on that it got out of control. The first time I saw them, that wasn't a problem.'

It wouldn't be too long before it was, though.

With the UK tour a triumph, My Chemical Romance headed to Los Angeles to begin work on their second album. The death of Mikey and Gerard's grandmother was still at the forefront of the brothers' minds.

'After our grandmother died, getting back to the practice space was the only place that made us feel good,' recalled Gerard. 'I think by the time we got to LA there had been some closure. But when she died, that's when the drug and alcohol thing started to develop into a problem. I carried that with me to LA and I definitely allowed it to flourish there.'

Conversations with their Warners A&R man Craig Aaronson had brought them to a shortlist of producers. Aaronson says the band's first choice was Butch Vig, who had produced Nirvana's *Nevermind* and The Smashing Pumpkins' *Gish* among many other albums. He was busy though, and so they worked their way down the list until they came to Howard Benson. 'I knew he could do a great job with them,' says Aaronson.

On the face of it, Benson's experience seemed an unlikely fit. His work in the nineties had taken him from the thrash punk of Motörhead to Less Than Jake's ska and on to the million-selling, though critically questionable, likes of Christian nu-metallers POD and the glossy post-grunge of Hoobastank. He had a reputation for focusing on singers. Viewing them as the centrepiece to any band, he would work for hours on melody lines with them, teasing up their performances and allowing the band to fit in somewhere behind. And in Gerard, he saw a star he wanted to work with.

'It was him. It was all about him,' Benson admits. 'I always look for a star in a band and Gerard is an incredible frontman. He's very humble and smart but he understands what he's doing. He's a ham, which means he's always good in front of the camera. Any producer who couldn't spot that in him must be kicking themselves.'

My Chemical Romance handed the producer the demo they'd recorded. Using the Queen-ish, camp-punk stomp of 'Headfirst for Halos' as a reference point, they had embraced a flamboyant yet direct sound, aiming not so much to kick-start their sound as to high-kick it. They had also channelled Gerard's grief and anger over his grandmother into the music. That lent it an emotional intensity that the singer heightened with what he called a 'pseudo-concept' about a man coming back from the dead to find the woman he loves by embarking on a killing spree.

'There were songs on the first album that allowed us to go into the second album,' said Gerard. 'We wrote some punk-metal songs on the first album but we also wrote "Headfirst for Halos" which meant no one could ever say, "Oh, that's not who you are" when we moved on.'

'I remember one of the conversations we had when we started the band was that nothing should be taboo,' said Ray. 'If it was a great song, or had great lyrics or a great melody, then we had to do it. You can't have a "too cool for school" attitude with a great song – if it's great you have to do it.'

Benson's first thoughts on the demo, though, were not encouraging. 'I thought, "Man, there's nothing here at all". But it did have the one thing I always look for and that was intensity. It sounded fearless. When a band is fearless then you know there's something to them. That's why I met up with them.

'They played some songs to me and they weren't great. But I sat and talked to Gerard and looked him in the eye – and I'll never forget this because it was a special moment in my career – and I asked him, "How much do you care about the fans you have now? Are you willing to go far beyond that? Are you willing to possibly piss off your current fans in order to make a big, huge rock album?"

'Sometimes bands aren't willing to do that, in which case I'm probably not the right guy for them. But Gerard said he was willing to make the best record he could, he was willing to work, he wanted me to teach him whatever I could.'

The band knew that Benson was right. There was, after all, little point in signing to a major label and working with a million-selling producer if all they wanted was to play to the same old crowd. '[Benson] definitely knew that we were going to go far,' agreed Gerard. 'We wanted that and we just had to figure out who was going to let us go that far.

'All of our favourite bands had made a second record where they had truly harnessed everything they were great at. We didn't want to retreat and make anti-music. The bands we loved were unafraid and they wanted to make the ultimate distillation of their band.'

'The demos for *Three Cheers* showed a lot of promise to me,' says Aaronson. 'But I could see how the songs needed a little work with a producer though. They needed to work on the arrangements with someone and so that's what happened. Ray and Gerard are very smart and want to be the best they can be, so they were very open to listening to other ideas and, if it worked, they would try it out. Credit to them to have the confidence to try out other ideas and be open to Howard or me.'

In LA, they lived in the Oakwood Apartments, a cluster of buildings near the Warner Bros headquarters in Burbank, which were regularly rented by actors and musicians due to their proximity to both film and music studios. Gerard says he enjoyed observing some of the sleazier elements of Los Angeles, feeding the experience into some of *Three Cheers'* seedier lyrics. But he also liked the vibrancy of the place – because My Chemical Romance's mood was high in Los Angeles. They were excited. It was, after all, the first time they had been in a recording studio that wasn't the basement of someone's house. There was a part of them that couldn't believe their luck.

'It felt like we snuck in there and someone was going to realize and go, "Hey, these fucking assholes are in here! Get 'em outta here,"' said Frank of their exhilaration. 'We felt like we had to get our shit done as quick and as well as possible so that nobody caught us.'

But while that drew Gerard, Ray, Frank and Mikey closer together, it also dragged them further from Pelissier. Frank admitted as much later. 'Going into it, I don't think we were as confident as we thought we were,' he said. 'There was definitely inner turmoil. It was mostly between us and [Pelissier]. You could tell that just from our living arrangements. He was the only one who lived alone. Some personalities just can't see eye to eye on everything. As much as we wanted to make it work, you just can't live with certain people.'

But as much as the issues with Pelissier were a worry, they were not a full-blown problem. In fact, Gerard had welcomed the drummer's support in the wake of his grandmother's death and so, though they had struggled through the UK tour, and though Pelissier was living alone, the recording process would not be affected.

'My relationship with Matt was actually very good when we made that record,' said Gerard. 'I know we had stuff in the past and that we didn't always get along but he was there for me when my grandmother died – that's not something I'll ever forget. When she passed away, he was at the funeral, the wake and the service. He gave me a hug and then we went to make this record. He could be difficult occasionally but I remember saying, "I want this song to be about my grandmother," and he was right up there with everyone else in agreeing with that.'

Soon after arriving in Los Angeles, they began to restructure their music in a practice studio. 'We wrote another ton of songs,' said Frank. 'We trimmed some stuff down, turned it around until it really made sense to us and we could be clear about exactly what we wanted to put across.'

At first, things did not go well. They recorded one song in advance after being asked to do so by the label as a test to see how they were coming along. 'None of us had ever been in a real studio,' Frank said. 'The producer they put us in with told us, "You guys aren't ready." We were like, "Oh shit!" So that was a fucking horrible experience. So when we went in with Howard, we didn't know if it would be terrible or fun because the only time we had been in a real studio, someone had told us to get the fuck out again.'

Benson wanted them to work on their basic songwriting and arrangement skills, concentrating on building big choruses and immediate vocal lines while essentially leaving the guitars to do their own thing. 'You hear stuff on that record that Ray and I were getting away with,' said Frank, 'because we were a little more under the radar. We were doing a lot of "chorus-teasing" on that record. I think it was a phase we were going through – you can hear it on "It's Not a Fashion Statement, It's a Deathwish" and "I Never Told You What I Do for a Living". Howard was not a fan of that at all. He thought that, if you had a chorus, you should put it out there. Sometimes that works, sometimes it doesn't.

'Howard really likes to work on singles. Early on, he decided which songs would be the singles and he really worked hard on them. He kind of says, "You know what? This is an album track and I don't really care about that so you guys go ahead and do what you want to do with it." We were like, "Wow … all right, I guess." Sometimes that sucked but, hey, whatever. To tell you the truth, in the writing process, he was there every day and he heard the songs. If he didn't like something and we did, then we still did it, you know.'

Benson wanted a big-sounding, big-selling record. It meant that his ethos sometimes jarred with the band's, and particularly Frank's, underground-punk leanings.

'The thing with Howard was that there was a part of me that completely understood why it worked and another part of me that couldn't understand how it had,' said Frank. 'He knows his shit, but he's very much from a different world. There were a few things we really butted heads on. I remember saying something about the Misfits one day and his reaction to the conversation was to say, "Yeah, well how many records did the Misfits sell?" I was like, "What the fuck? Are you crazy?"'

My Chemical Romance spent three weeks in pre-production – nearly three times longer than it took to record the entire of their debut – as they fine-tuned and wrote the remainder of the songs they needed to fill *Three Cheers for Sweet Revenge*.

'I think we had about half a record, then we got really inspired and ended up writing a whole bunch of songs, tweaking sections of songs we previously had and fragments became songs,' remembered Gerard. So it was that, with their songs reworked, they were ready to record. They moved into Bay 7 Studios out in The Valley on Magnolia Boulevard. Benson remembers that it was Ray who took charge of the musical side of things – as he had done on the band's debut – and that Frank, making his first record, would look to him for guidance.

'As far as the music's concerned that record has a lot to do with Ray,' says Benson. 'He came up with a lot of that stuff; he's like the musical director. Ray dictates a lot of what happens musically in

the band. Frankie takes a lot of his cues from Ray. The best thing
about the bass player is that he offers stability to Gerard and he's a
great guy too.'

The recording was quick – the budget not allowing for unlim-
ited time – but intense, and the band surprised themselves with how
good they sounded. After they'd recorded the first track, it was
edited and put through Pro-Tools. The next day, when the band
were back in the studio, they listened to their work with Benson.

'Who did you bring in to play this?' Ray asked. 'You must have
brought someone in, this isn't us.'

'What do you mean?' asked Benson, surprised

'We don't play this good,' Ray said.

'It was a very funny moment,' Benson remembers. 'They played
a lot better than they thought they could because they really didn't
think they were that good then. But they improved a lot.'

The only problem Benson could lay his finger on was the relationship with Pelissier. It seems clear the drummer polarized opinions
and everyone had one. Sometimes his rawness worked, but there
were times people found him hard to work with. 'It was funny –
nobody liked the guy but he still played a great record,' Benson says.
'He knew the songs, he'd lived with them and he could do it on the
record. The problem was live – he was so inconsistent. You can't be
that way live because there are too many other problems going on.
There's too much other shit to deal with. In the studio he either
didn't play very hard or he played too hard – he was all over the
place but he still did a pretty decent job.'

Benson, as was his way, concentrated on Gerard. The producer, like
Geoff Rickly on *Bullets*, had noticed that the singer created characters in his lyrics and was using these imaginary worlds when turning
in his vocal performances.

'Gerard is one of those people who can translate the emotions
of those around him very well,' says Howard. 'When he gets in front
of the mic he turns on that thing. He jumps into his brain and, when

he's done, he can jump out again. Most great artists are like that because if you live that life of the artist the whole time, then you basically self-destruct. Look at Kurt Cobain. He tried to be a real person but it was pressed upon him so much that he was a saviour that he couldn't deal with it. He had no other way out.'

Gerard first got into character when the band were recording 'Vampires Will Never Hurt You', aided of course by Alex Saavedra's punch. However, creating different personas was something he had been doing all his life, certainly since he started writing stories and comics. Alongside the imaginative leaps he took, he would also use props to create a mood.

'The method acting,' he explained. 'Well, "Vampires" was definitely the first moment of that. It's something that I've done time and time again while I've been recording. For example, when I sang "You Know What They Do to Guys Like Us in Prison", I was running pornography in the room.

'Each song felt like a completely different colour palette. And each individual palette had to be just as good – but different – from the next one. I had to figure out how to make my part of each song great, which meant that it was like reinventing the wheel for each song. I never wanted to go into a song thinking, "OK, let's just do this one like all the others." Each song had to have a completely different approach and a lot of times that involved method acting. I think, during "Prison", I wasn't wearing very many clothes either. I was in an attic that nobody was allowed into. I do remember Howard encouraging me to get pretty weird in there and I think I got weird in my own ways too.'

It was the relationship between Benson and Gerard that came to dominate *Three Cheers*. Reasoning that if the man up front can fill the spotlight, the rest of the band and their music will follow, the producer was determined to get as much from My Chemical Romance's frontman as he could.

'His main psychology is singers,' said Gerard. 'He has a way that he operates with them and he knows how to get what he wants from them. He knew how far someone could go, he knew when you couldn't continue and he would stop you. He would be like, "You're shot, we're done, you're not coming in tomorrow."

'He would push you in a very encouraging way – even though there were times you wanted to fight against him. He would push me by playing a harmony on a keyboard that was way out of my range and then he'd look at me and go, "Just fucking do it." He was very much like that. He's great with singers, that's his forte.'

Despite Gerard's claims that Benson had encouraged him to 'get pretty weird', the producer says he tried to avoid relying on tricks to access the singer's emotions. In fact, he says, touching on Gerard's feelings was the easy bit.

'That wasn't a problem at all. That's the part they came in with,' he says. 'That's the part they have to come with. I'm not going to be the kind of producer who's going to scare them, insult them or play passive-aggressive mind games to get things out of them. That's not the way I work at all; that's called, "I don't know how to produce, so I'm going to try something else." You might get emotion like that but you don't get good songs or arrangements that way. I didn't have to do any of that with My Chemical Romance.'

But that's not to say Gerard wasn't doing it himself. In fact, as *Three Cheers* progressed, the singer felt more and more that he needed to get into the character of a nihilist rock singer. And it wasn't necessarily a healthy place to go.

'There was a lot of hiding,' said Gerard of his drinking back then. 'A big part of it was creating a persona of this wasted, reckless, street-drifter. I was hiding a lot behind all of that. I wanted to keep people from knowing anything about the real me. But slowly the real me was disappearing.'

Behind the scenes, as My Chemical Romance recorded *Three Cheers for Sweet Revenge*, they were indulging in a certain amount of extra-curricular activities. But it was something they kept hidden. 'When we were recording that record, we were all kind of partying a little,' said Frank. 'We'd get home from the studio, have a few beers and then maybe take a few pills. It happened especially if we had a weekend off. Let me put it this way, there are some weekends that I don't really remember – I took a bunch of pills and woke up on Monday. At points I thought, "This is out of control," but most of the time I thought, "Ah, whatever, I'm just trying to get my head out of this record, there's too much going on for me to worry about this."'

'That was the same for a few of us,' said Gerard. 'When we weren't making music, there was such a fog. I couldn't tell you if we were all experimenting with pills or it was just some of us, because we'd all just vanish for days when we weren't in the studio. We'd be professional in the studio, and we wouldn't drink in there – although I tried to sing drunk once and it was the worst take I ever did.'

The track was called 'Desert Song' and it didn't make the album but can be heard on the *Life on the Murder Scene* documentary. 'To record that song, Gerard just got wasted all night,' said Frank. 'The final recording was just drunk. It fitted the mood of the song though. It was more like he was playing a character and, in order to play that person, he had to get fucked up.'

Gerard's own chemical romance with The Used's Bert McCracken continued during the recording of *Three Cheers*. It seemed fitting that McCracken should sing backing vocals on the high-kicking, flailing stomp of 'You Know What They Do to Guys Like Us in Prison', a song inspired by the two singers sharing a kiss in a game of on-the-road truth or dare. ('When you're kissing a guy with a beard,' Gerard said, 'it's different.') Written from the point of view of cellmates, the song was informed by the idea of life on the road, of men cramped into vans and riding across America.

'Sometimes it feels like jail when you've got eight or nine guys in a van. It smells like jail, that's for sure,' said Gerard shortly after *Three Cheers* was released. 'Sometimes it feels like prison, but sometimes even the guys in prison, as fucked up and rough as it is, they buddy up and stick through it together. I think that's definitely one of the reasons I wanted Bert to sing on it, because he's one of the few people that I've met on the road and really connected with.

'He was like a cellmate in a way. He's already been through the crazy rock star shit and I'm just new to this. [The song is] definitely about that camaraderie and obviously touches on lost masculinity. I think that comes from being around dudes so much and you actually start to lose your masculinity. Especially because we're not the kind of band like Mötley Crüe where we fuck around with groupies or anything.'

During the recording sessions in LA, Ray was more abstemious. In fact, he was shocked to later discover what had been going on. Interviewing the band for *Kerrang!* in 2011, I brought the subject up. It was a balmy day in Lisbon, Portugal, My Chemical Romance had set aside an entire day for a photo shoot and a long interview that delved into the murkier corners of their history. Frank thought back to those days and said, 'Yeah that was weird. I'd wake up and not know what day it was.'

To my left, I noticed Ray squirm in his seat then look visibly confused. As Gerard and Frank talked about the pills they'd popped and the drinks they'd drunk, Ray interrupted and said, 'Really? I had no idea that stuff was going on.'

He shook his head again and shrugged his shoulders, still baffled by the revelation.

'I was so naïve at that point,' he continued. 'I knew there had been a couple of instances and I had a talk with Gerard after one major one, but I didn't see anything that different. I'm actually kind of surprised. I didn't know that until today. Frank was taking pills? I didn't know that; this is a revelation to me.'

Frank looked over at me and pointed a mock, accusing finger: 'Thanks a lot, Tom.'

'Yeah,' added Ray, 'you just sold Frank out!'

But Ray wasn't the only one who hadn't cottoned on. Benson, too, hadn't realized that the singer he was working with was, to all extents and purposes, a functioning alcoholic. 'A few months after the record came out, Gerard phoned me up and said, "I just want you to know that I'm clean and sober now." I was like, "I didn't even know anything was wrong with you!" He seemed fine to me. I think he hides a lot of things. There are a lot of things going on in the background that he doesn't let anybody see.'

Craig Aaronson too had no idea that anything other than hard work was happening.

'I never knew there were any issues with partying going on with that band,' he says. 'I was told about it afterwards at some point but I never saw them getting crazy. It's a great fucking album, so I always like to think that comes from a pure, drug-free spirit. But maybe some sex, drugs and rock 'n' roll did get into it.'

There was one night in particular – the night that Ray referred to when he said he had to give Gerard a talking to – that things threatened to get out of control.

'Well Ray and I did have to have a serious talk one morning because I wasn't able to sing after one night,' recalled Gerard. 'So maybe that was an early wake-up call. I realized: "We're not rock stars, this studio costs a lot of money and I can't sing because I did cocaine all last night." I couldn't sing, I felt awful and I couldn't go to work, so I went and told Ray. Because I went to him straight away, it wasn't a problem again until we were on the road.'

Frank thinks, in part, that the drinking and the pills stemmed from a need to escape. Scattered across the other side of the country from their New Jersey homes, they were cast adrift with little else to occupy them other than their work. And they went about their work with an intensity they sometimes needed to get away from. On top of it all, there was also the pressure of recording for a major label. Making *Three Cheers* was the biggest thing that any of them had ever done.

'We knew it was crazy, we knew it was out of control,' said Frank. 'Nobody else we ever knew well had ever been on a major label – we felt a little like we were in the big leagues on our own yet we were just five idiots from Jersey who had just been playing songs in basements. It was big stuff.

'A lot of it was maybe to do with that, trying to cope with things. There was depression at not being at home, missing your relatives and things like that. What it felt like, at that point, was that everything was changing but us. We felt the same but everything around us was different. We felt that we were the same people as always. We were the same kids from Jersey that loved punk rock and music, kids that liked going to the diner and smoking cigarettes until four in the morning. That's what we were – honestly. We were just a punk band from Jersey. If we'd have stayed there forever, we would have been happy. But, I guess, we got to the next level.'

They had few distractions too. Certainly Warner Bros were keen not to crowd them and so, to the band's relief, left them largely to their own devices.

'I wanted to be around during pre-production to hear what they were doing,' says Aaronson. 'Once I heard the songs and the arrangements, I stayed out of their hair. I'd stop by the studio to hear how things were going but not too often and we never sent any radio people or anything in there. We wanted to leave the band to do what they do. That was always our relationship with the band: creatively we let them do what they do and we supported that because they're fucking great. They had a very clear vision and Gerard's creativity always inspired the fuck out of me.'

Frank was particularly pleased when they got in touch with Keith Morris, the influential punk singer who had led Black Flag and Circle Jerks, to ask him to guest on the album. Both bands were groups that Iero and Hambone had adored. For Iero, having Morris sing on 'Hang 'Em High' was something of a highlight. 'When Keith actually sang on *Three Cheers for Sweet Revenge* and I got to eat Chinese food with him and talk for a little while . . . well, that wasn't a bad moment,' said Frank.

It marked a rare opportunity to take their heads out of the record they were creating, to pause and cherish what they had. Because the rest of the time, they were buried in *Three Cheers* – so much so that they no longer knew if it was any good.

'We lived and breathed that record, that's the way we are,' said Frank. 'There were times we got so attached to it that we wanted to redo the whole album because we wanted it to be so good that we thought everything sucked. There were times we had to take days out just to get away from it so we could have space to think. We were so involved in it. It was real intense.'

Gerard, like Frank, occasionally had crises of confidence about what they were making. 'When you make a record you go through every emotion you possibly can and one of those is panic,' he said. 'One night I totally freaked out – Ray and I were sharing a room and I was listening to the recordings on headphones. I leapt out of bed and was shouting, "Dude, I don't know if people are going to get this. Does this make sense at all?" I was worried about all of it – the fact there was a cabaret song on it ['You Know What They Do to Guys Like Us in Prison'] or that it changes from song to song, or that it's too aggressive – or will it scare the shit out of people? It wasn't sounding like anything I'd heard before.'

It turned out that was a good thing.

The song that allowed the album to fall into place wasn't one they had even really considered when they arrived in Los Angeles. Lurking on the demo they had recorded back in New Jersey was a long piece of music which, halfway through, contained one simple idea that was little more than a couple of guitars and a vocal line. It had been a song that had been lying around for a while, one of Ray's ideas that they had yet to spend much time working on. 'I'm not okay,' sang Gerard over Ray's guitars. It took Craig Aaronson and Howard Benson, to spot its genius.

'There was a chord progression that reminded me of The Smiths that came in around six minutes into the song,' says Aaronson. 'It just sounded so good and made me feel something, so I worked on them. I can't take credit for the song, but I can take credit for pushing those little fuckers into working on it.'

Benson, too, had spotted the appeal of Gerard's melody. To appease both producer and A&R man, the band agreed to go through the song. 'Ray played the chords on a clean guitar and Gerard just sang "I'm not okay",' said Frank and suddenly they all realized what

Benson and Aaronson were talking about. 'It was just the most beautiful song we had heard. We went, "What the fuck are we doing? Why haven't we put this on the album? Why haven't we written this yet?" So we did.'

'We simplified the chords, and concentrated on that amazing melody,' said Ray. 'That's actually the genesis of a lot of songs: they start out as something completely different, then there's one bit you latch onto and develop. If you heard the original of "Helena", for example, it has no chorus or bridge but it had that one melody you could latch onto.'

'I immediately knew we had a hit song,' says Benson. 'I didn't need to hear anything else, it was just perfect.'

In the studio, they set about fleshing it out, holding on to Gerard's central melody, and leaving Ray's guitar line that floated underneath it. Having worked through most of *Three Cheers* by that stage, the band were already moving on from the punk that had informed some of the early songs and were allowing more of the Queen references that appealed to Ray.

'A lot of the Queen influences you hear on *The Black Parade* were things that we came up with during that song,' says Benson. 'It was like a prototype for that album. The guitars and harmonies . . . Gerard could have said that he didn't want to do any of that but, instead, he said, "Yes, give me as many vocal parts as you want to give me." I just kept throwing stuff at him. I was going, "Try this, try this, try this," and he just sang them all. And, wow, he could really sing that stuff. Harmonies are hard for a lot of lead singers because they can't always hear much beyond the lead vocal so it was so cool that he could pick up harmonies and run with them. It was a real turning point for the record – we went back to "Helena" and "Ghost of You" and did the same to them too.'

They were buzzing about the song, experimenting with it and seeing just how far they could push the boundaries of its catchy, fizzing punk. Frank came up with a suggestion he thought was ridiculous, before realizing it worked.

'Nobody does this,' he said to his bandmates, 'but, if you listen to Cheap Trick's *Live at the Budokan* there's a part where everything breaks down. It would be really funny to have that on the recording – like a live moment but actually on the record.'

'So we thought "Fuck it" and did it,' Frank remembered. 'I can't believe we got away with it because, although it's beautiful, there's stuff on there that's so over the top. There's so much that shouldn't work on there, yet it does.'

Gerard, too, realized the power that song would come to have. 'That song was like an infiltrator,' he said. 'On first listen people would think, "Oh, that's catchy, it's nice. Maybe it's punk, maybe it's pop." Then, on the second listen, they realized what it was about and got a sense that there was a lot more there than a simple pop-punk song. A lot of people assume we hate playing it because it was the first hit and it was the catchy one but, actually, it's one of our favourite songs to play live.

'It was definitely an anthem. The straight-up lyric "I'm not okay" was a declaration from me, it was a declaration for kids who would become our fans, who would realize that, "You know what? Everything's not OK." The odd thing was that it wasn't the outsiders who got that – it was normal people, people who were tired of pretending to be something they're not. That song became almost an anthem because of that.'

It would be a song that made them stars.

7: PARTY POISON

The way My Chemical Romance tell it, they had barely spoken to Warner Bros during the making of *Three Cheers for Sweet Revenge*. Once it was finished, they marched into their offices, put their music on the table and said: 'There you go – there's your record.'

'They didn't know what they were going to get,' said Frank. 'They told us they liked us, they liked the direction we were going in but they didn't know what they were going to get. If the record had been horrendous, they might have had something to say about it. But we felt like we'd written the record we wanted to write and we couldn't give a shit what anyone else thought.'

Craig Aaronson loved it. But he was one of the few inside Warners who did, because it met a decidedly mixed reaction when it was played to the rest of the label. 'They were all like, "Oh, you know what? This is going to be tough. This is very left of centre, it's not what's being played on radio right now,"' says Aaronson. 'They liked "I'm Not Okay" and they said they'd give it a run, but no one was jumping up and down at all. The expectations for it were very moderate – low to moderate, I'd say.

'I was like, "Are you guys fucking kidding me? This is a top five single." I knew it in my bones but the company was not so sure. They wanted to dip their toe in the water and see how people were responding.'

It might have been cause for concern but My Chemical Romance wouldn't have time to worry about it. Because, from March 2004, they were doing one thing only: touring. From the middle of that month until the end of the year they would play nearly 200 shows in 290 days. It would be a defining period for the band, and a harrowing one. In that time, though the world would begin to see their potential, their singer would drink himself to crisis-point and their drummer would be kicked out of the band.

Three Cheers was still unmixed when they hit the road. With My Chemical Romance in a van and Howard Benson back in the studio finessing the sounds they had made, it was hardly the ideal process. 'I was left having to do a lot of the mixing myself,' says the producer, 'and that caused a few conflicts because the band has to be there for that because I can't read their minds. I didn't know where I was going for a moment there and we were very lucky that [respected mixer and producer] Rick Costey mixed four of the big songs. I was left mixing the rest and I could follow what he'd done.'

The first leg of My Chemical Romance's tour was in the US from March until the end of May. The band relentlessly criss-crossed the States with, variously, Avenged Sevenfold, Thrice, Alexisonfire, the short-lived Moments In Grace and Funeral For A Friend. And as they did so, Gerard and Mikey's drinking began to accelerate. Funeral For A Friend's then drummer, Ryan Richards, remembers their tour with My Chemical Romance.

'It was one of the first tours in the States that we did,' he says. 'It was us, My Chemical Romance and Avenged Sevenfold. It sounds like a decent bill but there were nights we were playing in the Midwest to only thirty or forty people in shacks on the edge of town. Those people didn't really care at all. But about two months later My Chemical Romance absolutely blew up.

'Gerard was still as charismatic in front of a tiny crowd as he would become in front of a massive one. He's one of the most charismatic frontmen I've ever seen. When we were playing those little shows, I'd always make sure I watched him every night just to see what he would say and do onstage. It was always pretty interesting.

'They were very friendly guys. There was a family vibe with them. Ray played me a rough version of [*Three Cheers*] and I just knew they were going to do it. I heard "I'm Not Okay" and told them that song was going to be huge – not that it took a genius to work that out. There was definitely a confidence to them then. You could tell they were really proud of their record. They weren't arrogant but proud.'

Richards also remembers that it was then that Gerard's drinking began to cross the line from prop to problem.

'I think it was something that went with performing for him,' he says. 'The more he drank, the more unhinged the show would be. He would start drinking well before going onstage. It was very compelling when it started; watching him drink was almost like watching a car crash. You couldn't take your eyes off him. Everyone was talking about him, about the band with the crazy frontman.'

Gerard remembered that tour too; he remembered that My Chemical Romance's manager, Brian Schechter, would deliberately not include alcohol on the band's riders in a bid to control his drinking. So the singer would simply drink Funeral For A Friend's instead. 'I had to apologize for that sort of thing a lot,' said Gerard.

He and his brother Mikey were beginning to earn themselves a reputation. 'We were pretty wild,' said Mikey. 'People were giving us nicknames – they called us The Chemical Brothers. I'd roll into places and people would always ask me if I had any drugs, because that's what they were used to. Me and him got a reputation for it; we had this aura of trouble around us; people thought we were dangerous.'

There were stories doing the rounds of Gerard sharing lines of coke with the road crew – stories he denies – but it all added to the aura of a singer who was out of control and on the edge. 'The coke with the road crew wasn't true. I never did coke that much,' he said. 'There were only four or five incidents of me going on coke binges. I only got totally into coke after I'd been drinking all night.

'The vodka thing is definitely true though. I was such an alcoholic that I was living off it. It would take me about an hour to finish a bottle of vodka. I was definitely drinking one of those small bottles before shows. But there weren't that many instances of me taking coke. I remember once at a house, once at a hotel, once at another house and I can't remember many more times. It was never during the shows it was always afterwards.

'There are a lot of stories floating around from those days and sometimes I wonder if I did do some of the things I'm supposed to have done because I don't always remember! I just know I was nice to everybody that I met.'

Three Cheers for Sweet Revenge came out on 8 June 2004 shortly after My Chemical Romance had completed another short UK tour, squeezing in dates in Portsmouth, London, Manchester, Leeds and Glasgow with the Arizonan metalcore band The Bled and the Welsh hardcore band Hondo Maclean. Oddly enough, two people on the road with them on that trip would go on to later play drums for the band. One was The Bled's powerhouse drummer, Mike Pedi-cone, then touring his band's *Pass the Flask* debut. The other was My Chemical Romance's soundman, Bob Bryar, who was such a fan of the band that he was prepared to work for free.

Bob was aware of a tension between Matt Pelissier and the other four members. As they travelled through the UK – tired and pushed to the limits by their schedule – he saw there was a disconnect and a rift growing that could have had disastrous consequences on the eve of the release of *Three Cheers*.

'They were definitely going to break up at that point,' he said. 'I noticed that things weren't right between them all. The mood around them was ruining them and I think it came from the old drummer. You have to be able to get along when you're in a band because you spend so much time together and they just weren't.

'They wouldn't even look at each other when they played. They just weren't happy. They'd get in the van, put their headphones on so they couldn't hear each other and couldn't talk to each other. It was just miserable.'

Ray was frustrated about inconsistencies in the band's perfor-mances at that time and said the difficult atmosphere increased uncertainties within the band.

'There was a feeling that anything might happen next and that wasn't good,' he said. 'There was a lot of shit going on then. At least once a week one of us wondered if the band would last.'

It was not ideal, given that the album was about to come out. But, when it did, they found themselves swept up by its success. Their only aims on its release had been for it to sell more copies than their debut. It actually sold twice as many copies – on the first day.

'The funniest thing about *Three Cheers for Sweet Revenge* is that the label and I had agreed that if we could sell 300,000 copies we would be happy,' Brian Schechter said. 'And then, you know, the first week of sales I had predicted 3,000 and we had no idea what was going to happen. In the very first day we kept getting phone calls about how great things were going and I think right about then is when we realized something weird was going to happen. The fact that [on] the very first day [we] had sold twice as many as the previous record had sold in its whole lifespan at that point – I think we realized that something big was about to happen. They sold, like, 120,000 records through that summer.'

It sold 11,000 records in the first week. 'I think my mom bought 10,999 of them,' said Mikey. And suddenly the staff at Warner Bros who had been sitting on the fence about My Chemical Romance took notice. 'At that point,' says Craig Aaronson, 'everybody got a bit more supportive.'

In *Rolling Stone*, Kirk Miller said *Three Cheers for Sweet Revenge* was reminiscent of the Misfits in its goth-punk style, its 'shout-along choruses, speedy drums and horror themes' but that it also added 'cool metal licks and a sneaky sense of humour'. He concluded that it was 'a hell of a good time' in a three-star review.

The *Kerrang!* review pointed out that 'lyrically, Way is far from a happy bunny, but as on his band's debut he's clearly having fun piling on the B-Movie imagery,' before deciding 'it's nevertheless a fine, thrilling mix of sounds and ideas from a band with the potential to go deep and far.' But few predicted quite how well it would be received.

The reviews were largely positive, though one negative one would stick in Gerard's mind. 'There was one criticism that I still remember,' he recalled. 'It said something like, "Why would you want to watch this guy run around onstage whining about his nana?" It was the one thing I read that made me think, "I hope this guy falls under a bus." How fucking shitty a human being do you have to be to say that?'

It was a review that missed how much else was going on in *Three Cheers for Sweet Revenge*. 'To the End' mirrors the William Faulkner short story 'A Rose for Emily', before the vaudeville melodrama of 'You Know What They Do to Guys Like Us in Prison' explores comradeship on the road. 'I'm Not Okay (I Promise)' was the stand out, as the singer issues a cry for help, before the sensitive 'Ghost of You' arrives.

Throughout, from the Smiths-referencing 'Thank You for the Venom' to the spaghetti westernisms of 'Hang 'Em High' or the suicide-referencing 'Cemetery Drive', there is a sense of the macabre. Riddled with horror references, and the poetry of doomed romance, it contained a blackness and bleakness amid its punk.

But mostly what *Three Cheers for Sweet Revenge* has is chorus after chorus after chorus. Buoyed by a phenomenal sense of melody – something to which My Chemical Romance owe Howard Benson a partial debt – there was something immediately catchy about the album. It offered listeners an instant way in to discover the rich layers underneath.

On the night of 11 July 2004, My Chemical Romance played their official record-release show at the Starland Ballroom in Sayerville, New Jersey. 'It was sold out, and I remember there was something like 2,500 people there,' remembered Mikey. 'Seeing that many people moving in unison and singing along was so overwhelming.'

And from there, it grew and grew. Initially, the band toured locally with Boys Night Out, Nightmare of You and Drive By, playing reasonably near to home in Pittsburgh, Baltimore and New

Jersey before setting out on the Warped Tour – which is where things really started happening.

The Warped Tour has long been the proving ground for punk bands across America. Once a year, it rumbles into the outskirts of every major (and some minor) American towns – a vast caravan of lorries, trucks, buses, cars and vans that rolls from one car park to another as its cast of bands and crew set up to play. The crew will build seven stages before 11 a.m. each morning, then the gates will open as the vast sprawl of American suburban youth pour in for the annual dose of vicious riffs and snarling attitude.

Run by Kevin Lyman since 1994, it's a punk-rock institution where bands play in bullet-point half-hour slots. There will be local bands, fast-rising bands, freefalling bands, multi-platinum bands, and who-the-fuck-invited-them bands. But they'll all largely get the same half-hour slot; they'll all be victims of the famous egalitarian Warped Tour lottery that means each act gets a randomly selected time to play every day. It's why megastars may open to ten people at 11 a.m., and why nobodies might 'headline' at 9 p.m.

On bare stages, they'll play in natural light only. With costs pared down and set-up kept to a minimum, there are few stage lights, so each show ends at sundown. Then, once it's night, the crowds leave and the whole carnival becomes the bands' domain. Around the phalanx of tour buses and vans, impromptu barbecues are sparked into life, beers are passed around and the idiocy begins. Beer bongs, shots and cocktails are downed, drunk and invented. Singalongs, shout-outs and silliness erupt from all parts. Poker tables are set up in bus-back lounges, computer consoles burn hot with overuse and guitars are strummed as bands mingle and merge. The old war stories come out – tales of the past – and on into the night it goes, the party alive for as long as there are bodies to stoke its fire.

Then, deep in the early hours, the buses nose their way out of the car parks and onto the American highways. Hundreds of them set off with the hissing of airbrakes and the swooshing shut of doors. And once again the great caravan is on the road, ready to roll into the next venue, ready to do the same all over again.

Every year, there is a break-out band, one act who will be the highlight of the day no matter what time they play, no matter what stage they are placed upon. In 2004, it was My Chemical Romance. They owned the place. Gerard would walk out onstage dressed in an increasingly stinky suit, black and white tie draped around his neck, and then deliver performances of such searing, white heat that people could only stop and stare. Like a demented preacher, he would scream and howl his way through the band's set, throwing himself into the characters he had created in his songs, his sweat-soaked hair clinging to his face.

Alongside him was Frank, ever the most physical player on My Chemical Romance's stage. He would spin, head-bang then collapse to the floor, playing while lying on the stage and pedalling his feet furiously. Mikey was at the back, feeling Pelissier's beat, while Ray was always to one side, keeping things tight and sending jarring riffs out to the crowd.

Anything could happen onstage. It would be nothing for Gerard to walk over to Frank and kiss him full on the mouth before spinning off to the other side of the stage and wailing into the mic. Increasingly, it became part of the act – until they noticed that people were beginning to write sexual fan fiction about them on the internet.

'The whole thing with me and Frank doing stuff onstage together was really just to irritate people,' said Gerard. 'And it was funny for a brief period. If you boil down the DNA of My Chemical Romance, the base would be this: what do you want us to do? – because we're going to do the opposite. But people started getting into it, so we stopped.'

'You'd see these quintessential jock dudes beating each other up to our music,' said Frank, 'and you'd think, "Wouldn't it be funny if they turned around and saw that they were beating each other up to us two kissing?"'

Kissing aside, every day for the month they were on the Warped Tour they gave their performances everything. And every day Gerard would be drinking himself into the act before he went on, then sending himself to oblivion afterwards.

Footage of that tour has Gerard as a wreck backstage. Happily slurring and stumbling around, it was nothing for his trousers to fall down onstage and for him to fall down offstage. He would puke in car parks, then reach for another beer. He would drink to get up, then drink to go to sleep, medicating himself with anti-anxiety medication along the way. It led to some wild performances, but he was increasingly a mess. His bandmates would pick him up, dust him down, then set him on the bus.

'We're best friends,' said Frank. 'If you see your best friend fall down, you pick him up. You don't want to see anyone take advantage of him when he's in that state, so you make sure it doesn't happen. I've been there before and he's picked me up.'

Slowly, though, it dawned on them all that it was getting a little more serious.

'While I was tour managing The Used and managing My Chemical Romance at the same time, Gerard drinking was just Gerard drinking,' Brian Schechter said. 'That was what he did and he progressively got worse and worse. He would drink more and more and would just get loaded. That was the beginning of his downward spiral. Intervention wasn't working at that point – my discussions with him just weren't, the band's discussions with him just weren't. He wanted to be drunk. OK. He was a growing boy with this weird position he was in where he was singing in this band that had grown up a little too fast.'

Gerard was in thrall to the idea of the tragic, demonized frontman. 'I think people want you to self-destruct in a way,' Gerard said. 'I might be making excuses but I think people at times want you to play the character of the fucked-up drunk singer, so you start playing it for a while and then suddenly you realize that you're not playing it any more, you are that character.'

He was heading for trouble.

8: I'M NOT OKAY

Gerard Way was in Kansas City on the night of 19 July 2004 when everything came to a head. That evening, he went to see The Killers at The Hurricane club, shortly before their *Hot Fuss* album made them stars. Gerard estimates that, at the time, he was drinking a bottle of vodka a day and taking $150 worth of prescription pills a month. That night, he also scored an eight-ball of cocaine.

'That day was really the beginning of the end,' he said. 'That's when the feelings of suicide and depression got real bad. That was the explosion. I did so much [coke] that I was completely out of my mind, I was throwing up in the street and my head was going to explode. I lay in my bunk and couldn't sleep and I'd never felt more suicidal in my life. It was just a chemical thing, that was what the drug was doing to me.'

As he tried to sleep on the tour bus, Gerard hit a wall. Lying there, wide awake but emotionally and physically exhausted, he began to mentally tear himself apart while his heart pounded so hard he thought it might burst through his chest.

'I just felt so empty. I felt so much despair, more than I'd ever felt in my entire life. I felt completely desperate. I wanted everything to stop; I wanted it to all be over. I wanted to go home, I wanted to freak out and smash things, I wanted to hurt myself doing it. I wanted it all over, all of it . . . everything.

'Until that point, I had mostly just done pills and booze. Booze to get ready, to continue the high after the set and then pills to bring me down again. I was constantly trying to artificially control my brain and my moods. I thought I could have a real handle on it. Then, occasionally, I'd start dabbling in other garbage – but nothing major. Just enough that I got to the point where I realized that, in another few steps, I could go over the edge. I knew it was bad but it wasn't as bad as it could have been . . . yet.

'It all got too much. I was going mad from everything and one thing leads to another. You have to be careful in a band; it can make you an alcoholic very quickly. The booze leads to the pills, the pills lead to the coke – it's all interconnected.'

As night became day in Kansas and he lay there in his bunk, he realized he had a problem. It would be the start of a troubled week in which he would call Brian Schechter who was back in Brooklyn, and wrestle with his emotions.

'When he hit rock bottom, there was about a week's worth of rock bottom-ness,' said Schechter. 'There were a lot of 5 a.m. phone calls. The first couple of times were him opening up a little bit and saying, "I have a problem." The second couple of times were him fighting that he had a problem. And the last time was him wanting to kill himself.'

Gerard was at his lowest ebb. The problem was that his band were primed to explode. It was not the time to take a break. And so, though Gerard was telling the band's manager that he felt suicidal, My Chemical Romance remained on the road and his bandmates were oblivious to the extent of his issues. They played first with The Bled and then with Funeral For A Friend from late July into August. Immediately after that, they flew to Japan to play the Summer Sonic Festival in Osaka and Tokyo. Gerard was in no state to go. He felt so low he genuinely thought he would take his life in Japan.

'Sometimes, when you make the decision, you're at your most calm,' Gerard told me shortly after the band returned from the trip. 'I've read a lot about suicide. They say that the reason people often can't see it coming is because you've actually already made the decision. That was what happened to me in Japan. I didn't pack anything – stage clothes and a couple of changes of underwear at best – because I didn't think I was coming back.'

The rest of My Chemical Romance hadn't realized things were so bad. Or, if they had, they weren't in a position to cope with it.

'People in Gerard's state have a way of hiding it,' said Frank. 'But, at the same time, we knew he was hiding it but didn't want to deal with it.'

'We knew he drank a lot,' added Ray, 'but I don't know if we realized how severe the problem was.'

But it was on that Japan trip that Gerard crossed a boundary. Suddenly, it was all too obvious to each of them that he had a real problem.

'I was wasted there permanently,' he said. 'I was bombed out of my head on sake and I just kept going. I was waking up severely depressed – it was very, very bad depression. I didn't think I could ever climb out of it.'

His performances were shambolic, drunken and messy. One was recorded by the band's Japanese label to be released alongside *Three Cheers for Sweet Revenge* as a bonus disc and Mikey was horrified when he watched it later. 'I was like, "This isn't even us. We don't look anything like that, we don't play anything like that and we don't act anything like that." It was like a completely different band.'

The worst performance was the final one in Tokyo. As My Chemical Romance staggered to the end of the show, Gerard walked offstage and began to throw up painfully and copiously at the side of the stage. The band knew then that they could no longer ignore the crisis in front of them.

'Suddenly it was very obvious and blatant,' said Gerard. 'I was vomiting into a garbage can and, at that point, everyone knew there was a problem. I threw up for ten minutes straight and that was it, I had to make a change.

'Ray turned to our manager, Brian, while I was vomiting sake, and said, "You've got to get this dude some help. He's sick, look at him." By sick, he didn't mean I was ill either. He meant sick like I wasn't going to make it. When I heard him say that, I realized he was right. I realized I was sick and that I wasn't going to make it out of there. That was it.'

On the flight back to New York, Gerard made a decision. He said, 'I've got a problem, I'm gonna go fix it so we can be a great band.' Soon after they landed, he went and got help. He didn't have much time – within days of that return from Japan, My Chemical Romance would be on the road in the US again. He had to act quickly and decisively.

'My therapist was just a normal guy, I can't stress that enough. He wasn't some rock-doc who worked with musicians,' Gerard said. 'It was a chance encounter that I ended up being his patient. I had such little health coverage that I went to a clinic where they pick a dude for you at random – he was just a normal dude, a family guy; he liked Paul Simon. He was just the right guy for me. And I had that determination that this thing just wasn't going to fucking beat me.'

The therapist talked to Gerard, asked him about himself, and listened. And he realized something early on – it was that Gerard was unable or unwilling to draw a line between the singer onstage and the person off it. Gerard felt he needed to perform twenty-four hours a day and it was beginning to destroy him.

'I can't remember the exact quote he came up with, but it was something like, "When the music stops, the rest is silence,"' said Gerard. 'He was trying to explain that when the show is over, it's over. He wanted me to understand that the show is a show and my life is my life and that they were two separate things. He was saying I was so high on performance because I thought it was what kept me alive. He said that I was trying to continue the performance all the time. He said I was permanently in character but the character was going to kill me. He told me to just stop it, that I had to figure out how to do this without being that character the whole time.'

He also spoke to Gerard about his depression and about his sui-cidal thoughts. Certainly, the singer had considered it an escape route – an easy way to knock his problems on the head. Possibly, too, he was attracted by the idea of being the fucked-up singer in the band, the tortured frontman who had just released a brilliant album and who went down in a blaze of glory. But Gerard once told me that he doesn't know how serious he was about killing himself.

'I've always wondered whether I was flirting with the romanti-

Left to right: Jet Star, Party Poison, Fun Ghoul and Kobra Kid,
aka My Chemical Romance. London, October 2010.

Even at the very beginning the band were full-throttle live. Supporting Thursday at Irving Plaza, New York, February 2003.

Gerard gets in to 'character' recording *Three Cheers for Sweet Revenge*, Bay 7 Studios, Los Angeles, November 2003.

Frank takes a tea break during recording.

And Matt Pelissier lays down the drum tracks.

Gerard, Mikey and their mother, Donna,
at the family home in Belleville, New Jersey, February 2004.

My Chemical Romance Mark 1
on Gerard and Mikey's grandparents' sofa, February 2004.

At home with the Toros. Ray in the bedroom he shared with his two brothers, February 2004.

There is always a standout Warped Tour band each year. Mikey and Matt let San Diego know that 2004 was My Chemical Romance's year.

The happy drunk: Gerard on the Warped Tour, 2004.

Gerard getting into the character of 'the reckless street drifter'.

All smiles backstage
in Sacramento on the
2004 Warped Tour.

Frank is wistful
in Boise Idaho,
Warped Tour, 2004.
My Chemical Romance
owned the place.

Sober, focused and beginning to think hard about their image.
My Chemical Romance recreate their look from the 'I'm Not Okay (I Promise)'
video for a *Kerrang!* cover shoot. London, February 2005.

A brief and explosive friendship: Gerard and The Used's Bert McCracken.
This was the moment that My Chemical Romance began to really make waves.
Taste Of Chaos, February 2005.

About to parade through the streets of Soho before playing the Astoria, April 2005.

cism of it or whether I really wanted to do it,' he said. 'I've never truly been able to figure that out. The fact is, either way, it's dangerous.'

As Gerard sought help, the rest of My Chemical Romance had another problem they needed to address. Pelissier had long been an issue in the band, with Ray concerned that he could be unreliable onstage. Offstage, it was also clear that the relationship was not working as well as it could have. Gerard, Ray, Mikey, Frank had secretly been talking to Schechter in the summer of 2004 about sacking him. By the time they returned from Japan, the decision had been made.

A new drummer – Bob Bryar, the band's old front-of-house soundman – was in place to join but despite that quick transition it was clearly a turbulent period. In fact, Schechter was beginning to think that the band's issues at that time might prove too much for them all. He said: 'When that decision was made [to replace Pelissier], and Gerard was wasted, and the record was starting to do what it was doing – which was make an impact – all I could keep thinking in my head was, "Fuck, here it goes. This is going to be one of those legendary records that never was because the band is not going to make it through."'

The task of telling Pelissier that he was out fell to Ray and the manager. 'It was like the moment that you break up with someone you've been dating for three or four years that you used to love in the beginning of the relationship and things went sour, but for some reason you're still together,' Ray said. 'There are obviously things that went along with that, like a lack of getting along with him and a lack of being able to play the songs the same way every night. But the main reason was that we weren't having fun being in the band. He had to have known in his heart – whether he'll admit it or not – that he wasn't performing up to the way we needed to perform. You had to have been fucking blind to not see the relationship problems between each of us and him – that we just didn't get along.'

One of Pelissier's first moves was to go straight onto the message boards on the band's website and post a lengthy statement about his treatment.

'I just wanna clear some things up with you all. I'm not looking for pity, I'm not looking for the band to bring me back because I don't think I could even play with them again for a million reasons,' he wrote. 'I just want to say my side of the story to you all personally before Brian puts a post up sugar-coating or making light of what actually went down. Whether or not you believe me is up to you.

'I got home two days ago from the most exciting two shows we've played in a while in Japan; we all had an amazing time there. I get home the next day and Brian has a big band meeting and I have to be there. He was supposed to pick me up. Instead it was Ray and Brian alone in front of my house.

'They told me to take a walk, and told me I'm out of the band because, "they are uncomfortable with me onstage and they are afraid I'll mess up." I've had some whoppers on a few occasions – I'll never deny that I'm human and we all make mistakes.

'Their other reasoning was I never wanted to use the click track (a device to help me play in perfect time). The only reason I never wanted to is because I truly believe no show should be perfect. If someone wanted a perfect show they'd listen to the CD.

'They said they've been planning this for two to three months. They already have another drummer lined up. They never acted or implied that this was the plan in those two to three months. Just acted like they were my brothers. I still haven't even heard from Gerard since I saw him at the airport. I never got a band meeting to discuss this, just the boot for messing up.

'Do I think I've been shafted? Yeah. What I want to know though is what happened to the five brothers that loved each other more than anyone else on earth, that no one would come in between. I loved those brothers with all my heart, I would have gone down in a plane crash, taken the bullet for any of them. I gave up everything for each one of them. This is the thanks I get. Someone please tell me what happened to my best friends. Because they are lost.'

He went down to the band's rehearsal space to try and remove his drums, to find that he couldn't get in. He left a note, pointing out they were his drums and that he wanted them back and got a call back from Frank in return telling him not to be so immature. '[I] told him to grow up and to call me when he did. He hasn't called yet,' said the guitarist.

'We always wondered whether it was going to be a good show or a disaster,' said Frank of playing with Pelissier. 'No one was having fun offstage and even on sometimes. I don't think about those times because they were bad times.'

Pelissier has since gone on to form his own band Revenir but declined to be interviewed for this book or to respond to what the band have said about him. He made it clear, though, that he is still angry about his treatment.

Frank believed there was fault on both sides, saying that My Chemical Romance tried to make the relationship with Pelissier work but that things had run their course.

'You could say that compromises need to be made, that both parties can change, but it had got to the point where we had compromised too much and we were changing ourselves to make something work that wasn't ever going to work,' he said. 'For two and a half years we tried really hard to make that relationship work. And we recorded two really good records and, even through the frustrations and bad times we had, there were definitely some good times there. Maybe the split [with Pelissier] should have happened before we made [*Three Cheers*], maybe it should have happened when it did – I don't know. Hindsight is 20/20, I guess.'

The decision to recruit Bob was in some ways simple but in others a risk. He was a friend of the band, they knew they could tour with him as they had spent time on the road already and he was available immediately. The only thing was, no one in My Chemical Romance had actually heard him play.

Bob, born on New Year's Eve 1979, grew up on the outskirts of

Chicago and started playing drums aged four. 'I didn't really know what the hell I was doing at that age – but there are pictures of me beating drums,' he said. 'I was fucking around. But when I got into grade school I joined the school band. I picked the snare drum and took lessons and went from there.'

He played in the jazz band, the marching band and the orchestra at Junior High but then quit all three when he got to high school simply because he felt no one else was taking it seriously enough. There was also a certain amount of peer pressure involved – playing in school bands was hardly cool. 'The whole band-dork thing came in,' he said, and so he had a change of heart.

'There was a group of jazz guys who would get together and play coffee houses and parties, so I would do that a lot,' he said. 'Then I joined a punk band and a rock band. I joined a King Crimson cover band for a while because we wanted to have two drum-kits onstage. It was fun but a little ridiculous – nobody wanted to come and watch us.

'Then I formed my own band, which was kind of a punk-rock band. I was of the mentality that you play as many gigs as you can when you're in a band. You buy a van and you tour as much as possible. Other people in my band had girlfriends, they wanted to go to school and that kind of stuff and so I gave up for a while. I went off and got a degree in recording and sound-engineering and did that instead.'

He trained in Florida and briefly played drums at Disney World in the Little Mermaid and Aladdin shows, before returning to Chicago and working at the House Of Blues venue as their soundman. After doing that for a couple of years, touring bands realized his skills and would ask him to go out on the road with them. He went out with the post-hardcore band Thrice and then became The Used's soundman, which is where he met My Chemical Romance's future manager Brian Schechter, who was then The Used's tour manager. While on the road with Thrice, he met My Chemical Romance for the first time and immediately fell in love with their sound.

'It was weird, we clicked right off the bat,' he said. 'We hung out together all the time. They knew I played drums but I don't think they ever heard me play them.

'The first time I saw MCR play was in Irving Plaza in New York. When they were finished, I thought, "If this band ever need a drummer, I'm there." This was before *Three Cheers* was out; hardly anyone knew them and not that many went to see them. But, from that day, I knew I wanted to play for them. We became really good friends. Then, when the opportunity came up, I was in the middle of another tour and I just baled on it immediately.'

So desperate was he to join that, when the band asked him to replace Pelissier, he didn't tell them he had broken his ankle. He reasoned that, given how tight time was with My Chemical Romance when he was recruited, if he were to mention that he could barely close his hi-hat pedal, then they would be forced to ask someone else to come on board. 'I was worried people would think I sucked because I couldn't use my foot,' said Bob, 'so I pretended it didn't hurt. It really fucking hurt.'

His first act as a member of My Chemical Romance would put his injury to the test. The band had a video shoot scheduled for the performance part of 'I'm Not Okay (I Promise)' and would then be going out on the road again. Within days of replacing Pelissier, Bob was behind the kit shooting the video for the single that would become the band's breakthrough hit. A few days later, he would be touring.

Given that My Chemical Romance hadn't yet played with him, it was a brave move to include him in a video for the first single from *Three Cheers for Sweet Revenge*. Had things not gone well, it would have been odd to see a drummer behind the kit who did not play with the band. Beyond the video, it was likely the forthcoming tour would have had to have been cancelled. 'It was the riskiest thing this band has ever done,' said Bob. 'If it hadn't worked with me, it would have been a disaster.'

Directed by Marc Webb (who would go on to direct *The Amazing Spider-Man* feature film), the 'I'm Not Okay (I Promise)' video itself was a satirical swipe at rights-of-passage high-school movies, and

was presented as the trailer to a film. Split between the band performing in their rehearsal space, and high-school scenes in which
Gerard, Mikey, Frank and Ray play preppy, weird and croquet-play-
ing nerds bullied by the school jocks, it is funny at first, before an
underlying darkness emerges. 'People thought it was going to be a
pop-punk teen video and then they realized it was very dark and it
was referencing things like [the Wes Anderson film] *Rushmore.*'

The school scenes were intercut with footage of the band playing in their rehearsal space – Bob doing an admirable job of
appearing not to be in agony. The video wouldn't be released for
another four months and, by then, Bob was a firmly established part
of My Chemical Romance. The others immediately enjoyed having
Bob in the band. They liked his commitment – an example of which
came one night when, shortly after joining, he drove their van for
seventeen hours straight – and they liked the fact he could play. The
only thing was, they completely forgot to tell him he was actually,
formally in.

'It was odd because they never really said, officially, that I was a
member of the band,' said Bob. 'About a year later, when we were
hanging out in the bus, they came up and said, "I don't think we
ever said you were actually in the band, we just kind of assumed it.
You are in, by the way . . ."'

Bob found the attention that came with being in a successful
band awkward at first. Nervy, self-conscious and, as a soundman,
unused to being the focus of attention, he tended to keep himself to
himself – viewing himself as a worker in the band's engine room
rather than a star. 'I remember the first time we did a photo shoot
and I was shitting my pants,' he said. 'It felt so weird to do that kind
of stuff. Walking outside and meeting kids who want my autograph
was very weird to me. I could understand why they would want to
meet Gerard – and he was able to just walk straight up to them and
know that every one of them wanted to have their picture taken. I
would doubt whether they knew who I was and I couldn't figure out
why they would want to talk to me. I didn't want to seem like a dick
and not sign something for someone but I needed to be called over

because I was never sure they wanted to talk to me. I didn't really know why they would want to meet me. I think that's the way I grew up. I never expected anything like that.'

The late summer of 2004 was a period of significant change for My Chemical Romance but it was one when their star was very much on the rise. I first interviewed the band at that time in New York – thirteen days after they had returned from Japan and ten days after Gerard had stopped drinking. In fact, it's likely that the first photo shoot that Bob was so afraid of was for the *Kerrang!* article I was writing.

Bob was quiet and nervous, speaking mostly just to Mikey, who also tended to take a back seat. Ray and Frank talked passionately about the band's music, but Gerard seemed to have something he wanted to get off his chest.

I had no idea of Gerard's recent history at this point. His drinking was not something he had talked about with anyone but his band, their manager and his therapist. But as we talked, he became more and more open. He talked about how he struggled to fill the time off the road because he didn't know what else to do with himself. I asked him if he drank a lot – not because I suspected anything, but because it was something other bands had told me they did to kill boredom.

Gerard stopped, and he looked at the rest of the band. Then he plunged right in and revealed what he had been going through.

'Not any more but certainly in the past,' he said. 'It was heavy drinking too. I've completely stopped drinking now because it all got too much. I was going mad.'

And then the whole story came out, that night in Kansas, the thoughts of suicide and the collapse in Japan. All the darkness, the depression and the black days on the road, the puking, the self-loathing and the unpleasantness of that time. He talked of therapy, of despair and emptiness, as his band looked on, uncertainly. He said that the only thing he was leaning on right then was the fact he felt he was on top his problems. 'I feel like I'm in control,' he said. 'Control is important to me, because musically we're so out of control. We're so on edge in this band that I want everything else to be very controlled. I need it to stay sane.'

It was the first time he had told an outsider about his problems and it was difficult for the rest of the band to watch. They shifted uncomfortably in their seats. There was a feeling that he had said more around this table, and in more detail, than he had ever confessed to a stranger before. They seemed a little shaken.

Later that night, when they played New York's Irving Plaza, it was interesting to see how they performed. It was Bob's fifth show with the band and Gerard's fifth sober one. At the start of that tour, they had been nervous about whether the singer would be the same visceral presence onstage without alcohol and whether the new drummer would fit. 'I remember, for those first couple of shows, I was thinking, "Oh man . . ."' said Frank.

However, that night in New York, My Chemical Romance were spectacular. I had never seen drunk Gerard perform, but sober Gerard was a revelation as he preached, wailed and howled at the crowd. I remember thinking that My Chemical Romance would do just fine, as long as they could hold it all together.

Gerard's big struggle was that he had to figure out how to stay sober on the road. It was one thing to avoid alcohol while at home, but quite another to steer clear of it in the bars and clubs in which they would be spending their days and nights while on tour.

My Chemical Romance were on the verge of real success too – their shows were getting bigger, better and busier, while demands on their time for interviews, promo spots and the general hyping of their record were getting more demanding. Gerard was going to have to find a dividing line between his on- and offstage persona, while out on tour, with a new band member, and surrounded by alcohol in venues. It wouldn't be easy.

'That was one of the hardest things,' he said. 'The actual physical addiction was the first part. I went through the sweats; I was lying in the bottom of the van shaking. I was sweating it out on tour.

'But then came the mental part because I thought, "Drinking is what I do in a club." I had to make these fake drinks – cranberry juice, Red Bull and ice was one – and I would nurse them constantly. It's something I've seen a lot of alcoholics do – they're always holding these bizarre non-alcoholic mixes for a long time when they first get clean. That's what I had to do. It was the first thing I did in a club. I had it on the rider. It was a ritual.'

And then there was the pressure of performing. Since their first show, alcohol had been the prop that got Gerard onstage and, so he thought, made him the frontman he was. Now, though, he had to be that frontman sober. Worse still, there was so much hype surrounding *Three Cheers for Sweet Revenge* that the spotlight was particularly bright. Critics were writing up My Chemical Romance as the band with the wild frontman: sober Gerard had to find a way of living up to drunk Gerard's reputation.

'In the very beginning I had this obsessive, weird vibe. I felt like I lived it every day, that I was always the person you see onstage. I used to have this extreme confidence where I felt like nothing could touch us,' said Gerard. 'Becoming an alcoholic kind of ruined that. Then quitting it made it worse for a while. I didn't have any confidence, I felt bizarre onstage a lot of the time. I wasn't confident about how unhealthy I looked, about how bloated the pills were making me. I didn't want to look like a washed-up dude.

'One thing I noticed about quitting drinking and pills was all the free time I had offstage and on. Onstage I had free time and I would stand there not knowing what to do with myself. I also felt like I'd created this character so well, that it was all I had. When I stopped drinking it felt like I'd defeated the purpose of Gerard from My Chemical Romance. I felt I had to live up to the drunken Gerard. I felt invalid, like I'd lost the thing that made me me. It took a whole tour to sort that out.'

Sober, Gerard took a good hard look at himself. 'That period where I'd just quit was the first time I'd seen myself clearly and I saw it all,' he said. 'Losing my grandmother was the worst moment in my life. This was the second. I'm sure the two are connected.'

Frank thinks Gerard struggled at first but says that, once he worked out how to get onstage without alcohol, he became a much better frontman.

'[Drinking] was Gerard's way to get onstage and deal with playing in front of people. Then it turned into something he thought he had to do. Since he stopped he realized the booze wasn't the reason he was performing; it was his talent. Realizing that was definitely a confidence booster for him.'

Still, Gerard's sobriety was a work in progress and for the next year he would struggle. Two weeks after the Irving Plaza show, the band were in the UK again on a short tour that culminated at the now demolished Mean Fiddler venue in central London. Gerard remembers that he found it difficult to be onstage, that he was forcing moves while sober that had come naturally to him while drunk.

'There was a review from the Mean Fiddler show that said, "If he's sober now, I can't imagine what he was like on the booze,"' recalled Gerard shortly afterwards. 'That night I was consciously thinking to myself about how I could defeat the old Gerard, how I could defeat the drunk Gerard. Every day I destroy that person a little more.'

Gerard's battle to get sober and Bob's arrival in the band coincided with My Chemical Romance's explosion on both sides of the Atlantic. 'I'm Not Okay (I Promise)' was released in September and by December the band had played on *Late Night with Conan O'Brien* twice (with Frank taping 'Hi Mom + Dad' to his amp); by January 2005 they had appeared on *Late Show with David Letterman*, playing to a US audience of over three million – with Gerard describing the feeling of playing on TV as like 'being a Martian'. Soon afterwards, they played on the influential *TRL* show on MTV and their performance was beamed onto massive TV screens on Time Square in New York – the band requiring a police escort to get back to their van. Things were happening, and they were happening fast.

The band toured constantly again – playing 230 shows in 2005, with days off filled with travel, promo and very little rest. The year began with a January tour of the UK in support of Taking Back Sunday, including a show at the renowned Brixton Academy, and it was arguable as to which band had drawn the greater number of fans. They played their own sold-out headline show at Islington Academy on 4 February at the end of that tour, a powerful and explosive performance that saw the entire room drenched in sweat and a subsequent *Kerrang!* review that started with the line, 'This is fucking astonishing.'

Next came dates in Japan and Hawaii, before they joined the Taste Of Chaos tour with old friends The Used, plus Killswitch Engage and Senses Fail across North America. It was then that *Three Cheers* went to yet another level. 'When that tour happened,' says Craig Aaronson, 'it was game-fucking-on.'

'When they did that US tour with The Used, Taste Of Chaos, that's when we really started to see it taking off,' says their booking agent Matt Galle. 'They started having huge crowds come out for them every night in those arenas. They were going on before The Used and a lot of people were leaving after My Chem played. We were like, "Wow, what's going on here? There's some kind of move- ment here." Right then, it really hit us.

'What was it that connected? The sincerity and the message they were sending across. They were hitting a lot of real topics and some of them were uncomfortable for people. They were going into areas that not a lot of other people were going. They were just dudes from New Jersey who didn't give a shit about anything. They just wanted to play great music and spread their message. And people could tell – people could see they weren't out to just grab a cheque. They never were.'

Though Gerard and The Used's singer Bert McCracken were friendly on the tour – and posed for pictures together, still looking the closest of friends – something changed in their relationship sub- sequently. Later in the year, McCracken was talking of a falling out and saying that he didn't speak to Gerard any more. 'A friend is like a grilled cheese sandwich: it's nice when you first get it but when you leave it there for a bit, it gets soggy and fucking not worth it,'

he said later, adding that he 'couldn't give less of a shit about My
Chemical Romance or any of those other bands that sound exactly
the same.' Gerard, when asked about it, would sigh wearily and
wonder who McCracken was now mouthing off to. It seems relevant
that the pair's relationship was first forged when both had a taste for
alcohol, and changed after Gerard lost his. It was also on Taste Of
Chaos that My Chemical Romance began to eclipse The Used, the
band they owed their first ever European tour to. Some suggested
the change in status grated with McCracken but he denied it, saying,
'It's got nothing to do with their success.' However, as late as
February 2013 he was adamant that Gerard and his band owed The
Used a debt.

After Taste Of Chaos, My Chemical Romance noticed that
things felt different. They had gone from being a band with a shot,
to one that appeared to have hit the bullseye. *Three Cheers for Sweet
Revenge* was becoming a phenomenon. Meanwhile Gerard was still
battling to stay sober.

'It was really crazy to be inside the band then because everything was going mad and I had just chosen to get clean,' said
Gerard. 'Not only was I dealing with all this new stuff with the
band, I was also dealing with getting a new body by getting clean.

'People don't always know this about addiction but, when you
get clean, you have to re-learn how to do everything. You don't
know how to cook for yourself. You don't know how to do your
laundry, you don't know how to do things because you're so used
to doing them fucked up. You don't know how to talk to people.
Meanwhile, we were having to go on TV, give interviews, get our
pictures taken and give our opinions on world events or bullshit
celebrity-gossip events. I was thinking, "Oh my God, I don't even
know how to dress myself."

'I was trying to figure out how to deal with everything and
having to talk to journalists about world peace. It was enormously
hard to deal with. It was such a trial by fire. The benefit was that
getting through that made us realize we could do anything.'

To keep his mind off alcohol on the road, Gerard focused on

where the band might go next. He thought about looks, he thought about their image, and he thought about what they might do onstage to heighten their performances. He would also draw, scribbling art-work and pondering where he might take his comic book art. Anything to fight his urges and to fill the time.

'I had to concentrate on being creative, I had to let the creative side take over the alcoholic side,' he said. 'I got excited about writing songs again as opposed to just shredding them out live. I got really interested in doing things apart from the band to help [get some] separation. Writing the whole time, and not necessarily for the band, occupied my time then, so I had a good separation where it didn't really feel like a job for me to be in a band. I could turn it on and off.'

He thought about the band's image and slowly My Chemical Romance became more stylized. Frank would wear a flak jacket onstage and for photo shoots – something that eventually the rest of the band would come to adopt. It was the start of a more cohesive style for the band – in photo shoots they (or Gerard, to be specific) were becoming far more interested in how they came across, hence they might dress as the Droogs from *A Clockwork Orange* or in stark black suits with bright red ties in others. Slowly, Gerard's comic book influences were inspiring their look, their videos and their ideas. In a post-hardcore scene populated by bands in jeans, T-shirts and matching haircuts, they stood out a thousand miles. And it was a look that was key to their appeal – something they would work on much harder and more grandly on their next record.

'We have started to do things in a more theatrical sense,' Gerard said then. 'I like things that bring that element back to rock 'n' roll, showmanship and theatre. I miss that stuff; you don't see it any more at rock shows.'

By April 2005, they were back in the UK briefly after *Three Cheers'* second single 'Helena' went into the Top 20 having already gone into the US Top 40. Evidence of My Chemical Romance's increased attention to theatricality came in the video, which was dark and gothic but camp and kitsch. A cast of mourners pay tribute to a young girl lying in a coffin in church, as Gerard stands above, playing the preacher in the pulpit. As the song explodes, so too do a troupe of dancers, jazz-hands held high as the funeral begins. The girl is revived, dances, then dies again, collapsing back into her coffin – a stark visual statement and one that Gerard found a little unnerving to film, given the song was written about the death of his grandmother and his anger at himself for not being there for the end of her life.

'It was extremely cathartic at first,' he said. 'But the video was the hardest video we have ever made, because of that. I think that might be why it's our best. It was almost torturous to make. I showed up and the coffin was the same [as his grandmother's]. I watched Tracey Phillips, who was the dancer, do the dance segment and I had to leave. There were a lot of moments that I had to leave that video. There was a very sombre mood. It was very quiet. We all sat in the church very quietly.

'Maybe that's where the magic is in that video – because it came from a completely raw place. My grandmother's funeral was very hard and that video was like reliving it again. That video was very special, really personal.'

Again directed by Marc Webb, it was nominated for five MTV Video Music Awards and was so beautifully and sensitively shot that it heightened My Chemical Romance's visual appeal. Where other bands filmed videos showing them simply playing, My Chemical Romance were making statements with theirs. And once made, they followed them through. The band's show at London's Astoria on 9 April 2005 was preceded by a funeral procession through Soho with Victorian mourners marching behind a vintage hearse. It was a record company stunt that the band were fully behind, or at least they were until the hearse broke down and had to be pushed.

Their short UK tour was followed with a massive jaunt around America, supporting Green Day at what was arguably their peak as they toured their *American Idiot* album. The experience would have a profound effect on My Chemical Romance. Watching Green Day's singer Billie Joe Armstrong control these vast arenas struck Gerard in particular. He saw how Green Day's stagecraft could inspire and how a band could hold the attention of so many people.

Green Day, for their part, were just as impressed with their support act, and they would hang out with them when not onstage, even getting into fancy dress together. 'I remember one time we went to see the last *Star Wars* when it came out, and we all dressed up,' Armstrong said to *Kerrang!*'s Ian Winwood. 'Gerard went with the dark side. He didn't go as one particular character, he kind of did his own thing. But he looked cool. The whole evening was pretty funny.'

On that tour with Green Day, Gerard turned to Armstrong for advice. On top of attempting to remain sober, Gerard was also having difficulties with the increased attention he was receiving as the singer in such a fast-rising band. Initially, he had thought that attention was what he wanted – then, once he started getting it, he thought again.

'I can be kind of a parody,' he said. 'I'm like, "Pay attention to me, pay attention to me!" Then, when they do, I'm like, "Don't pay attention to me any more!" That's the role I've been fighting forever.'

It was something he discussed with the Green Day frontman, asking him how to come to terms with fame, how to behave in public. Armstrong told him something very simple – that he was a rock star and he should embrace it.

'When we were on tour with them I had conversations with Gerard,' said Armstrong. 'He was feeling a bit uncertain at the time and I just told him not to be afraid. I think he was shying away. He was at that point where a band reads too much of its own press, and they start to internalize everything. To the point where they become boring. So I told him that it's OK to be a rock star. It's OK to be that, because the world needs good rock stars. We've got enough boring people. And he took that to heart, I guess.'

Gerard did. 'That's exactly what he said to me,' he remembered. 'It's a cliché to say "I'm a rock star but I'm really not a rock star because rock stars are lame." No, people look up to us. We should give them hope; we should empower them and give them something to believe in. I'm not afraid of that any more. I'm not going to pretend that's not what we are. I'm going to embrace it and run with it. We're going to give them something to believe in. We like playing to 20,000 people, we're into that now.'

Soon there was a new purpose to Gerard as he went out onstage. He was increasingly comfortable in front of the spotlights, his movements and speeches no longer feeling as forced as when he first tried them sober.

'The coolest thing is that it doesn't take me all day to get into character any more, it doesn't even take me an hour,' said Gerard. 'An hour before the set I put my make-up on but even then I'm joking around, I'm the same dude and I stay that same dude until they turn the lights off now. It's the first time in my life I've had that. I used to have to punch mirrors, spit and curse at myself, yell at God and everything.'

By June, My Chemical Romance would be on the Warped Tour again as, increasingly, their thoughts turned to new music. As they toured in the summer of 2005, they began to give some serious thought to what they might do after *Three Cheers for Sweet Revenge*. They hired another bus, ripped out the back of it, and put a makeshift studio in there. In the daytime before shows, they wrote new material in it, working through the songs that would later make up *The Black Parade*. With Ray operating the recording equipment, they sketched out the bare bones of where they would go next. A new flamboyance entered their sound. And throughout it all, Gerard worked hard to stay off the booze. He dealt with the issue by refusing to socialize, burying himself on the tour bus, avoiding temptation and seeking solace in creativity.

'I'm sure I made a lot of enemies on Warped Tour and I'm sure I lost a lot of friends because I couldn't hang out,' he said. 'I wouldn't leave the bus. I knew people were going to think that I'd changed and that I'd become a "rock star". I knew I just had to fucking deal with that because if I had left the bus and one more person had waved a bottle of alcohol in front of me – which had been happening since the first day – then I knew I would have gone crazy and would have had to have gone home. I had to be the asshole on the bus. So that's what I did and I'm very proud of it. It's quite hard to make the decision to be disliked.'

He relied on his bandmates and My Chemical Romance's crew to support him, to prop him up and to tell him he would get through it. On the Warped Tour, recovering alcoholics in the tour crew would chat to him too, passing on their experience of going through Alcoholics Anonymous.

'There are a lot of people who deserve a medal for keeping me clean on that tour,' he said. 'A lot of stage managers helped me out and a lot of good people checked on me every day. Without them, I wouldn't have made it through. They knew why I was on that bus.'

It wasn't wasted time. The music he and his bandmates were making in their makeshift studio would take them to yet another level.

9: BURN BRIGHT

Evidence of quite what a stunning year 2005 was for My Chemical Romance came when they returned to the UK to tour in November. Three dates into the run, they played Brixton Academy – the venue where they had started the year as Taking Back Sunday's support act. This time they headlined the grand old hall. And they did so for two nights in a row.

I joined them on that tour and discovered a band who were delighted that life was going so well, but who were also approaching burnout. They had released the third single, 'Ghost of You', from *Three Cheers for Sweet Revenge* in August and there was some pressure to justify the fact they had spent over $1m on the thrilling video that accompanied it – hence they were touring again. Set in World War II, the video reimagined the band as wartime crooners and mimicked the opening scene of *Saving Private Ryan*, with the band storming ashore in boats while being shot at from gun towers. It hadn't been easy to persuade Warners to part with the cash so near to the end of the album cycle, but Craig Aaronson – who describes his A&R role as to 'keep everybody's dick up' – had finally convinced the record company to think of it as an investment in the band's next record.

It meant that My Chemical Romance needed to prove they were worth it, though. So, as they arrived in the UK for the last time on the *Three Cheers* tour, their schedule was so tight that there was barely time to draw breath. They played their first date in Wolverhampton at Wulfrun Hall only hours after getting off their flight. 'Our bus was supposed to pick us up from the airport,' said Ray, 'but it wasn't there. There was some kind of mix up I think, so we had to rent a mini-van.

'We all jammed into this thing with all our gear and luggage piled all over us. It was actually pretty cool; it brought back memories of the first time we toured England in a splitter van. It was kind of funny to be back in one when we were doing a headlining tour. But Wolverhampton was the first place we ever played in England too so it all fitted. It was actually really exciting to go back there and headline.'

They didn't even spend the night in Wolverhampton, driving straight down to Portsmouth that night in a whirlwind. Life was changing fast for My Chemical Romance at this point – they were going from contenders to stars, and with that came almost constant calls for their time.

The following night was their double London date, and the build-up included a trip to Radio 1 to record a cover version of Blur's 'Song 2' for DJ Jo Whiley's Live Lounge sessions – a song Gerard and Mikey had loved growing up. 'We wanted to do an Oasis song,' said Ray, before revealing the exalted circles in which they were beginning to operate, 'but the Foo Fighters had already recorded it.'

Those two nights in London were a career highlight – 'two of the best shows we've ever played in our entire life,' Ray told me. 'Seeing kids making circle pits in between songs makes us play better because we can see how much they're having a good time and it fuels us. Brixton is a legendary venue too, so to play two nights there in front of such an incredible crowd is so great. It was one of the best times we've ever had onstage.'

A day off followed, and all five of My Chemical Romance headed to Camden in North London and trawled the vintage clothes shops, comic book stores and markets. Constantly they were stopped and asked for autographs and photographs and, good-naturedly, they obliged. Gerard bought himself a vast leather jacket and, swirling around while wearing it, he looked like a pimp, albeit a pasty one, in a Camden backstreet. His bandmates were horrified, especially since they had all been telling me how good it was to see Gerard so settled after a turbulent year of sobriety.

'Are you fucking kidding me?' howled Ray on seeing the coat.

'You look like a poodle,' laughed Bob.

'How much did you spend on that?' asked Frank, disbelieving.

'Erm . . . £60,' said Gerard, his expression increasingly sheepish.

'Dude, what are you thinking?' replied Frank.

'We were just talking about how you've settled down!' said Ray.

'How you're not a crazy asshole any more!' added Frank.

'Un-fucking-real,' muttered Ray before Frank shook his head and chuckled. 'You need a cane, a pimp hat and some bitches with that,' he said finally. To the best of my knowledge, the leather jacket was never seen again.

The laughs they were having made a marked change from their experiences of touring the UK with Pelissier. Back then, they were tired and miserable. This time, they were still tired but they were happy and successful.

'Our childhood dreams are coming true,' said Frank. 'Touring with Green Day, seeing the world, headlining shows in Japan and England – if someone told me we'd be doing that four years ago I would have told them they were lying.'

Even the exhaustion of touring for so long was something in which they could find positives. This was their twenty-first straight month on the road – and they still had another month to go in Canada and Australia – and though they moaned when extra dates were added, or further rounds of interviews were scheduled, they knew they were reaping the benefits.

'When you've been on tour for a year and a half straight and you're given a little time off, then it gets snatched away from you when someone books another date, you can feel haggard and in a routine and like it's a job,' said Frank. 'But if you go onstage and flatten a crowd then it's such a release after that. It's unlike any drug or any other experience you can have. There's a special feeling in knowing that you've given your all, that you're left on the floor, that you're completely done and you're going to do it the next day too.

The feeling you want is that you have nothing left. If we can get up onstage and destroy everything, it doesn't matter where we are. You could put us in a dark room and never let us out and never let us know where we are if we could kill every night.'

My Chemical Romance spoke a lot about wanting to feel dangerous in those days. It was how they motivated themselves, how they pumped themselves up before a show. Perhaps more than most bands, there was a mindset and an adrenalized spirit they needed to find before they hit the stage.

There was a very intense psychology at work between the five of them then, something that was fostered and distilled by the amount of time they had spent with each other in alien situations. Alongside their crew, they had found themselves in strange places all over the world – in venues in Japan, in arenas in the States, being lauded and screamed at in England – and they had turned to each other for support, hunkering down and developing an unusual mentality. Given Gerard, Mikey and Ray's sometimes lonely childhoods, they had been forced to adapt quickly to being in the public eye.

Gerard compared touring in those days to 'going to war'. It's part of the reason that the 'Ghost of You' video portrayed the band as World War II soldiers under fire, but it spoke volumes too about the passion in what they were doing then. Simply, this was becoming an all-consuming, all-powerful thing for them – not always healthily so. Gerard spoke of wanting to prove wrong all the people who had told him he wouldn't make it.

'I became obsessed with revenge ever since I heard the Black Flag song "Revenge",' he said. 'Then, later on, revenge started to mean something to this band; we thought we could get even for all the shit that's happened to us in our lives, for being raised by good parents in a really bad area and wanting to break out of that and see the world. And revenge on all the people who never believed in us – because there were tons of them.'

He said he obsessed over death, that shows were life-or-death affairs in which the results were victories and defeats. He talked a lot about fighting.

'A victory is a thousand kids throwing their fists in the air and screaming the lyrics to a song. That's a victory to me,' he said. 'I always think in terms of victories and defeats. I'm glad we haven't lost that about ourselves. But this is still a fight and I think we have a lot more fighting to do.'

Given the band had just played two nights at the 5,000-capacity Brixton Academy, the fact he felt there was still something to fight for – that they hadn't made it yet – showed his intense drive. If they hadn't yet won, surely they must have felt they were at least winning?

'We feel like we have the sons of bitches by the balls!' Gerard said, grinning wildly. 'That's the best way to describe it. We're not ready to let go at all. There's a feeling that there's shitty music and we want to defeat it by the throat or by the balls. We're a little punk-rock band that may not get artistic critical acclaim, but we're going to fight so much that we can't be ignored. We won't be ignored any more, we're just too loud.'

The UK tour continued through Glasgow – where each of them was given a pair of personalized underpants by fans ('Mine said, "Frank the zaniest",' revealed Frank. 'I don't know if that's a compliment') – and on to Newcastle and then Manchester. By then, the dates were beginning to wear them out. Gerard had a streaming cold, and he wandered around the Apollo with both hands clamped around a ginger tea rather than the more usual cigarette. Still, just watching them that day was interesting – a glimpse of who they were and how they behaved behind the scenes.

By the time of the soundcheck, the mood had improved a little, and the band spent time working on a new song, 'Disenchanted'. They sped it up, slowed it down, reworked a passage then played it all over again. But after the soundcheck finished, the atmosphere grew strained again. It was clear the months on the road were beginning to take their toll – the pep that had existed in London was ebbing, the November cold in Manchester was seeping into their bones, and some eyes, perhaps, were on the end of December, when they would finally be getting a break.

In their dressing room before show time, every surface was littered with cans of drink and bits of their rider. As their support band Every Time I Die went through their set, Gerard and Ray bounced on the spot, doing jumping jacks to get the blood pumping. When show time arrived, they high-fived each other and headed for the stage. Their intro music on that tour – The Smiths' 'Please, Please, Please, Let Me Get What I Want' – blared over the PA as the excitement built. And then they launched into their set, looking on as an ecstatic audience swirled and seethed in front of them. The tetchiness and streaming cold became a distant memory then.

'When the lights go off before you walk on, that's when the excitement builds,' said Gerard later. 'That's when you have those little moments with each other. You look at each other and you know what you're about to do. Then onstage it's all body chemistry. Onstage it's all looks. We read each other. We always know where each other are at all times onstage.

'It's so incredible and so addictive up there. We were home for a week recently and, by the fifth day, I was saying, "I need that crowd again." Without it, I feel powerless. It's a reason to live. I need a reason to do this.

'The point is to become something extraordinary for an hour a day. That's the reason for this. When we write music, it's to become something extraordinary onstage. The whole point is that we're jerk-offs and losers but, onstage for an hour, we become untouchable and that's what's special.'

Though their set was not the best that night in Manchester, the crowd were exceptional. Security guards at the front of the stage were pulling out crowd-surfers and fans who were passing out. The band knew it wasn't a perfect set, yet as they left the stage before their encore, all five were pumped from the energy of it all.

'We're chatty as hell when we come offstage,' Gerard said. 'It's probably the silliest moment you'll ever catch us. It's the biggest release – you're offstage, you're all sweaty and just talking about all the stupid shit that happened onstage. You're always apologizing for making mistakes that no one else noticed.'

That night they talked about Mikey, who managed to get hit by chewing gum that one crowd member had thrown and had also slipped over backwards – 'It wasn't my night,' he smiled. They talked too about a trick that Bob performed with his drumsticks, which the rest of the band pretended they had seen just to stop him talking about it.

'Bob is always talking about something he fucked up that no one heard, or about the trick he does with his sticks,' said Ray. 'We have to tell him we saw it even if we didn't just to keep him happy. Drummers are the most sensitive people . . .'

They headed back out to finish the set, their last dregs of energy seeing them to the close. Two more songs, and they were done – collapsing in their dressing room before showering and towelling down, then ignoring the piles of pizzas the promoter had ordered for them. The tiredness they had felt before going onstage returned and they buried themselves in their laptops, playing *World of Warcraft* on their computers and barely chatting. The tiredness was getting to all of them then.

'After the show we're not the band to be going out to all the strip joints,' said Gerard. 'We all just sit together; we're like a bunch of little old men. We reflect for a bit, that's a custom, then we shower and go back to the bus and do the same shit again. Then we're in bunks reading comics, playing video games.'

'If it's been a good night you don't have to try to come down from the buzz of being onstage at all,' said Frank. 'If it's been good, you're totally spent, you have absolutely nothing left. That feeling of being completely drained means you've played well. I don't think about going out to a bar afterwards because I've already achieved what I was supposed to be here to do – play the show.'

Still, the five of them looked beat that night in Manchester. They were worn out and it meant that they knew they weren't at their best. Frank admitted as much.

'By the time we got round to doing [that] headline tour, we were so exhausted,' he said. 'We felt done. I felt like I had nothing left. Looking back, a lot of that tour is a blur. I didn't know where I was most of the time. I thought that if I gave any more then I wouldn't be the same again. There was a whole month of that tour when I couldn't move. I felt bad because, although I was giving everything I had onstage, I knew it wasn't as much as I could have given a year ago. I felt like I was cheating people, I felt like a jerk because I didn't have a hundred per cent to give. I didn't have time to regenerate, to sleep, rest and heal my body. I still had injuries from months earlier that hadn't had time to heal.'

Part of the problem was the fact that, though they had always wanted to tour as much as possible, they hadn't realized the added pressures that came with playing in bigger venues, to bigger crowds, with a big record to support. The relentlessness of it all was becoming problematic. 'Nobody tells you how to take care of yourselves,' said Frank. 'Nobody tells you that you need to take a break.'

After they came offstage that night in Manchester, and after tiring of *World of Warcraft*, Gerard wearily left the others to it. He wandered out of the backstage door to the band's tour bus where, even several hours after the set finished, there was still a big crowd waiting for him. He spent fifteen minutes signing autographs as something like a frenzy built – fans clamouring and yelling, squeezing and shoving past each other to get near him. It got a little too much. When one fan grabbed at him a little too forcefully, he had to calm them down. It signalled the end of the impromptu signing session.

'Sometimes you feel like an object during those moments and that's one of the biggest drags,' said Gerard. 'Of course it's flattering too, but you get worried that they'll hurt themselves because it's hard to stop them shoving each other.'

Other times, though, he enjoyed the attention and played along with it. 'I actually have a lot of fun because, sometimes [people have] built me up as something,' he said. 'Then they say, "Oh, you're really quiet, your voice is different than I expected, you're really nice." The big one is, "You're smaller than I thought." Everyone says that.'

Such attention – whether welcome or not – was a sign of how much the band's stock was rising and how passionate their fans were becoming. My Chemical Romance were famous now – not something they had ever expected. A little later, after the others had come back to the bus with Gerard, they chatted about the change they had noticed.

'Those moments are weird,' said Ray. 'You feel like you're in a cage sometimes, that you only exist for their amusement and that's an odd thing to feel. People will run along the side of the bus and shout, or they'll be yelling at you to take your hood off or make a face.'

'But you can't be rude to them, unless they're rude to you,' added Gerard. 'If I don't get a good vibe from someone, then I won't help them out. Often I won't do the things they tell me to do because I don't want to become a puppet.'

Mikey found it hardest of all. 'I have social anxiety. I find it hard to talk to people that I don't really know. Sometimes I feel like people think I'm a dick. When I get approached in the street I get freaked out, I get nervous. I get funny around large groups of people. It's hard at night when you have to go from the venue to the bus. I sometimes get really freaked out about that. I know those people have been waiting for hours though, so I should go and see them, but it's quite overwhelming at times.'

Gerard had another reason for feeling a little uncomfortable with the attention. He had already struggled with switching off the rock star he became onstage – it was what had led to his round-the-clock drinking on tour in the summer of 2004, and it was why his therapist had told him he needed to come up with a method of turning off when not performing. 'I think of ways to not be "Gerard Way from My Chemical Romance",' he said. 'A lot of my day consists of me trying to be as normal as possible. I want to go out and get coffee and do those mundane things. It's very important for me to do those normal things because of what I went through before.'

Though there were times they struggled with the attention, they were also flattered by it. They remembered touring *I Brought You My Bullets, You Brought Me Your Love*, when they would appear at out-of-the-way venues to a hostile crowd. Now, they were headlining vast concert halls packed to the rafters with fans howling for them.

'It's less us against the world – now it's us and the fans against the world,' said Gerard. 'And when we get a great crowd that understands that attitude then it leads to the best shows. That's how it's been recently.'

It was the same the following day in Dublin. Queues of fans lined up outside The Ambassador at 6 a.m., partly hoping they might see My Chemical Romance arrive, but mostly so that they could charge to get to the front when the doors opened.

The journey from Manchester the night before was an odd one, with hardly any of the band sleeping despite their tiredness. They were up until 8.30 a.m. in the back lounge of the bus, watching Ray play *Grand Theft Auto* or picking at his guitar. Frank, an absorber of thrillers and horror novels, read all night. 'I brought a bunch of books over here and I read them all in the first few days,' he said. 'I was freaking out that I had nothing to read so I started reading anything – toothpaste tubes, cereal packets, whatever I could find.' Gerard and Mikey spent the night tapping out messages on their SideKicks – handheld emailers that were a precursor to smart phones.

'Frank never sleeps. He's always up till six or seven in the morning watching movies,' said Ray. 'I don't know how he does it.'

'Mikey is always on his SideKick,' added Frank. 'But, no matter where we go, he will find something that he's so psyched about – weird stuff that he thinks he needs. By the end of the tour he's curled up in a ball in his bunk with shit piled up everywhere – books, toys, T-shirts, movies, everything.'

At 9 a.m. they arrived at the ferry to take them to Dublin. They headed to the on-board restaurant and immediately ordered the full English breakfast, a tradition. Keith Buckley, the singer from their support band Every Time I Die joined them.

'He was horrified by what we were eating,' said Gerard, 'So we made him have one too.'

It wasn't a good decision. Within minutes of the boat leaving the port, it hit a rough sea. Bottles fell off shelves as the boat pitched and rolled; standing became impossible without clinging to the

walls; and Ray and Buckley were soon throwing up while hardened
Irish drinkers looked up from early-morning pints with amusement.
The rest of the day was spent as normally as possible. My Chemical
Romance looked around Dublin, stopped in a comic store to browse
the racks. They headed out for a coffee, dodging the fans outside the
venue. Then began the ritual of preparing for the show, playing the
gig and decompressing afterwards – the endless cycle of the road.

The following night, in Newport, was the end of the line – their
last date in the UK on the *Three Cheers* cycle, and the last really serious touring they would do for nearly a year. Their UK promoter,
Johnny Phillips, marked it by hiring out a swimming pool in the
Welsh town with a wave machine and slides. And so My Chemical
Romance's slaying of the UK came to an end with all five of them
in swimming trunks bombing down water flumes. They were cele-
brating.

'Craziness absolutely ensued,' said Frank. 'We swam, we drank,
we jumped off the water slide, we did the beer snake – it was glorious. Definitely a highlight. There's nothing like having fun with
your friends. We have the best job ever.'

But for a few dates in Europe, Canada and Australia (including
stadium-support slots with Green Day), they were finally off the
road. On the way they had gone from being five guys with a good
album to becoming stars.

'It's been really special,' said Gerard. 'Whenever you tour, you
hope it will feel like a victory lap. This is the first time we feel we've
earned that. For the first time it's felt like everyone in the crowd
wants to be at our shows. No one's here to ridicule us, no one wants
to tell us how much we suck now, these crowds feel like they're
behind us. These crowds want to be here because they feel they've
earned it just as much as us. That's special.'

They knew they had achieved something great. Their next move
was to make the album of their lives.

10: HEAVEN HELP US

When My Chemical Romance returned home for Christmas 2005 at the end of the *Three Cheers for Sweet Revenge* tour, they were tired out. What they weren't expecting was to be returning to a landscape that had changed. In the time they had been on the road, their friends and family at home had moved on too. The band hadn't realized how much the five of them had changed either, or how differently they would now be viewed by those around them. When they had left New Jersey, they were a little band with big ideas. On their return, they were stars. Things were different. Initially, they struggled to adapt and it was a measure of how intense the experience was that they repeatedly, and possibly insensitively, compared themselves to returning troops.

'You're like a soldier that's come back from war – you're completely shell-shocked and you're having a hard time even relating to other people,' said Gerard, who had first gone on holiday in Japan before returning home. 'That's something we noticed a lot at first.'

Mikey found it particularly hard and was living on antidepressants and alcohol. He was engaged to his girlfriend Alicia Simmons, who he had met earlier in the year when she was the touring bass player of the band From First To Last. But he struggled without the routine of being on the road. It was a peculiar and unwelcome experience to be without his bandmates. It would be the start of a turbulent period for him.

'I had moved to Brooklyn just after we had got home from touring *Three Cheers for Sweet Revenge* and it was the first time the band had got the chance to be home for any length of time and be normal human beings for a while,' he said. 'That was a hard hit to me. It felt weird. I just couldn't get used to being home for two or three months. I just didn't get it. Everything was supposed to be stable and great but, the thing was, it wasn't. I had all these chemical dependencies and I had turned twenty-five and that depressed me. Life was just getting to me.'

Frank too took a while to adjust. He was surprised that his friends, his family and those around him had not simply trodden water for the period he had been away.

'Coming home was real hard,' he said. 'It's hard to relate to people, even your friends and family. You don't know how to talk or relate to normal life. Sometimes all people ask you about is touring, they ask you about work constantly and you don't have any answers for them.

'You realize that life didn't stand still. People change, people move on. The neighbourhood changes, the roads are different. It's a weird thing. You come home to find mini-malls in places you didn't expect, or that other things have closed down. You realize you've missed a year and a half. It takes a little getting used to.'

Gerard felt the same: 'Stepping into normal life is actually terri-fying. I couldn't cope with it or deal with it or adjust. I couldn't be normal. I'd go out to a restaurant and I couldn't even have dinner like a normal person. That's not because people were bothering me but because I couldn't remember what it was like to do those things.'

In this, he touches upon something else that was happening. When My Chemical Romance returned, they could no longer blend in anonymously. They were famous now, and people were beginning to treat them as such. 'I don't walk down the street picking my nose, just in case someone does know who I am,' said Frank, half joking. Ray added, also laughing, 'You're always aware of that! There could be a camera around at any moment, just trying to ruin the My Chemical Romance mystique!'

But laughing or not, having built up such a rabid, loyal fanbase it simply wasn't possible to turn things off for a while. 'When people treat you like you're not a normal human being it is very odd,' said Gerard. 'It gets tough then. There's a fine line between being treated like a demi-god and a circus monkey. It's almost the same thing. People who don't even like your music want their picture taken with you and I find that strange. I'll have a picture taken with one of our fans any day but you find that you're signing things and doing things for people who couldn't care less – a lot of them are there because they see you in a teen magazine that you don't have anything to do with.'

Which was another thing that was beginning to grate. Determined to preserve the credibility of their music, My Chemical Romance were always adamant that they would only work with magazines that they viewed as serious music publications. Even then, there were times they shied away from photo concepts or interview topics they found to be gimmicky or too lifestyle-focused. While it stopped the teen press from getting too many original interviews, My Chemical Romance were powerless to stop those magazines from writing cuttings-jobs from other interviews. The band began to feel as though they were turning into a commodity, a money-spinner for people who couldn't care less about their music.

'It feels weird,' said Mikey. 'Because we're the most un-heart-throb band in the world.'

Away from the clamour of the crowds when onstage, and with time to reflect, they began to question and second-guess their success rather than just enjoy it. They started to worry that they might have been a flash in the pan. Increasingly, they found the negatives easier to absorb than praise. The doubts led to uncertainty and to a sudden lack of confidence, despite the fact they had just recently returned from sold-out arena shows.

'You never quite know what you're doing in an arena,' Gerard argued. 'You never quite know why you're there. You hope it's because your fans are behind you. But you don't know whether it's because you're on TV or in teen magazines. That's when you're at your most nervous, because you're selling out arenas but you don't know why.

'*Revenge* was written when we were playing in basements. We wrote it to play in basements and, even though it had a bit of an arena attitude, we had no idea we might be playing bigger clubs with it. So when you do start playing bigger places and arenas, it feels different – as though it's not yours any more. It feels out of control very quickly. We really got put through the wringer on that record. It was like boot camp for becoming important.'

Gerard's big fear was that their success was built entirely on the outpouring of emotion that was at *Three Cheers for Sweet Revenge*'s heart. It was a record that was written in such a rush of booze-soaked self-loathing and pill-based necessity, that he was frightened that – now he was sober and had not been through the same kind of grief as he had when his grandmother died – he might not have anything else to offer.

'That record spilled out of us,' he said. 'It was an emotional reaction to something so it was surprising when people told us that it changed their life. Maybe all those arenas were full of people who wanted therapy. Maybe that's all it was.'

There was also the fact that they felt there were those who were expecting them to fail, to not be able to pull off another hit record. On internet message boards that the band said they did not read (but secretly did), there were those who dismissed them as sell-outs, losers and dilettantes. 'A lot of people didn't like *Revenge* and they thought of us as a flash in the pan, they wanted us to be a fad,' said Gerard. 'They thought [another album] would just be *Revenge* all over again because that's how most bands follow up a successful record. So we had to process that – it was hard for all of us. We found it hard to realize that we were better than what some of the press was saying we were capable of.'

'There was a lot of pressure,' added Frank. 'A lot of eyes were on us at that point. It was just dark all around. And the band had changed. We had a new drummer, Gerard was sober, everything was different but we were still expected to live up to this level that people had set for us. The thing is: we didn't know what we wanted and we had to figure it out under a microscope.'

As it turned out, Gerard would rediscover that emotional rush that so fed into *Three Cheers*. But without the more obvious inspirations of grief and alcohol, their third record would be a far more psychological process. Put simply, My Chemical Romance ripped themselves apart.

At the start of 2006, the band listened back to the songs they had written in the makeshift studio in the back of their bus while touring *Three Cheers for Sweet Revenge*. At the time, they had been pleased with the results but now they realized that they had not been ambitious enough. Gerard admitted the songs they had worked on were basically '*Revenge* part two', which was something he had no intention of releasing.

Only a few songs made it through from the bus recordings – 'I Don't Love You', 'Disenchanted' and 'Dead!', which would become the next album's second song. It was this song that says the most about the My Chemical Romance mood as they finished up with *Three Cheers*. Though musically inspired by the bounce of Electric Light Orchestra's 'Mr Blue Skies' and guitar-wise by Cheap Trick's 'I Want You to Want Me', its dark lyrics speak of defensiveness, isolation and, that default My Chemical Romance attitude, defiance.

'It's about being dead and about people not liking you – it was a commentary on the band and how some people feel about us,' said Gerard. 'We wanted to say, "You may hate us but we're still here." We wanted to say, "Here we are, and we're better. Here we are and we're more daring and more defiant than ever."'

It was with that mindset that they went into S.I.R. studios in New York in early 2006 to write the rest of the record. There they sifted through the scraps of material they had and focused on writing. 'I Don't Love You' was finalized very quickly in New York as My Chemical Romance tried to channel the spirit of Creedence Clearwater Revival's 'Have You Ever Seen the Rain'. 'The End.', initially titled simply 'Intro', was finished there too before being beefed up later in the recording studio, while 'Dead!' was almost completed at S.I.R. 'Disenchanted', meanwhile, had already been written and aired on tour – but would receive a lyrical overhaul in the coming months. Another song, 'Teenagers', would sparkle to life in New York, fittingly perhaps, since it was inspired by Gerard's fear of after-school youths on the city's subways.

As they worked, Gerard in particular began to examine where their sound was heading. He came to a realization: that the best way to follow the success of *Three Cheers* was not to shrink away from it, but to exceed it. 'We did the opposite of what everyone thought,' he said. 'There were all these expectations about what we'd do, so we did the only thing that nobody had thought of. People thought we'd make a low-key album, they thought we'd make a back-to-our-roots basement punk album, people thought everything . . . except that we'd make a batshit crazy album. So that's what we decided to do.'

Early in the writing sessions, Ray had been bet that he couldn't write a polka – the Eastern European, oompah-ish folk dance. Building on the cabaret of *Revenge*'s 'You Know What They Do to Guys Like Us in Prison', Ray began to piece together his Russian dance while Gerard worked on a melody with the aim of creating something cinematic and fun. It would become 'Mama', one of their third album's key tracks: flamboyant, over-the-top, camp and wildly original. It was the song that told the band they could take their music anywhere they wanted – even if it was 'batshit crazy'.

In S.I.R., My Chemical Romance talked about what they wanted to do. And they were ambitious. They wanted to make a classic album, one that would last for decades and which parents would hand down to their children. They wanted to make something sig-nificant. They weren't messing around.

'We almost had homework to listen to,' said Frank. 'We were listening to the classic albums that underlined the concept we were working on. It was always about maximizing melody – that was always the main thing, even though a million other things were going on. When Ray and I worked on *Revenge*, we would each have our parts, throw them together, and that was it. On [the third album], we would talk more and work much harder to blend our ideas.'

Gerard had a Broadway, vaudevillian concept in mind – one that included marching bands and wild ideas about a hospital patient, cancer, illness and decay, and it was something he sent his band away to explore.

'We actually really researched what we did,' said Frank. 'We were thinking about all the different themes and different artists. If we were thinking about the cabaret theme, we would go to a store and buy movies on cabaret, watch them and get into the mindset to get into the feeling. We didn't want to half-ass anything. It was so precious to us.'

The record's working title was *The Rise and Fall of My Chemical Romance*. Gerard plotted to do something that would set his band completely apart from the current punk and emo scene that they had been thrown in with. He saw his contemporaries singing about their problems and he wanted no part of it – or at least, he didn't want to be so literal about things. He figured that, if this was to be their landmark album, he might as well deal with something big, something important. This record, he decided, would be about nothing less than life and death itself. But within that, buried under layers of pomp and circumstance, and swaddled in metaphors and concepts, were his own real fears.

'Partly I was processing the death of my grandmother still,' he said. 'But I also felt that nobody was telling the truth. There were a lot of bands who wanted money, and so they'd sing songs about their girlfriends and other dumb, suburban, white-kid problems. Nobody was talking about life and death, they were just talking about dumb, dumb shit. So I felt a responsibility to do that.'

And in doing that, it gave him an in. It gave him something to access and to channel. Slowly, he became obsessed with death – an endless source of inspiration for him, but not necessarily a healthy one. 'I wanted the record to be painful for people at the same time as they enjoyed and loved it,' he said. 'So I thought it had to be painful for me too.'

The Ways' father, Donald, had also recently suffered a non-fatal heart attack while on their tour bus during the *Three Cheers for Sweet Revenge* cycle – something Gerard had seen first-hand. 'It was terrifying, and he's young too, which made it worse,' said the singer. It too played into the themes of the album. 'All of that stuff was interlinked,' said Mikey. 'We were still dealing with the death of our grandmother and, soon after, my dad had a close call. So we both developed these strange obsessions. We were dark, morbid people. We were festering.'

He might have been festering and dark, but Gerard was also determined to do something big and universal. He didn't want to fall into the same trap as many bands do when trying to follow a successful record. A hit record means, generally, a great deal of tour-ing. It can lead to bands having little else to inspire them other than what they have been through on the road – hence they write a record about travelling, about tiredness, about life away from home and about becoming well known. They can be majestic records, but they can also be hard to relate to for fans who have not been through something similar. Gerard was determined that he wasn't going to make that mistake. He was going to go somewhere else – he was going to write a story.

'We could very easily have bitched about people snapping our pictures or being hassled,' he said, 'because that's what our life was like for two years. Or we could have bitched about forces trying to tear us apart because they want to see you fail. But we didn't want to talk about the band or fame or anything like that.

'It was important that the record wasn't about us getting famous. That's why the metaphors are so strong and it's partly why the record is about a character. We also wanted there to be lots of colour so that people would actually feel like they were in a hospital or on a battlefield.'

Typically, though, Gerard was not going to address things head-on. Instead, he envisioned a concept record. First he visualized it as a comic book story, complete with plot and character-arc and then slowly it became an album. It was this that was vital to him – having been an artist, and still finding it as easy to express himself visually as lyrically, he needed their third album to be a multi-sensory piece of work.

He envisaged a character called The Patient, dying tragically young in hospital, whose strongest memory was of his father taking him to a parade when he was a boy. It was a fiction based on truth, in that one of Gerard's own earliest memories was of him and Mikey being taken to a parade as boys. He could still see the giant floats and great inflatable balloons, but saw his fictional parade as a perfect metaphor for a story of life and death – in that it might represent either a funeral procession or a celebration. His procession would march flamboyantly towards The Patient's hospital bed while other characters would litter the narrative – Mother War, Fear and Regret, The Soldiers, The Escape Artist – as the concept became more elaborate still. It became a fully fledged world inside his head, complete with sights, smells and sounds. It would take him a while to hit upon the title to it all, but when he did it would sum everything up. My Chemical Romance's third album would be called *The Black Parade* and it would be the grandest album released in a decade.

'When we started the band, music was all about people's girlfriends; there was no storytelling, settings or smells,' said Gerard. 'I want people to see the confetti when they listen to *The Black Parade* or to see a marching band when the piccolo and glockenspiel come in. I want them to be able to see a hospital when we sing about one. *The Black Parade* has a structure. There is a beginning, middle and end. There are acts in it.'

But first they had to record it. And that's where things got interesting – because their heads were all over the place. In the space of the few short months since wrapping up the *Three Cheers for Sweet Revenge* tour, they had been through post-tour exhaustion and pre-recording anxiety. Gerard had become fixated on death and they had become wracked with doubts before being reinvigorated with grand ideas. They were bouncing from one emotion to the other.

Yet that was the moment they decided to head into the recording studio. No wonder *The Black Parade* is a record that they say nearly killed them.

11: WELCOME TO THE BLACK PARADE

If My Chemical Romance were going to make a landmark album, then they knew they needed the right producer. With a hit record in the bank, there were few who were off-limits in terms of budget or ability. Rob Cavallo, the man they eventually settled on, remembers that there were any number of people keen to work with them.

'I think I got the job because I won a shoot-out,' says Cavallo. 'It was like an old-fashioned shoot-out at the OK Corral. There were many producers gunning to get in there. I can't remember who they all were, but at one point as many as eight or ten people were being considered. The band did research on all of them, took meetings with all of them and then they narrowed it down to, I think, me and one other guy.'

Cavallo was a big name to be getting involved in a shoot-out. The son of a music manager, he started his career working in A&R for Warner Bros and made his reputation when he signed Green Day and then produced their multi-platinum major-label debut *Dookie*. His career was largely stellar from there on. The meetings he had with My Chemical Romance came just two years after he had helmed another multi-platinum Green Day album, *American Idiot*, making him arguably one of the top five rock producers in the world. It was an example of the level at which My Chemical Romance were able to operate.

Cavallo flew to New York to meet with them and to hear the songs they had written. His reaction to the music they played him was all the confirmation My Chemical Romance needed that he was the right man.

'They played me some new songs in New York, as they had been doing for the other producers, and I remember one moment,' recalls Cavallo. 'They played that song "Mama", which was on *The Black Parade*. I just loved the sound of that song so much. I thought it was so haunting, dark and scary. It had this essence of World War II coming over it too. I just stood up in the middle of the performance and started pumping a fist in the air. I just thought it was the greatest thing I had ever heard. I think they liked my enthusiasm . . .'

They did. The band felt his reaction made it clear that he would be a producer who would believe wholeheartedly in what they doing. They went out that night for a steak and asked him to produce their album. But it wasn't just Cavallo's response to 'Mama' that clinched things. The band were impressed by his production with Green Day and even more delighted that he had worked on the US post-hardcore band Jawbreaker's *Dear You* record – an album that had greatly inspired *Revenge*.

By April 2006, four months after they stopped touring *Three Cheers,* My Chemical Romance were on a plane to Los Angeles to begin recording again, having barely caught their breath. In terms of their health, they perhaps should have taken longer. But none of them felt it was a record that could wait. 'By the time we adjusted to being normal, we had to leave again,' Mikey ruefully reflected.

And what they left for was nothing like normal life. Rather than record in a studio, they hired an old mansion that overlooked Los Angeles. There was still a lot of work to put into *The Black Parade* – Cavallo remembers that only about a third of the record was written when the band flew out – and so they decided to write and record in the grand old Canfield-Moreno estate, a great Mediterranean-style villa also known as The Paramour Mansion. They didn't realize that it was as spooky as hell.

Built for a silent-movie star Antonio Moreno, who had married the oil-heiress Daisy Canfield-Danziger in 1923, the 22,000 square foot mansion became a key part of the glamorous Los Angeles image of the twenties and thirties. Until, that is, Moreno and Canfield-Danziger divorced and her car plunged into a canyon from Mulholland Drive a few years later. It has become Hollywood folklore that she has haunted the mansion's halls and corridors ever since. Spooky enough, but the place had also been used as a school for troubled girls and a nunnery. Then, decaying and decrepit, it fell into disrepair in the eighties before being restored by a developer and hired out as a movie set and recording space. When My Chemical Romance arrived in April 2006, it scared the shit out of them.

'I think the band had said to us that they wanted us to find some weird house in LA to record in that they could get for cheap,' says Cavallo. 'It was perfect for that – but it wasn't until we started spending nights there that it got freaky. It was fun for me but wasn't fun for them at all. The house was kind of haunted and some of the members – I think Mikey in particular – were seeing ghosts.'

'Oh man, that crazy fucking house,' is how Mikey remembered the place. 'We had to get out of that house by the end of it. That place was just a storm cloud in the shape of a house. The sun never penetrated that property.'

The bassist instinctively disliked the place, especially the room he was sleeping in. He would often wake in the middle of the night terrified, then go and curl up in his brother's room.

My Chemical Romance had set themselves up in the main living room to work on demos. Cavallo had brought in a PA system, a desk and some other recording gear, and there they would work on songs. Gerard says they would play from 11 a.m. until 3 a.m., sleep, then do it all again. All of them are convinced that The Paramour Mansion's peculiar feel bled into their music.

'The demo tapes are really crazy to listen to,' says Cavallo. 'You can almost hear the haunted house in the background. You can almost see the ghosts flying around the room when we recorded those songs. Especially that "Mama" song. When we played that at Paramour, we were in a giant living room with forty-feet-high ceilings and big windows overlooking Los Angeles, and it was cold. It felt like the dead of winter and we're not used to being cold in Los

Angeles. I would wear a ski jacket into that house because the heat didn't get in there. It was freezing. Thinking about it, why did we subject ourselves to that torture?'

But it was the fact that they did which made the record. Having based *Three Cheers for Sweet Revenge* on an emotional outpouring, Gerard particularly was of the opinion that, in order to create great music, he had to be cutting himself open. It was exactly what he had done on the first album too, screaming raw thoughts and howling dark fears into the microphone as some form of primal therapy. And so, he reasoned, he needed to up his game for *The Black Parade*. It made the writing and recording of the album a particularly bleak affair – more so given the weird ambience of The Paramour.

'It was a dark time,' Gerard said. 'At times it felt like the record was trying to kill us. At times we were seeing how ugly we were but, without that, you can't make a good record. A lot of bands who make bad follow-up records perhaps aren't willing to go that far. If your previous record is big, then you have to go even further – you have to push yourself right to the edge.'

The process of tearing himself apart started before pre-production in The Paramour. When the band first flew out to LA to start the record, they stayed in the same Oakwood Apartments in which they had lived when they recorded *Three Cheers for Sweet Revenge*. And it was there that Gerard really began to live inside *The Black Parade*.

'I remember going into G's room and he had all these signs up on the wall that he had drawn and painted,' said Frank. 'They were the song titles, and there was this one big piece of paper that said "Cancer" on it. He was so submerged in it. I remember thinking to myself, "Shit, man. I hope he's not too deep."'

'I had a conversation with Ray around that time about the fact that we should have somewhere to get away from things. He was like, "I don't know – I just want to really get into this one." But I remember thinking Gerard was in a little deep.

'There were multiple times in the band's career that I would say to G, "Hey, you know that you can just write a song? You don't have to kill yourself." He was always like, "Yeah, yeah, maybe I will. You're right." But I knew what he really meant was, "All right, whatever. Shut the fuck up." Ultimately, you need to do what you need to do to get the best out of yourself. But I wanted him to know he had an out. I wanted him to know he was allowed to have a little bit of fun.'

Gerard didn't take it in. Without booze to lean on, without pills to escape with, he got locked inside his own mind. He became ever more obsessive about the record and, after moving from the Oakwood Apartments and becoming secluded in The Paramour, began to further examine his emotions. He put what he found onto the album, but camouflaged it with layers of swagger and flamboyance.

'I wasn't depressed but I was extremely intense though,' he said. 'I was very edgy, almost like I wasn't living a normal life in Los Angeles. I was living inside the record. It really did feel like a black parade in the haunted house we recorded in. It felt like something was coming after us. Every time we turned a corner, it was staring at us – we couldn't escape it, we couldn't go to the movies, we couldn't listen to any music or read books or watch TV.

'It wasn't the happiest times of our lives. We were questioning our mortality. I think it's a very human record underneath the bombast and the theatrics. The sound is very large and grand but it's a very mortal record. It's an interesting duality because there are a lot of lyrics that examine ourselves – not just as a band but as human beings. We were examining each other and hopefully it will encourage listeners to examine themselves. We were putting our lives under a microscope. We wanted listeners to put their own lives under the microscope too.'

Gerard would struggle to sleep and would go on to suffer what he called 'night terrors' in which he said it felt as though someone was gripping his throat and squashing his lungs. He used it as inspiration for the song 'Sleep', written in the studio around the same time as 'Famous Last Words', but it pointed to the intensity of the experience. He became obsessed with Joan of Arc, and considered shaving his head as she had once done. He bought countless films about her and would watch them alone in his room, prompting nightmares in which he watched her burning alive.

It was a mentally difficult process to go through – and this was just the writing stage. There was one evening, in particular, that it began to get too much for Gerard. He wandered outside onto the estate, a cigarette burning in his hand and turmoil blaring in his head. He stared out at Los Angeles below him, a million twinkling lights, a vast city of different people leading different lives, and he felt completely lost.

'I was wondering what the hell I was doing with my life,' he said of that moment. 'I was examining every awful thing about myself. I was cutting myself open, taking all the parts out and examining them. It was like an operating room. Every day we were finding something new and ugly that we didn't like about ourselves. We found all the cracks, we found all the chinks in our armour and it made me realize, "Wow, I'm not that likeable a person." I found out that I was a coward. I found out all these things about myself.'

Such was Gerard's state of mind, Mikey began to wonder if his brother was going through a collapse. During the course of the recording, he and Gerard would make reference to The Smashing Pumpkins' classic double album *Melon Collie and the Infinite Sadness* but in a darkly self-referential manner. 'I went through a crisis,' said Gerard. 'Mikey called it my pre-mid-life crisis. He actually refers to the record as Pre-Mid-Life Crisis and the Infinite Sadness. I went through a very weird thing. We were in the middle of making this record and it was a crisis.'

The thing is, he was far from the only member of the band to feel like he was losing his mind.

Though Gerard felt utterly consumed by the album, it was Mikey who had the most extreme reaction to it. Deeply uncomfortable in The Paramour, and feeling cut off from outside life, he slipped into an all-consuming depression.

'I was drinking at the time,' he said. 'I had reached an age where a lot of emotions and hormones affect you. It was really tough for me. I was at odds with myself. The band had engulfed all of us and I found it overwhelming. There were some things I had never addressed about that and they were festering away too. The combination of all of that was beginning to eat away at me. Recording *Black Parade* was the moment it all came to a head. I just had to go fix myself.'

He and his brother – the old Chemical Brothers, as they had been known on the touring circuit – had both suffered their share of substance problems. But while Gerard had cleaned up, Mikey was mixing alcohol and anti-depression medication – a complex, unhealthy cocktail. It came to a head in The Paramour.

'There was the pressure,' he said. 'People were saying, "You guys are making your follow-up, you've got to beat the last one." That was in my head the whole time. Then I started worrying about my own abilities in my head too. But it wasn't just that. It was everything – life in general. Everything was in my head.'

The Paramour was about the worst place he could be. Freaked out, depressed, isolated, unhappy and surrounded by bandmates who were in the middle of the most intense experience of their lives, he became prone to panic attacks and sobbing fits.

'Being in that house was like being in another country,' he said. 'You couldn't get cell-phone service, the internet was really bad too so it felt like all my lines of communication were down. I didn't have my driver's licence at the time so it felt like I was stranded on the property and it was miles from anywhere – there's nowhere you can walk to from there. We had these long, vigorous practice schedules. We were waking up at noon and playing until midnight. Mix all that with the fact that I was manic depressive. It was like pouring gasoline on all my problems and setting fire to them. I almost didn't get through it.'

Midway through the writing process at The Paramour, the band had to take a break to play at Emo's nightclub, as part of the South By Southwest music convention in Austin, Texas. They had been making good progress until then, having got 'The End.' and 'Dead!'

more or less laid out. Their show was a success but when they returned to The Paramour, something had changed. They hit a wall, creatively. As they did so, Mikey's problems came to the fore.

Mikey first told me about his experiences over a year later. Initially he and the band had kept them under wraps. But, once the bassist decided to talk about the mental issues and depression he suffered at The Paramour, he was clear about how serious things had been. His answer to a question about whether he had considered suicide was stark.

'I was really close,' he said. 'I certainly knew that I was going to leave the band or maybe just leave planet earth altogether. I felt like it was either one or the other. I just thought, "I can't deal with this." People aren't all wired the same. My brother and I have a history of depression, it's a genetic thing. Me and him were born like that. It's the curse of the Ways.'

With his state of mind as fragile as it was, Mikey and the band thought it best for him to get away, to escape The Paramour and to get some help while they carried on recording. It wasn't an easy decision, but once it was made, My Chemical Romance's longstanding lawyer and close friend Stacy Fass took Mikey into her house in LA and forced him to see doctors for his depression.

'Everyone helped me,' said Mikey. 'My band, my brother, my parents, my fiancée, all my best friends. Stacy saved my life. She got me out of the house, she put me up and kicked me out of bed and made me go to my doctors' appointments. She made me get active help.

'I was seeing four different doctors a week. They were two steps away from putting me into a hospital and I think Gerard wanted to check me into somewhere. It was really bad. I thought I was stronger than that. Personally, I knew that being checked into somewhere wouldn't help.'

With medication and therapy he slowly returned to an even keel. He stopped drinking and used his medication properly – 'It's not the cure,' he told me, 'it's just a little thing like putting on training wheels' – but it was a slow process. The rest of the band, with their heads buried in the record, were not as sympathetic as they might have been. In fact, for a while, there was resentment that Mikey's departure had halted the recording.

'It started out as anger towards Mikey, because, like, doesn't he know that he is causing things to come to a standstill?' Ray said. 'But that was completely the wrong reaction to have – we were just upset and confused. He needed time to get better.'

In 2011, five years later, Mikey felt comfortable enough to talk about his experiences of that time some more. In an interview with the whole band in Lisbon, Portugal, the topic arose again. 'I think it was always going to happen,' said Mikey of his depression. 'I don't think there was any way of stopping it. There were just some screws loose upstairs that needed to be tightened.'

Gerard looked immediately concerned. Jumping in to protect his brother, he said, 'I don't think you had screws loose, Mikey. I think that was just how you were processing everything that happened to us. You were at that critical age [twenty-five] – that's the age I went nuts and started the band – and it's a weird breaking point. The band had got really big and people looked up to Mikey, which put demands on him. There was a lot of pressure: we were being scrutinized because we had become big.'

Ray then did something that day in Lisbon that was very brave. In full knowledge that the interview was on the record and that this was something that would go into print, he very publicly apologized to Mikey for the way he had driven him in the studio. It was a very touching moment, one that the whole band knew the significance of.

'I know I contributed to what Mikey went through,' said Ray. 'How I got affected by the microscope we were under was that I felt we had to be a hundred per cent perfect a hundred per cent of the time. But I think I confused perfect playing with great playing. That added to some of the stuff Mikey went through. I've never gotten the chance to say this to him properly, actually: I'm sorry, Mikey, I'm sorry for creating that atmosphere. I think I lost my mind a bit.'

Nevertheless, Mikey's departure from The Paramour threw them off balance. Already at a creative dead-end following their trip to South by Southwest, and now frustrated and worried about their bassist, My Chemical Romance began to doubt themselves again.

'It opened us up to fear and pressure in a big way,' Gerard said. 'It started to seep in and rise up, and the next thing you know you're waist-deep in the fear. Are we gonna make a shit record? Are we crazy? Are we gonna break up?'

Mikey's absence brought about a period that Gerard would later call 'the darkest period in the band's career – people were losing their minds, having giant personal problems and mental issues . . . it was the darkest days.' My Chemical Romance couldn't get back on track creatively, and while Frank wrote 'House of Wolves' at that time, they all struggled for direction. Though Frank's guitar tech, Matt Cortez, played bass during a few rehearsals, the mood was not there.

Gerard said they felt like they were drowning and burning at the same time. He said he would haunt the house, like one of the undead, barely showering. One week, he says he didn't even bother to get out of his pyjamas and had to resist the temptation to simply walk into The Paramour's pool and hold his head underwater until he could no longer breathe.

At their lowest ebb, though, they reached a turning point. One night at 4 a.m., two weeks after Mikey's departure, Gerard heard Ray playing around with a song then called 'The Saddest Music in the World'. Gerard says Ray would often play alone late at night at that time and that 'it sounded like he was fighting his guitar, frustrated that he couldn't play our songs.' This time, Gerard joined him. The two of them started working on Ray's music while Gerard emptied into it his fears and frustration about Mikey.

And then something magical began to happen, something they both felt. It was as if Gerard's feelings about his brother had been the cork that was blocking their creativity. Once he let those feelings out with Ray, music began to flow once more. It was an important moment and they both knew it. They went to bed in the early dawn, drained but with a feeling they finally had something.

The four members still at The Paramour continued to work on the song as, gradually, it took shape. Heartfelt, brutally honest and anthemic, it would become known as 'Famous Last Words' and would eventually close *The Black Parade*. It was a hell of a thing to write about your struggling brother, as Gerard's lyrics sharply challenged Mikey's spirit over angry, soaring guitars. But it came to take on more meaning as Gerard wrote. It evolved from being a song about Mikey, to being a song about the band in general. It became something very powerful.

'Right away I felt like I was singing about the thing I was most afraid of,' Gerard said. 'It felt like what it meant to be in this band, it felt like it was about Mikey, and it felt like it was about our lives, thinking of yourself as despicable or hated.'

All it lacked was a chorus. That came later, when Gerard was alone in the studio. 'We all left to get coffee,' said Ray, 'and we came back an hour later and Gerard had done this awesome layered chorus. It was so inspiring – the words that he was singing, the melody, it came out of nowhere really. It tied the whole song together and ties the whole record together.'

It would be the chorus that offered the song some balance. While the verses questioned and criticized, the chorus was uplifting and proud, offering some hope amid the despair, as Gerard defiantly and pointedly sang that he would keep on fighting for life. It was a line that would define the record.

With such conflicting emotions, Ray was keen to ensure his guitar solo captured the fraught mood. He had long been influenced by Ozzy Osbourne's late guitarist Randy Rhoads and turned to his playing for inspiration. He knew he needed to write something that mirrored the emotion of the lyrics, something frantic but fraught. He went to bed that night listening to his favourite Rhoads solos and, on waking up, immediately reached for his guitar and laid down the first thing that came to him. His spontaneous guitars became vital to the song.

'Famous Last Words' would get *The Black Parade* sessions back on track, despite its bare emotions. 'We all got a shot of inspiration when that song came together,' said Frank. 'It gave us a new life, a new hope. It really put us back in the mindset of making a great record.'

Even when Mikey returned to The Paramour and heard what the band had been working on in his absence – essentially, a song that was inspired by him – the mood remained high. Because despite its subject matter, the bassist realized quite how glorious 'Famous Last Words' was. He told them it was an anthem.

If 'Famous Last Words' got My Chemical Romance back on track musically, it did little to lift the intense mood. Midway through the sessions, Gerard broke up with his girlfriend. Cavallo remembers that the singer was screaming, saying his reaction to the split 'actually manifested itself in physical agony'. It only increased the blackness and despair which was feeding the record. Several months after the album came out, Gerard opened up about it – nervously.

'I have to approach this with kid gloves,' he said, before taking the plunge. 'I'd rather not get into too much detail about it, but I was alone for the first time in ten years. It was really hard. I was not used to it. I've had girlfriends since I was seventeen or eighteen. I was thinking, "Oh my God, who the fuck am I going to meet now?" But it makes the record make more sense to me. It makes it count a lot more.

'It was a six-year relationship that ended. It was practically marriage,' he continued. 'It was with someone that knew me before all this and knew me before the band. Halfway through tracking – literally just when I had finished tracking the vocal parts and chorus line to "Famous Last Words" – I broke up with her. I realized the lines in there were the truth and that I wasn't telling myself the truth any more. The record was so much about the truth that I knew I had to [end the relationship]. It was the hardest thing I had to do, harder than making the record. I had to fly back and talk to her. I had to move my stuff out. It was brutal.

'She was fucking amazing. I loved her and she was awesome but she couldn't deal with this. When I finally understood that I realized, "Wow, people can't deal with this."'

Already emotionally fragile, it made him even more of a mess as he recorded. He says the song 'Welcome to the Black Parade' was also tracked in the middle of his relationship problems and he believes his state of mind bled into the music. Originally entitled 'The Five of Us Are Dying', and sketched out as early as sessions for the first album, it had evolved to the extent that only the verse survived. It went through revision after revision in the studio, a painstaking process of trial and error. Singing it, Gerard felt he was close to complete breakdown. 'It felt like the pressure was tearing us up,' he said. 'It was the hardest song on the record to make. I was going through some very difficult personal things. I was literally going through them as we were tracking the song. Originally it was sort of a plea for help.'

My Chemical Romance definitely bled to make *The Black Parade*. They set aside one room in The Paramour Mansion and it became dubbed The Heavy Room. Inside it, they tore each other to shreds. They made a rule that they would be absolutely honest with each other in there, sometimes brutally so. They would have no-holds-barred conversations about the record, their playing, their personal lives and their relationships with each other. It was an utterly draining form of bloodletting but they felt this honesty was vital.

'Mentally, we were beating each other up,' said Ray. 'We were getting to the root of some really deep problems. We would spend hours and hours in that room, having long conversations while the little demons we all carried inside of us came out. As close as we all are, we all have things within us that we hold to ourselves. No matter how much time we spend with each other, we all have our little demons inside the closet. Sometimes you have to let those things go. That's just one of the things that was going on in The Heavy Room.'

'There were times when it got so hard making this record,' said Gerard. 'It was nothing personal between band members but we felt like we were all going through something hard and that became daunting, so we'd say to each other, "Well, we're going to have to have another talk in The Heavy Room." It was a room that drained our souls out. It drained everything out of you. It took all your energy because we just talked and talked in there. We talked about everything.'

Rob Cavallo – who Gerard would come to describe as 'as our therapist, big brother, dad and uncle all rolled into one' – and the band's lawyer and friend Stacy Fass were the only people outside of the band who were allowed in. Cavallo would oversee their conversations, half a concerned onlooker, half understanding the necessity of the procedure. He thinks that the band's blunt honesty in The Heavy Room helped them avoid making compromises because they were more concerned about the work than protecting egos.

'All of them together are the nicest bunch of guys,' he says, 'but sometimes being nice isn't necessarily the thing that helps you. Sometimes you need to dare to be really honest and to confront those feelings so that everyone knows and momentum isn't lost. So we would go into that Heavy Room to do that.

'Whether it was Gerard breaking up with his girlfriend, or guys having certain feelings about what other guys were playing, or the direction of the record, we would go into The Heavy Room and talk it out. It was a safe place for people to say the truth without wanting to kill each other.'

While some of the truths were hard to hear, the airing of them served to focus minds. The conversations in the room were not pleasant, nor were they easy. But there was something about the absolute honesty there that brought them closer.

'We became so protective of each other when we were making the record that everything became different,' said Gerard. 'We became a different band. We had always loved each other – we're all like brothers – but this was something different. We became completely protective of each other. We felt that we had to live behind a shield.

'What got us through this record was putting our personal problems aside in order to help the other guy. You'd realize, this guy is going through some serious problems and so I have to forget about my issues and help him. I had to forget my anxieties, depression and nightmares to help my brothers. We all went through that. That's what had to be done. That's why there were so many talks in The Heavy Room, we just had to be there to listen to each other.'

The question that struck me when I interviewed them shortly after the sessions ended was 'why?' Why tear themselves apart to make an album? Why drive themselves to the edge? Gerard had no hesitation in answering.

'In order for us to make something great, we have to give up normality,' he said. 'I certainly feel you have to suffer for your art. I feel that if we don't suffer, then it's not going to be sincere and honest. If we don't suffer then the songs don't come from a real place. The songs are always about extremely dark things; we can't fake that. I guess the chaos that comes at us and surrounds us and occasionally tries to tear us apart is maybe self-created. So I guess there is a little masochistic side to us but it is the willingness to suffer for our art that's more important. We don't feel like we've made true art unless we've suffered a great deal. Only people who have suffered a great deal have something to say.'

Cavallo entirely understood why they had to do it. He became a trusted confidant and had quickly got into their mindset. He knew exactly why they had to suffer so much to make the record. 'I think it was absolutely central to who they were at that point,' he says. 'It's central to why they ended up breaking up too. They probably didn't know how to do anything other than what they did. The art was flowing through them and they were on a mission that they had started when they were younger. It was very pure, I can tell you that. None of their creative output was wasted. They tore themselves apart because we were on a mission. I think you have to die a little to make a great album. You just have to die a little.'

Gerard wanted to be involved in every detail during *The Black Parade* sessions, living inside the bubble of the record. With his relationship over, he had very little else to occupy himself and so became fanatical.

'I was aware that people thought I had gone crazy. There wasn't a minute that I wasn't behind the [mixing] board,' he said. 'There were times, to our detriment, that I was trying to oversee everything. I don't remember a minute that I wasn't watching everything. That was how I processed it all. I felt I had the vision, which was why I felt I had to be the lunatic behind the board. And I'd be changing things constantly: a song would start one way then, the next day, I wouldn't like it so I'd try to force everyone to change it.

'Nobody was watching us, nobody was paying any attention to us. Nobody from the label checked in and I think *Kerrang!* magazine were the only people who wrote a studio piece about us. We were left alone to be fucking crazy madmen in that crazy house and so we became madmen. I got obsessed with death. I was repeatedly playing *The Passion of the Christ* with the sound off for days. I couldn't get things grim enough. I ended my relationship – in fact I was so obsessed with *Black Parade* that my entire personal life got destroyed.'

To Craig Aaronson, Gerard's obsession with the record was vital. He was one of the few from Warner Bros to check in on them – and he did so only sporadically. He immediately noted the intensity and fervour with which they were recording. But he also knew that was the way Gerard worked best – and he considered Gerard to be the vital cog.

'There was definitely some turmoil going on. There was some dark energy. They seemed very, very intense,' he says. 'They had a very strong vision and they came across as extreme. They wanted to do something that would really break down boundaries. They wanted it to have a super strong point of view. Gerard told me the vision for the record and he was so clear about it. He was inspiring. I'd ask him how he could see it all, and he didn't know – he could just do it. He had it all in his head.

'Gerard's ability to do that was key to everything. That guy is a fucking ninja when it comes to creativity. He just opens up and I don't even know how he does it. How does he see that shit? But that's the magic of Gerard right there. They made some rough mixes early on and I knew they were in the midst of making a masterpiece. I knew it, knew it, knew it.'

Gerard's creative urges were whirring at full speed and Cavallo remembers the singer as a thrilling, inspirational force in the studio.

'The guy is a super-genius,' he says. 'Sometimes I think he's a slightly tormented genius because he's the nicest, sweetest person in the world but I think he has the plague of too many ideas in his head. It's hard for him to organize them all because he gets bombarded by them. They're all such brilliant ideas that it's hard for him to know which one to select.'

But as much as Gerard was directing things in terms of the big ideas behind the album, Ray was equally as obsessed with the music. He was exploring his influences, and his character explodes across the record in Queen-esque guitar licks and the technically brilliant musicianship that counterpoints Frank's more instinctive playing. So while Gerard may have had the vision, Ray had the talent to make it come to life. But he was a hard taskmaster.

'Ray was intense, for sure,' says Cavallo. 'It was hard for them, I think, to find out what their roles were in terms of what they were to contribute musically and what they were to contribute personally. The good news on that record was that we did actually figure it out. Everyone found their slot and I think that's why the record is very cohesive. You could feel the flavour of all five of them on the album.'

'Everyone was trying to make it the best it was, and the pressure was so heavy it was weighing everybody down,' said Frank. 'People would have moments, freak-outs. Ray and I would write parts together, but that was the first time we had gone through parts with a fine toothcomb. Ray wanted things perfect, and we would go through parts a hundred times.'

Despite the brilliance of the music he was writing, though, Ray believes his focus was unhealthy. At the time, he didn't realize it but, later, he regretted how absorbed he became in searching for faultlessness and precision in My Chemical Romance's playing.

'I think we benefited from it in the end. If you'd heard what Parade started as and then compare that to how it finished up, you'd agree,' he admitted. 'We certainly went into it with the best intentions – but I know that, in my case, those intentions expressed themselves in the wrong way. The discussions we had in The Heavy Room created the atmosphere that ran through the recording.

'I guess I'm glad we went through that because, to jump ahead, it meant the attitude on [fourth album] *Danger Days* was completely different. I learned so much about what not to do and who not to be. You can be intense in such a way that you inspire people, or you can do it in a way where you intimidate people. And I think on *Black Parade*, I did it the wrong way. I wish I could have done things differently because [my attitude] led to some heavy talks. It was a tough time. Everybody wanted to make the best record they knew how and that caused all of us to lose our heads a little bit.'

Naturally humble and polite, this was Ray's way of apologizing to the band for his intensity. However, he deserves a lot of credit too. For without his talent and technique, *The Black Parade* could never have come to life. Still, it wasn't perhaps the best way to make an album. Gerard, like his guitarist, subsequently vowed never to make a record the same way in the future.

'Ray was a perfectionist and I was a fucking lunatic,' he said. 'I never want to be that guy again.'

The intensity with which My Chemical Romance recorded *The Black Parade* makes it sound as though there was little room for positivity in the experience. That wasn't completely the case. On 25 May, Frank proposed to his girlfriend Jamia Nestor, who he had been with since high school and who had sold My Chemical Romance merch on the road with the band. He was delighted when she said yes.

Bob Bryar, too, was settling in well. This was his first experience of recording with My Chemical Romance – and, indeed, of recording at this level. Frank said that, at first, the band had understandable nerves. 'It was the first time we had written with Bob, so we wondered whether it would happen in the same way.' But soon, the drummer became a vital cog.

'Honestly, if Bob hadn't arrived – this band wouldn't still be going,' said Frank. 'I don't want to blow him too much – and I'm not sure he'd want me to – but I swear to God, he's one of the key ingredients in bringing this band to the next level. We never could have made *Black Parade* with our old drummer. Bob has come from such a diverse background and is so talented that he can play anything.'

Bob, for his part, was delighted to be involved in the creative process. He had previously spent his time in the band largely playing Matt Pelissier's parts, gradually shaping them so that they better fitted his style. Now, though, he would be able to get in on the ground floor and stamp his own playing onto a record.

'It's not that playing the other songs live didn't mean anything to me – because I was always a fan – but it was stuff that I didn't have any part in creating,' he said. 'But on *Black Parade*, I was playing drums that I recorded and that makes it so much better.'

The bulk of that recording happened away from The Paramour. Once writing and demoing sessions were finished, the band moved into Eldorado Studios in Burbank, Los Angeles, to track the album.

There, Cavallo proved his worth as both a producer and a musician. He played the piano on the record, often operating as a foil to the band. On occasion, it led to some thrilling moments. One of them was on 'Cancer', the haunting piano ballad at the centre of the album in which Gerard imagines himself as a dying patient.

One night, Gerard was talking to Ray and mentioned that he had a song. He began to sing it and Ray grabbed a guitar and placed chords underneath his melody. Ray said his fingers were determined to find patterns and notes he wouldn't normally play until, instinctively, he knew it was a song that needed a piano rather than a guitar. The following day, Gerard was waiting for Cavallo when he arrived at the studio early in the morning, itching to show him the song.

'He said, "Quick, come with me to the piano, sit down,"' says Cavallo. 'He just started singing and it was really crazy. This has never happened to me before but it took maybe eight minutes to write that song. He sang, I played the piano and it was written. That was it. It just came right out. He directed me, told me what sort of chords to play and, all of a sudden, my fingers were doing the talk-ing. I had no idea what the fuck I was doing and "Cancer" came out eight minutes later. The engineer showed up half an hour later and we recorded it. Done.'

It was a song that struck the entire band. Heartbreakingly tender and almost overbearingly real, it details the pain and invasion of chemotherapy, in part a metaphor for the end of Gerard's relation-ship, and became almost too hard for My Chemical Romance to listen back to. Ray, who played bass on the song, found it difficult. He was worried it might upset people, so stark were its tones, and fretted for a few days as to whether they should include it. He talked to a friend who had been affected by cancer and that person eased his worries, saying it might act as a tribute to those who had died from the disease.

Cavallo would greatly influence other songs too. On 'Welcome to the Black Parade', he had an unintended but vital effect. It was a song they had struggled to complete and had been playing around with from the very earliest days of the band. By the time they were working on it in S.I.R. studios in New York, Ray likened it to Green Day's 'Jesus of Suburbia'. Once they got to The Paramour, they fid-dled with it some more, speeding up the tempo until they felt they had got into shape to record. But, once they had tracked a version they all liked in the Eldorado Studios, Gerard decided it wasn't as good as it could have been. The rest of the band were not happy – Frank, particularly was unconvinced about reworking the song again. Yet the singer convinced them to keep at it until eventually a new version emerged. The key to the whole thing became some-thing Cavallo had recorded for an entirely different song.

'For the intro to the album we had this original idea that you would hear a parade coming down the street,' says Cavallo. 'You'd first hear it in the distance then, as it got closer, you'd hear it getting louder and louder and crazier and crazier. You'd hear the crowd and all sorts of different instrumentation as it goes by. Then it would get quieter after it passes you by.'

Cavallo thought the idea would take shape as an instrumental, a curtain-raiser with which to unveil the album. He told the band his idea, then he was forced to leave them to their own devices for a few weeks.

'I had this vacation planned and I had to leave town with my family for a bit, so the guys asked me to play the piano to give them an arc of this parade idea. So I started with those piano notes – ding, ding, ding, ding and so on – and I did that twice. Then I harmonized it high up the keyboard, then I made it louder and louder until I was playing it Rachmaninoff style. The whole piano was screaming and then I worked it back down to being quiet. It lasted three or four minutes. They said, "Oh, that's great! That'll be the basis of the parade coming towards us and going away." I was really excited about that idea and I thought I had played it really good too. Then I went off on vacation.'

On his return, he discovered a slightly sheepish band.

'Er . . . we fucked with your piano. We didn't want to use it for something that was going to be an interstitial piece,' they said.

'Goddamn. I really liked that,' replied Cavallo, concerned they had thrown his part away.

'No, no,' they replied. 'We used the first half and stuck it onto this song called "Welcome to the Black Parade". Listen to this intro . . .'

Cavallo was stunned when he heard what they had done. He turned back to the band and said, simply, 'Oh my God! You guys! This is the greatest thing I've ever heard!'

The song would finally be completed by Ray's Brian May-esque solo, something which he had fleshed out as a rough demo but intended to re-record in the studio. But, on the final day of guitar tracking, his fingers just refused to fall into the right places. So instead, Cavallo chopped his guitar out of his demo – never mind the fact it was recorded on a low-quality SM58 microphone and a tiny Marshall amp – and it sounded perfect. In fact, it would be the final track added to a song that was positively towering with different instruments. When it came time to mix it, My Chemical Romance realized that 'Welcome to the Black Parade' – the grand statement after which they would name the album – clocked in at a massive 167 tracks. Ambitious was hardly a big enough word for it.

There were other times too when they were simply having fun with the music, pushing it to extremes to see just how much they could get away with. 'House of Wolves', and its lolloping jungle-blues kick, came from a dead day at The Paramour in the wake of Mikey's departure when only Frank was interested in playing. He borrowed one of the library of guitars that Cavallo had brought into the studio – in this case, a giant red acoustic – and simply started playing something he thought his dad might like. The giant tuba on the bridge of 'Dead!' was another Frank idea born largely from a spirit of experimentalism.

Listening to the music-hall stomp of some of the songs, the Broadway high-kicks and jazz-hands theatrics that they were blending with the dark music, an atmosphere of 'why the hell not?' emerged. 'Mama' was a case in point. Having started life in S.I.R. in New York as Ray's polka, it took on a life of its own in the studio in Los Angeles. Cavallo insisted that they enjoy themselves on it and layer sound after sound into the song – which is why, for almost no reason, there's a guitar synthesizer effect that's almost impossible for the human ear to hear as the crushing, slow and heavy riff booms doomily into life midway through. But more was to come.

Gerard had slipped into character on the song, singing in female voices as he sought to bring Mother War to life, but felt his efforts weren't quite working. He had been warming up for his vocal takes by attempting an over-the-top impression of the Broadway singer Judy Garland, and so when Cavallo and his engineer Doug McKean asked what he was striving for on 'Mama', he said it needed her daughter Liza Minnelli to guest on it. He was not being entirely serious.

So he was surprised to see Cavallo pick up a phone, have a short conversation, then say, 'I love Liza Minnelli' after ending the call. In just a few moments, the producer had convinced her to sing on the album – something which delighted the band.

'The reason Liza Minnelli ended up on *Black Parade* was because

I was thinking about who my grandmother would have wanted on it,' said Gerard. 'A lot of my decisions were based on me thinking, "What would my grandmother do?"'

But it was Minnelli's crackling, creaking, stagey and quite brilliant cameo as Mother War that stole the show. She recorded in New York, with the band listening in from Los Angeles, and though her role is just a few bars long, it makes the song. And with its completion, My Chemical Romance knew they were on track with *The Black Parade*. It had, after all, been 'Mama' that had convinced them to take risks back in the writing sessions in New York, and it was 'Mama' that had convinced Cavallo he wanted to work with them. Once it was completed, they felt they had the centrepiece to the record.

'About halfway through the record we started to say, "Hey, this is pretty good. There's some really epic stuff on here and if we can finish it properly, then it's going to turn some fucking heads,"' said Frank. 'That felt really good. When songs like "Mama" and "Black Parade" started to finish, we were excited. When Gerard laid down the middle section of vocals [on "Mama"] right before the solo – with that Orphan-Annie-type vocal melody – that's when it really hit me that we were doing something huge. You could really hear what he was saying. We knew that if it turned our heads, then people were going to have to pay attention to it.'

As the tracking sessions progressed, Gerard began to see the loose concept that he had worked up for the album come to life. The characters he envisioned in his head were taking shape and he found himself singing in different voices as he thought about what the characters might sound like. He was still playing with different personae as he recorded, just as he had done on the band's previous two records, and so he cut his hair short and dyed it bright white to look ill like The Patient and get further into the character's mindset. Not only was he obsessing over the record, he was beginning to live within it.

★

By August 2006, the difficult, troubled recording of the album was done. Mixed by Chris Lord-Alge, its credits would also state that My Chemical Romance helped produce it – something they were both surprised and touched that Cavallo had insisted upon.

'We hadn't ever discussed that and it was very flattering and moving,' said Gerard. 'I was quite emotional about it because I didn't expect it. I turned to him and asked him about it. He was like, "Yes, because we did all produce it. That's how I do it. You produced this record with me." It was incredible, it was such a partnership.'

It had been a difficult, gruelling and frequently emotional record to make. But the results would go on to make My Chemical Romance iconic. *The Black Parade* would bring glory, triumph and success. However it would also bring hospitalizations, fallings out, tiredness and trauma. Not that they knew it, but the band were in for a hell of a ride. That August, they had two months before the album would be released. It was a period of delicious anticipation as they prepared to let their record from their grasp. And they were well aware of how charged the atmosphere was.

'I'm happy. I'm excited, nervous,' Gerard said then. 'I'm almost violently happy. I'm edgy. But it's all good. It feels like the eve of an election. You don't know what's going to happen. You don't know if it's a set-up. You don't know if there are people gunning for you. There's a whole whirlwind right now and it's one of the most amazing feelings in the world.

'I have something in my hand that I'm cupping, it's like our baby and we're just about to let it go into the world and give it away. They're either going to love it or hate it.'

12: HANG 'EM HIGH

For all the pomp and bombast of *The Black Parade*, deep down it was a highly personal record. Gerard may have been singing about cancer, patients, hospitals and death, but he was really talking about himself. 'The End.' was riddled with self-doubt and concludes with a giant scream for help. On 'Cancer', he ostensibly sings about The Patient's disease but in reality he is singing about his own depression as it crawled over him like an illness and his relationship troubles. 'Mama', for all its high-kicking, chorus-line stomp (it was partly inspired by The Doors' version of Kurt Weil's 'Alabama Song' and by elements of Pink Floyd's *The Wall*), was actually about alienation on tour and, deep down, sometimes just needing your mother. 'Dead!' centred on his paranoia that the band were loathed, while 'The Sharpest Lives' was concerned with his former drinking, drug-taking and partying. There are references, too, to the end of Gerard's relationship – 'I Don't Love You' being perhaps the most clear. The album may have been wrapped in metaphors, characters and concepts, but at its heart it was more intense and private than anything the band had previously written.

'It's actually the most personal record,' said Gerard. 'I'm trying to say that I'm not this rock star, I'm sick. This one is intense. I worked out a lot of stuff on this record so there is therapy there.'

But it is therapy masked by the spectacular as the band drew on influences like *The Rocky Horror Show*, Queen, Pink Floyd and The Smashing Pumpkins' double album *Melon Collie and the Infinite Sadness* to deliver a dark cabaret of *The Wall*-esque proportions.

'I had to put a mask on to show people who I really was,' said Gerard. 'There was such a layer of fiction, costume and pageantry that perhaps I was hoping to hide everything I was saying – which was to use cancer to metaphorically talk about relationships and things like that, rather than cancer.'

Such was Gerard's desire to both deliver their bold statement and distract attention from the personal nature of the record, he and the band went into disguise. With the confetti and piccolo whistles of a parade in their minds, they decided that, for at least the birth of this album, they would no longer be My Chemical Romance – instead they would become a band called The Black Parade when they performed live. And in order to do that, they had to look the part. Gerard, again leaning on comic book inspirations, envisioned the band in the marching uniforms of a parade. But, rather than the celebratory costumes seen more traditionally, he had in his head a more apocalyptic version: his band would be something like a black-clad version of The Beatles' psychedelic Sgt Pepper's outfits.

He found the perfect person to make his ideas reality. He approached Colleen Atwood, the Oscar-winning costume designer famed for her work with the director Tim Burton, and told her his scheme, and she set about bringing them to life. He would check in with Atwood every day, forming such a close relationship with the designer that he would come to say that she was like a big sister to him. When she had finally made the outfits, he was breathless with excitement at trying them on.

The band met Atwood at an LA hotel. They wrapped themselves in their new uniforms and saw themselves morph in front of each other's eyes. They went from Frank and Ray the guitarists to two deathly Victorian sentries. Or from Mikey the bass player to a black-clad Napoleonic captain. Bob was transformed from drummer to an apocalyptic Union Cavalry soldier. And Gerard, hair bleached white and military jacket buttoned high, said he felt like nothing short of a 'super hero'. The singer, who had for so long played with personae in his head, now had the outfit to make those characters real. It was quite the look.

Warner Bros were thrilled, not only with the band's stylistic vision but also with the record. 'I thought, right away, that we had a flawless album,' says Craig Aaronson. 'It didn't get any better than *Black Parade*. The company's confidence was up about the band too, and they thought the same as me. There were arguments over the singles though. I had zero doubt in my mind that "Black Parade" should be the first single but other people wanted "Famous Last Words" and "Teenagers" even. But in general, everyone loved it. They just weren't sure how to get the campaign started. So I said, "Make a fucking statement, man. Go with the 'Black Parade' – that's the fucking tune." I knew and understood the band and I knew "Black Parade" was the right song.'

Not only was he right, but he also got his way. 'Welcome to the Black Parade' would be the statement first single to unveil the album, the concept, the band's new image and their bold, grand sound. With Warner Bros behind it, there was money for a bombastic, explosive video. Which is where My Chemical Romance really went to town.

They wanted to work with Sam Bayer, the video director best known for shooting Nirvana's 'Smells Like Teen Spirit' video. However, Gerard and Mikey had been more impressed by his work on the dark, nightmarish and heavily conceptual video for The Smashing Pumpkins' 'Bullet with Butterfly Wings'. They found Bayer to be a powerful creative force, full of drive, focus and, occasionally, mania. Gerard told him his vision for the video.

'When death comes for you, I believe that it comes for you however you want,' said the singer of the concept for the shoot and, in fact, the album. 'If it's a black sedan or a guy on a bicycle or a pretty girl, it's something. So our character The Patient's fondest memory of childhood is going to a parade with his father. So when he passes on in hospital at a tragically young, early age, he is then picked up by The Black Parade and brought along on this journey.'

Bayer bought into Gerard's parade idea and set about bringing it to life in a vast hangar, normally used to build space shuttles, in Downey, California. When My Chemical Romance arrived for filming, they were speechless. Gerard, in particular, was blown away at seeing his vision come to life. They were faced with the actual incarnation of all their ideas: a macabre marching-parade float, behind which a great backdrop unfurled as if a city of phantoms was rolling past. Meanwhile a marching crowd of men, women and ghouls, including the album's characters Mother War, Fear and Regret, trooped alongside the flatbed truck on which My Chemical Romance would play. Visually, it was stunning: a black and white, confetti-filled, larger-than-life apocalyptic pageant leading The Patient from life to death.

'This was our dream,' said Gerard as the shoot neared its conclusion. 'And this is the biggest we've ever seen the dream. It's a really amazing, special moment for us.'

Craig Aaronson says that Gerard – more usually self-critical and nitpicking – was unusually delighted at the shoot. 'He was very excited and proud of it,' says Aaronson. 'He wasn't always like that, but when that album was done and that video was done, he felt really good. He was very proud.'

The video was a powerful statement and exactly the sort of introduction an album as grand as *The Black Parade* deserved. There was just one problem. It cost so much money to make, that the record company insisted that another video should be tacked onto the shoot to make it better value for money. And so, having spent an age capturing the majesty of 'Welcome to the Black Parade', time was tight for the filming of the video for the second single, 'Famous Last Words'. In fact, it was so tight they had around three hours to get it into the can. Fortunately, its concept was nothing like as ambitious as 'Welcome to the Black Parade'. In fact, it was almost the opposite. On 'Famous Last Words', the idea was to burn down most of the set they had used for the first video. The band would play in front of the set's funeral pyre on a circle of dirt, as vast columns of fire erupted around them. The video would go on to look stunning – but its creation took a physical toll on at least two of the band.

So intense was the heat, Bob's back was coated in a flame-retardant jelly to protect him. But on the final take, as the fire roared, the drummer was forced to stagger from his kit at the end of the song.

'We need a medic on Bob,' yelled one of the crew.

'Is he all right?' shouted someone else.

He had a third degree burn on his leg – one which subsequently became infected to give him staphylococcus aureus. The bacterial infection spread and gave the drummer an abscess on the side of his face that put pressure on his brain. He required several stints in hospital, during which one or two doctors told him he could have died from the infection. It meant, too, the cancellation of a couple of early pre-album release shows. Bob, though, typically tried to make light of the situation.

'When you write it down it looks really bad but I didn't feel that bad,' said Bob. 'Although, it is quite scary any time someone tells you that you're close to death.'

'Bob even tried to check out of the hospital as he wanted to play the shows we were forced to cancel,' said Gerard. 'It was a scary moment as we were so engrossed in the [album's] notion of death that when Bob nearly died, it was like it was a dream, well, a nightmare.'

Gerard, too, was left walking on a stick following the video shoot. A playful tackle from Frank at the end of filming had accidentally floored him and strained ligaments in his ankle, briefly requiring him to use a crutch. The funny thing was that Gerard didn't mind all that much. He was still so obsessed with the album, and with its concepts of death, that he simply bought into the pain as something he had to go through to get the record out. 'When I broke my foot,' he said, 'I didn't get angry because that's how I wanted it. I certainly feel you have to suffer for your art. We're not faking anything.'

In August 2006, shortly before the release of *The Black Parade*, the journalist Sarah Sands wrote an article in the *Daily Mail* with the dramatic headline: 'EMO Cult Warning for Parents'. If My Chemical Romance needed further proof of the support of their fans, and of the fact that the mainstream viewed them with suspicion, then this article would prove to be the catalyst.

Sands likened 'The Emos' to goths and claimed that they rejoiced in self-harm, and would compete to show off scars caused by cutting themselves. She named My Chemical Romance and Green Day as the two central emo bands, then mentioned lyrics by an obscure group called Adam and Andrew, who were a parody act. Adam and Andrew's comedy track 'The Emo Song' is what bothered Sands the most. She reprinted its spoof lyrics – which make the joke claim that writing suicide notes and slitting your throat make you an emo – and called them witty, but neglected to mention they were intended as satire. Later in the article, she also managed to misspell the name of Kurt Cobain – arguably the most famous musician in the last quarter of the twentieth century.

Gerard was furious when the article was brought to his attention. He read it as a direct attack on the band. Having suffered depression and watched his brother's struggles so recently during the making of *The Black Parade*, he found the story insensitive and inaccurate. More to the point, he frequently addressed suicide onstage, preaching against self-harm.

So when he read what Sands had written, he fumed. 'That article was almost funny,' he said. 'It was badly researched and was very negative. As far as I could see, it wasn't actually based on fact. My Chemical Romance don't promote self-harm and, as people who have been to our shows know, we actually try to help people with those kind of problems. I would hate it if anyone thought they had to do something like cut themselves in order to fit in at one of our shows.'

Sands' article, which concluded by dramatically linking so-called emo bands with suicide, was later called 'shrill and barmy' by Alexis Petridis in the *Guardian*. She was deluged with complaints and admitted that, in twenty-five years as a journalist, nothing had ever caused such a backlash. Sands claims that her inbox was full and the *Daily Mail*'s switchboard received threats directed at both her and more generally at the newspaper. She says that part of her remit at the paper was to broaden their audience. Faced with the reaction of furious My Chemical Romance fans, she realized she had done the opposite: 'I went a bit quiet at that point,' she later admitted in an article for the *Times Educational Supplement*, further confessing, 'I know little of pop music or of cults.'

The *Daily Mail* would continue to misrepresent the emo genre – two years later they referred to it as the 'sinister cult of emo' – but they were not the only ones. In fact, emo is a genre that has frequently been misrepresented. And though My Chemical Romance in 2006 found themselves being touted as its leaders, it was a tag that was entirely inappropriate, unwelcome and which they always rejected.

Emo began its life as an insult. It emerged from the hardcore punk of Washington DC in 1985. There the former Minor Threat guitarist Ian MacKaye – a righteous and respected punk pioneer and the prophet of the empowering Do It Yourself punk movement – started the band Embrace. He wanted to continue to write personally, emotionally and truthfully, as he had done in Minor Threat, but he wanted to add colour to the stark, direct and furious punk of his past. With hardcore becoming a more violent and aggressive form of music, he wanted to write with intelligence and thought, pouring out emotion rather than solely aiming to stir up mosh pits. Hence Embrace were one of the first wave of post-hardcore bands – a genre sneered at as 'emo' by its detractors.

MacKaye says the term emo was always a form of abuse used to mock the more thoughtful and less violent punk he and his friends were making in the DC scene: 'We called ourselves hardcore punk as a term to differentiate ourselves from the nihilistic, self-destructive punk rock that people associated with Sid Vicious. At some point people started joking around with the term hardcore by adding "core" to anything – skacore, metalcore, gothcore and so on.

'Brian Baker, who was at that time in Dag Nasty, came up with "emocore". If I recall correctly, it was first used publicly in an interview he did in *Thrasher* magazine in 1985 or 1986. It was then seized upon by Tim Yohannon, the editor-in-chief of *Maximum Rock 'n' Roll*, which was probably the leading punk fanzine in the world in the early to mid-eighties. He got a hold of that term and just ran it into the ground in every review: "Get out your handkerchiefs: more emocore from Washington DC." It was a term we never, ever used. We were punk bands. We never thought about calling ourselves anything else. "Emocore" was purely derisive, it was meant as a put down.'

To some it became post-hardcore, to others it remained emo, and it grew in Washington DC almost in isolation in the late eighties. But slowly its influence spread. MacKaye formed the vastly influential Fugazi in 1987 while in New York other bands began to replicate the DC sound. Jawbreaker – who would go on to work with *The Black Parade*'s producer Rob Cavallo – became a key post-hardcore band, while Walter Schreifels formed Quicksand and Norm Arenas set up Texas Is The Reason.

As the nineties unfolded and grunge exploded, post-hardcore became its underground alternative. In Seattle, Sunny Day Real Estate (whose bassist Nate Mendel and drummer William Goldsmith would play in Dave Grohl's post-Nirvana band Foo Fighters) became a cult concern. In California there was Far and in Illinois there was Braid. All of them were wary of violence in hardcore punk and they wanted to express more emotions than just anger. Bands like The Smiths and Joy Division became as much of an influence as Minor Threat.

And as those post-hardcore bands began to find a sound, so the major label A&Rs flocked towards it. They were desperate to buy into alternative rock bands in the wake of grunge's explosion – no matter that few of these bands sounded anything like Nirvana, Pearl Jam or Soundgarden.

'We played our first ever show in our living room, and there were major label people there for that,' remembers Arenas of the hype. 'Word got around that three major label A&Rs were at our first show. Before we knew it we had deals on the table from fifty labels.'

Though post-hardcore was being talked up as the next great alternative movement by the labels, its members were all too aware they were not the next Nirvana. 'I thought we were a great band,' says Quicksand's Walter Schreifels, 'but I didn't see us as being in the running against someone like Pearl Jam. But that's how these guys were seeing us. It was going to lead to some disappointment.'

Still, the mid-nineties was probably pure post-hardcore's most popular period. As Mikey Way would later point out, 'There hasn't really been an emo scene since about 1995.' But the bands largely became elevated above their status by labels who wanted alternative hits. It meant most collapsed, though not before they had been an important influence. The legacy of Quicksand, Sunny Day Real Estate, Texas Is The Reason and others bred a new wave in post-hardcore towards the end of the nineties. There is a much more direct link from that new crop to the sort of music My Chemical Romance would go on to make.

Geoff Rickly's influence on My Chemical Romance was important. From providing early support to producing their debut, he was a key figure at the start of their career. His band Thursday, alongside others such as The Get Up Kids (whose keyboardist James Dewees would later play for My Chemical Romance), were one of those who picked up the post-hardcore baton towards the turn of the century. They became known as 'the second wave of emo', largely by magazines looking for a means to differentiate them from their predecessors. Though that too was a term that was largely dismissed by anyone within the scene.

'The second wave of emo is a term that's been bandied about,' says The Get Up Kids' Matt Pryor. 'We thought we were an indie band. What seems to make bands emo are the lyrics. But most of my lyrics were as a result of the fact I was eighteen years old and that's the raw way I was thinking at the time.'

Thanks to Rickly's inability to scream convincingly (as he said, 'we sounded like Joy Division doing hardcore'), Thursday's music ended up being more melodic than they originally intended – and it caught on. Perhaps as a reaction to the macho riffs of nu-metal that dominated heavy music at the turn of the century, the more sensitive post-hardcore found its place almost in opposition to the glossy bombast of the likes of Linkin Park. Thursday became stars. No one was more surprised than they were.

'I mean we even found it weird the first time we had to play on a stage!' says Rickly. 'So when we got big it was a real shock. It was nothing we had ever wanted, considered or thought possible. We didn't know how to deal with it.'

Labels like Deep Elm began to release compilations called things like *The Emo Diaries*, while other labels such as Victory and Drive-Thru began to take post-hardcore into more pop-punk territory and away from the sounds of Thursday and other key 'second wave' bands like Glassjaw, Thrice and those on the Jade Tree label. It was certainly a more commercial direction, and by 2002, the sound was mainstream. Jimmy Eat World went platinum with *Bleed American*. Dashboard Confessional's *Screaming Infidelities* was a hit and the lines between post-hardcore and pop-punk became blurred to the extent that emo was starting to become an all-encompassing genre that simply described an era rather than a particular sound. And of course, those within it still thought of emo as a nonsense genre – 'I always thought emo was a stupid term,' says Rickly.

As he and Thursday steered away from the more commercial aspects of the genre, along came The Used, Fall Out Boy, Panic! At The Disco, The Academy Is . . . and others to take up the cudgels. Their sound – pop hooks, chart-friendly choruses and slick production married to confessional lyrics – was far more easily consumed than Fugazi's complexities or Quicksand's visceral riffs but, despite sounding nothing like post-hardcore's early bands, they came to be known as emo nonetheless.

It was this watered-down, filtered, but rampantly successful genre that My Chemical Romance were supposed to be leading. The problem was that they were doing something very different to those more pop-punk-influenced bands like Fall Out Boy. They found the tag uncomfortable. 'Basically, it's never been accurate to describe us [as emo],' Gerard told the University Of Maine's student newspaper *The Maine Campus*. 'Emo bands were being booked while we were touring with Christian metal bands because no one would book us on tours. I think emo is fucking garbage, it's bullshit. I think there are bands that unfortunately we get lumped in with that are considered emo and by default that starts to make us emo. All I can say is . . . put the records next to each other and listen to them and there's actually no similarities.'

Unfortunately, whether that was My Chemical Romance's opinion or not, *The Black Parade* would make them emo's figureheads. They didn't like it, they certainly didn't court it, but it was how they would come to be seen. It would lead to something of a trial by fire one afternoon in late August 2006.

When My Chemical Romance were asked to play the landmark Reading and Leeds Festivals in the UK over the August bank-holiday weekend, it was an obvious show to accept. It would be the eve of the release of *The Black Parade* and they would be high up the bill on the main stage – third from the headlining slot under Pearl Jam and Placebo.

They unveiled *The Black Parade* concept at a warm-up show at Hammersmith Palais five days before they were due to play at Reading. The performance began with an announcement that initially brought dismay: 'Unfortunately, due to unforeseen circumstances, My Chemical Romance are unable to perform tonight,' boomed a voice over the PA. 'The band have asked some good friends of theirs to play on their behalf.'

At which point Gerard Way, dressed as The Patient in medical gown over his full military regalia, was wheeled out on a hospital gurney. Sick, tired and dying – or so the act would suggest – he pushed himself up and the bleeping heart monitor that opens *The Black Parade* album studded the auditorium with sharp dots of sound. As Gerard began to sing the album's opening song, 'The End.', the lyrics majestically unfurled behind him. As the song's great booming guitars kicked in, he ripped off his gown to reveal his marching uniform as, simultaneously, a curtain dropped to reveal the band behind – all in uniform, dressed as their Black Parade band alter egos. 'My

Chemical Romance?' Gerard sneered. 'Fuck those guys. We are The Black Parade!'

The show was triumphant – the initial shock that the band might not be playing overtaken by euphoria at the new music they were unfurling. So it was that they travelled to Reading on something of a high. There, though, things would be different. Not only were they not playing to an audience made up exclusively of their own fans, they would also be following the metal legends Slayer – whose fans were notoriously charged, especially after a set of furious thrash.

At that time, Slayer had recently welcomed their estranged, lynchpin drummer Dave Lombardo back to their ranks to make them an even more potent live force. Following a wild, whirling set, Slayer's fans didn't take kindly to what they saw as 'just an emo band' following one of metal's most iconic acts.

From the moment My Chemical Romance walked out onto the stage, the leftover Slayer crowd made their feelings clear. Gerard, with stark white hair and in marching uniform, became an easy target. Deciding that attack was the best form of defence, he did little to placate them.

'When we walked out, the aggression started from a very small group of people in the crowd,' he said, laughing years later about the incident. 'Then, unfortunately, I instigated it from there. It was a very large mistake to tell people to throw stuff at us. At its peak, there were even people in My Chem shirts throwing stuff at us.'

As Gerard marched about the stage, both arms up and ushering the bottles towards them, the crowd responded with everything they had.

'They threw everything at us: golf balls, bottles of piss, everything,' said Ray. 'What does it feel like to get hit? It sucks.'

'I was bobbing and weaving through the whole set and I was quite proud that I didn't get hit until right at the very end,' said Mikey. 'I think it was an apple.'

No one was spared the bottling – each member of the band came in for attack. There are those who say that being bottled by the Reading crowd is something of an honour, a badge to be worn with pride. It is, after all, a rare privilege meted out only to bands that manage to really antagonize a crowd. And if getting a reaction was the goal, then My Chemical Romance certainly got one. But it wasn't much fun at the time.

'It fucking hurt,' said Frank. 'I got hit on the bridge of the nose by a bottle cap. Everything shut off for a second.'

'My worst moment was at the end of one song,' said Gerard. 'We had made it through one barrage and, just when I thought we'd get some respite, I crawled back to the microphone. As I got there, I slipped and broke my ass.'

He told the crowd to boo and hiss – and they did. He introduced 'Thank You for the Venom' with the line, 'This song is called thanks for all the bottles, thanks for all the piss, thanks for all the golf balls, thanks for all the apples and thanks for all the sticky shit.'

Remarkably, though, My Chemical Romance turned it around. They didn't give up, they didn't back off and they didn't call for security. By the end of the set – though a little shaken – they had seen off the barrage and counted the show as one of their finest: a backs-against-the-wall performance in the heat of an inferno. In seeing it out, they turned the tide too: by the end of the set, the crowd were stunned by them.

'We did win that crowd over,' said Gerard. 'It felt like a victory in the end. Reading was one of my favourite sets because we've never faced that kind of adversity. And once a few things were thrown at us, it's our nature to say, "Go on then, throw everything." It was a big fuck you. Then everything started coming at us!'

'It's how you deal with it that matters,' said Ray. 'Do you walk off? Do you get pissed off? Or do you just play your show, enjoy it and make a joke out of it? We had fun with it. But it also grounds you – no matter who you think you are, something like that can always happen. It's up to you to make the best of it.'

There was a key moment when the set turned around. Gerard slowed the pace and took a minute to address the crowd, drawing upon the band's recent experiences with the *Daily Mail*. 'They wrote an article calling people who listen to our music or fans of us a cult,' he yelled from the stage to the very people the *Daily Mail* was talking about. 'They called us a fucking cult. Do you believe how fucking ignorant that is? And that we promote self-harm and suicide in our lyrics. Do you fucking believe that? So we're here to tell you that you, our fans out there, are not a fucking cult but an army! And that nothing is worth hurting yourself over. Nothing is worth taking your life over. Do you understand?'

And with that, he began to shout, 'Fuck the *Daily Mail*! Fuck the *Daily Mail*! Fuck! The! *Daily*! *Mail*!'. The entire Reading crowd joined him, a vast chant of 'Fuck the *Daily Mail*' roaring out across the festival site, a rallying cry for everyone there.

The bottling became a long and distant memory, while the chant itself has become an iconic Reading festival moment. My Chemical Romance would not forget the level of abuse that greeted them, nor would they forget the support they left with.

As they walked from the stage, Gerard made himself a promise: he would never return to the festival unless he was headlining it.

13: PLANETARY (GO!)

The September after their Reading festival appearance found the band hard at work being interviewed, playing promotional shows and telling the world about the bold, brave album they had just made. .And, despite their experiences at the hands of the Reading crowd, everywhere else they went it seemed anticipation was high.

I flew out to Philadelphia a month before the release of *The Black Parade*. My Chemical Romance were performing at the Trocadero to film a show for the MTV $2 Bill series. The queue to get into the venue had started at 2 a.m. the previous evening. Waiters and cooks from nearby Chinese restaurants had emerged with surprise to see a neat, orderly line of black-clad fans all waiting with wide-eyed expectation for a band who would not hit the stage for another nineteen hours.

Inside the theatre, closer to showtime, the venue was a tangle of TV cables, cameras and people with clipboards. It was a controlled chaos of schedules, interviews and endlessly circling runners and producers. In the middle of it sat My Chemical Romance, unsure whether to be daunted or delighted.

The launch of *Three Cheers for Sweet Revenge* had been nothing like this. For starters, they were already famous by the release of *The Black Parade* and this is what went with it. It meant many times the number of interviews, it meant much more work and it meant being recognized wherever they went. Some of the band embraced it. Some didn't. Gerard threw himself into it, desperate to ensure the album he had worked on so hard would be delivered as perfectly as possible.

'I've been doing press and TV for days,' he said. 'I don't really have time off. I actually love talking about this record and I actually love talking about things that are related to it – the chaos surrounding the band, our lives at the moment. It's all relative.

'Talking about this record is the furthest thing from work for me. It's a little different from *Revenge* in that respect. That wasn't work but that record was made at a visceral moment in time. We were just spilling everything out and putting it on a record. There wasn't a whole lot else to talk about besides my grandmother. Talking about that got a little daunting. It was also a pseudo-concept record, so we talked about the concept but I never really felt like it was a true concept record. There was always a grey area when we talked about that album but *The Black Parade* is so focused, so it's different.'

Gerard clearly believed he was at the start of something. 'It feels very intense at the moment. If you look at any band's career, or any band that makes an impact, then you find that right before a turning point in their career then something always happens. Actually it's probably like that in most people's lives. Right before something big happens then the air gets charged.'

He was confident My Chemical Romance had pulled off something daring and dramatic. They had been through hell to make *The Black Parade*, and when they came out on the other side, they were on a high.

He came across as incredibly ambitious. He looked on *Three Cheers for Sweet Revenge* almost as a little thing that they had done of limited significance. *The Black Parade* was different – he talked about it in terms of it changing the world. This was no longer a basement punk band; My Chemical Romance had set their sights on the major leagues.

'When you start to achieve the things that surpass your initial goals, then you find there are larger things on the horizon,' he said. 'You realize that *Three Cheers for Sweet Revenge* didn't change the world as much as you had hoped, so now we've got a second chance now that people are paying attention to us. Another record is another chance to say something bigger, to say something more, to reach more people. Everything is very primed right now. It feels like there's a pinhole that we have to punch through.'

Gerard was a dizzying person to speak to at that point. He was so entirely consumed by *The Black Parade* and so driven to ensure it would be given its due that he talked incredibly rapidly and with a powerful passion. It was an obsession born from the fact the band had given so much of themselves and that it had paid off. He was quite something to see as his nerves tautened in the build-up to the release.

'This album is imbued in us, it's so completely this band that, even if it fails, it will be such a glorious failure it will be spectacular,' he said. 'We would be going out with such a bang, it would be like lighting ourselves on fire. This record is us putting everything on black and then spinning the roulette wheel. Unless you're doing that, you might as well not play at all.'

But as much as Gerard was the one doing the bulk of the talking to the press, he wasn't alone in his excitement. The rest of My Chemical Romance felt similarly on the edge, fired up yet nervy.

'I can't wait to unveil this and have everyone be a part of it,' said Frank. 'Once the album comes out, it's going to feel like a huge weight has been lifted off my shoulders. It feels like I've just been to a psychiatrist and told them all my deepest, darkest secrets and they have it written on a pad and now everyone's going to read it. It's nervous but I'll feel like there are no secrets any more. I can't wait. It feels like my chest is going to open up. I do feel like we're on the brink of something. I don't know what's going to happen next but, whatever it is, I can't wait.'

'That's the feeling we've all got – it's excitement,' said Ray. 'Having to wait another month for the record to come out is excruciating. Having played a few shows and playing some new songs during those shows – the feeling we've been getting is that kids are so psyched to hear new stuff. That makes us feel so good. It feels like we're ready to take the next step.'

'It's a feeling of accomplishing something you weren't sure you could ever possibly do,' continued Frank. 'But it's more than that: it's taking it past what you even set out to do. That's what we're feeling – it's such pride about what we've done.'

At that stage, the thought of playing the album on the road was thrilling. It was all they could do not to litter their set lists with new songs that their crowd would not have heard simply because they were so keyed up about the new music.

In the anxious, energized months before *The Black Parade* was released, they lived in a kind of bubble of pre-show nerves. And everywhere they went, they met fans who were just as charged as they were. They were increasingly recognized and followed. Bob Bryar, used to being completely ignored from his years as a sound-man, was perhaps the least at ease with it all.

'When I first started doing this, kids didn't react to this band in this way,' he said in Philadelphia. 'But yesterday, we pulled up in front of a TV station to do an interview and this girl ran up to me and started screaming hysterically. She was saying, "I can't believe that you're real!" I was smoking a cigarette and I'd just taken a piss – it was really, really weird. That kind of stuff makes me quite uncomfortable. I'm the least comfortable person in the band when it comes to photo shoots, interviews and all that stuff. It's nice to know people care but, you know . . .'

'It's so weird. It's really bizarre,' agreed Frank. 'It's even weird to me that people want to know about our lives, about what went into making the record even. It's an odd place to be.'

Each member of the band would have different examples of incidents that made them uncomfortable – from Bob's hysterical girl to the day the band were invited to MTV's Video Music Awards (VMAs) and sat with the world's biggest stars.

'Nobody talked to us, we just didn't belong there,' said Gerard. 'Those things reminded us of where we stood too. There were all these famous people wandering around in really expensive clothes and we were thinking, "What are we doing here?"'

Even if they had felt comfortable in that world, My Chemical Romance would soon have found a way to alienate themselves. 'This band needs adversity,' Gerard said. 'If we don't have that, then we're not doing any good because we need something to fight against, we need people to win over, we need to be changing people's minds. That's the whole point of the band. The second we lose that, we become normal. If we're ever mundane then we can't be special.

'We don't want to be accepted. We want our music to be understood and we want it to touch people – which is a form of acceptance – but it doesn't validate us. We validate each other. Awards don't validate us. I like the fact that we can go to something full of famous people and we can still be those kids on the outside. There's never been a desire to fit in.'

He argued that they were still outsiders. Despite the fact *The Black Parade* suggested they were set fair for success, he pointed to their treatment at Reading and Sarah Sands' *Daily Mail* article. Though feted, he said My Chemical Romance were still looking in on a world they felt they were not a part of. What they did acknowledge, though, was that, on the eve of *The Black Parade*'s release, they were outsiders with an army of fans. And that changed things.

'This time around it feels like people want us to be the greatest band in the world,' said Gerard. 'It really feels like that. Before, people wanted us to be this messy, visceral band that the teens listened to. They wanted the singer to be fucked up and people loved that. Now, it seems people are rooting for us. They seem to want us to grow up and we've gladly accepted that. We're in a position where we can make everyone who supported us really proud.'

The Black Parade was released on 24 October 2006, and it met a curious reaction. At first, it seemed, people did not know what to make of it. The last music that people had heard from the band was the full throttle punk of *Three Cheers for Sweet Revenge*: this was something different. This was 'batshit crazy', as Gerard described it.

The high camp of *The Black Parade*'s more vaudeville numbers, the deep emotional core of songs like 'Cancer', and the thematic and lyrical left turns in the pounding Status Quo-esque 'Teenagers' initially baffled critics. And then it dazzled them. There was darkness,

Frank puts the spit into
My Chemical Romance's sound.
Warped Tour, Washington DC,
August 2005.

Ray works on ideas for
The Black Parade in the back lounge
of the band's tour bus, Scranton,
Pennsylvania, August 2005.

Gerard takes some time out on
the last day of the Warped Tour.
Randall's Island, New Jersey,
August 2005.

'Welcome to the Black Parade'. August 2006.

'My Chemical Romance? Fuck those guys. We are The Black Parade!' Unveiling the new look live, Hammersmith Palais, August 2006.

Bob Bryar in full flight. Frank: 'He's one of the key ingredients in bringing this band to the next level.' Denver, 2007.

Denver, 2007.
It took seven trucks
and four tour buses to
keep the full Black Parade
World Tour production
on the road.

Each night on The Black Parade
World Tour, Gerard would come onstage
dressed as The Patient, before casting off
his hospital gown. March 2007.

James Dewees: unsung
My Chemical Romance hero and
keyboard player. Denver, 2007.

Ever the band's most visceral live performer: Frank flat on his back as My Chemical Romance headline Download Festival, June 2007.

The last date of The Black Parade World Tour, Madison Square Garden, May 2008.

Above: Gerard, backstage beforehand with his wife, Lindsey.

Below: Mikey Fuckin' Way and Gerard bringing the curtain down on
The Black Parade. 'It felt like it was the ending credits . . .'

New album, new look: unveiling the *Danger Days* costumes, Sunset Marquis Hotel, Los Angeles, September 2010.

Pre-show smiles at the Hammersmith Apollo as the band prepare to air the new *Danger Days* material for the first time. London, October 2010.

Onstage at the Hammersmith Apollo:
Frank and Gerard (*above*);
Mikey provides the rhythm
with new drummer
Mike Pedicone.

Rehearsals in Los Angeles before the second leg of the
World Contamination Tour. January 2011.

there was light and there was also much more humour than anyone could have expected: from finger snaps to high-kicking guitar lines, from lyrical asides to smart one-liners.

In *Rolling Stone*, the revered veteran critic David Fricke drew parallels with David Bowie's *Diamond Dogs* album, saying it was 'a rabid, ingenious paraphrasing of echoes and kitsch from rock's golden age of bombast'. He referenced Alice Cooper, Queen, Danzig, Iron Maiden and the Buzzcocks, and pointed out that the record is littered with references to death, obsession and destruction. He concluded that Gerard is a singer worth believing in, and that the record is worth believing in too.

Reviewing it for *Kerrang!*, I heard Pink Floyd, Queen, Green Day and much more besides, but most of all I heard trauma. 'The spectre of something awful, some dark secret [hangs] over the writing and recording of this album,' I wrote. 'There are loose themes running throughout – a man called The Patient dying in a hospital bed, dreaming of death coming to take him in the form of the Black Parade – but more important is the theme of death itself. It's a common Gerard Way characteristic and here he seems to be standing up to it, fighting it, rather than letting it consume him.'

Amid all the pomp and drama, it was the core of the songs that held *The Black Parade*'s secrets. 'Underneath the imagery and the concept is where you'll find all sorts – hope, resignation, anger, defiance, self-loathing and a thousand more emotions besides. It'll take a few listens but, when *The Black Parade* reveals its secrets to you, you'll be dazzled by its brilliance.'

And then, for reasons I'm still not entirely clear about, I awarded it four out of the five Ks that make up the *Kerrang!* rating system. I still can't explain it – and I couldn't explain it to Gerard either when he took me to task on it.

'Four Ks?' he queried when I spoke to him a short while afterwards. 'Four?'

'Erm . . . sorry,' I said, eventually.

He let me off the hook.

'I know – I read your review and I read Fricke's review and I agreed with both of them,' said Gerard. 'I got Fricke's perspective. He said the album should have ended with "Teenagers" and maybe he was right. But then nobody would have heard "Famous Last Words".'

In the *NME*, Dan Martin – a long-standing My Chemical Romance fan – gave the record 9 out of 10 (I've not asked if he was similarly chastised by Gerard for the missing mark). He wrote: 'It's a piece of work that will challenge every preconception you ever had about the people who made it.' He said it was the, 'crisp, vast, and fiercely melodic kind of stadium punk that is barely emo in the slightest.' He concluded: 'Long live My Chemical Romance, the outrageously-camp, loud and righteous new kings of the world. Those bottle-chucking haters are just going to have to get used to it.'

Martin picked up on something a lot of reviews missed: that though it was created when the band were in a dark place, *The Black Parade* was riddled with humour. Just one listen to the secret track, 'Blood', should be confirmation of that. A music-hall piano ditty with Gerard singing about the fake blood in which they had been constantly lathered in photo shoots during the *Three Cheers* era, it was a funny swipe at those tired old photo concepts.

Not everyone felt the same about *The Black Parade*'s brilliance. In the *Observer Music Monthly* supplement, Jaimie Hodgson said the album 'reeked of a band with ideas above their station', saying their 'pseudo-theatrical feel' made them sound like 'Meat Loaf's spoilt nephews'. But while other UK newspapers printed nonsense articles entitled things like 'How to spot an emo' in the wake of the release, the *Observer Music Monthly* went on to run an article calling My Chemical Romance's fans the best of the year.

The Black Parade shone commercially. It went to Number 2 in the UK album charts, while its title track 'Welcome to the Black Parade' went to Number 1 in the singles chart on its release before the album at the beginning of October. In the US, *The Black Parade* went to Number 2 on the Billboard 200 chart and to the top of the Billboard rock album chart. It was, by every yardstick, a hit.

But somehow, inside the band, it didn't feel like it had got the reaction it deserved. For an album that had taken so much from its creators, the response was a little unsatisfying. They were expecting something extreme – both good and bad. What they felt they got was just nicely positive. Despite the plaudits, they felt short-changed.

'You have to understand the mindset we had,' said Frank. 'We went in to make a record that we were expecting everyone to hate because we had been successful with *Revenge*. So we thought, if no one else likes it, we better really like it. So when we put it out there, we were waiting for it to be torn to pieces. But, at first, there was no real good or bad reaction. People just looked at us weird. So we went on tour – and that was when stuff really happened.'

14: THE JETSET LIFE IS GONNA KILL YOU

Each night at the start of The Black Parade World Tour, Gerard Way would be wheeled out onstage on a hospital trolley. Dressed as The Patient, he would sing the first lines of the album's opener 'The End.' From fragile beginnings, as he lay supposedly ill on the bed, Gerard would build and build until Bob Bryar's great booming drums announced the rest of the song.

Gradually, unerringly, inevitably, the performance would grow, the band playing every song on the record in order and in costume. The stage featured the same city skyline backdrop as in the 'Welcome to the Black Parade' video while a giant, open house loomed over everything else.

Gerard, emboldened by his ringmaster-esque outfit, became even more the focused, demagogic frontman. He would bay at his crowds, demand more from them, abuse them, call them 'fucking animals'. 'Do you have the juice?' he'd yell. 'Then let's see you fucking dance!' The legions of the broken, beaten and damned My Chemical Romance were singing about on *The Black Parade* would bend to his will too: screaming, howling and fainting in the front row, delirious under confetti cannons, faces melted by pyro guns. Fans who had frequently queued overnight underwent something like a religious experience. Sweat-sodden and bedazzled, the murmurs that 'My Chemical Romance saved my life' would grow into something approaching chants as the band toured the US from February 2007.

And once they came to the end of the album – complete with its jaunty, jokey hidden track 'Blood' – My Chemical Romance would retire from the stage, the show apparently over, no one quite sure how anyone could expect more. But then they would return – an encore set that read like the band's greatest hits: 'I'm Not Okay (I Promise)', 'It's Not a Fashion Statement, It's a Fucking Deathwish', 'Cemetery Drive', 'The Ghost of You', 'Give 'Em Hell, Kid', 'Thank You for the Venom', 'You Know What They Do to Guys Like Us in Prison' and finally, inevitably and deliciously, 'Helena'.

With their sound filled out by the addition of the keyboard player James Dewees – an old friend who was formerly a member of The Get Up Kids and who helmed his own solo project Reggie and the Full Effect – My Chemical Romance set out for the world.

Though My Chemical Romance had already aired material from *The Black Parade* over the course of sixty shows since their Reading performance in August 2006, the album's world tour officially began in Manchester, New Hampshire, on 22 February 2007 after the band had taken a couple of weeks off. It would span the globe, a seemingly endless string of dates that – by the end of the tour on 9 May 2008 at Madison Square Garden – the band would reflect had nearly killed them. In total, they would play nearly two hundred shows in a little over four hundred days and would perform any-where from Buenos Aires to Moscow.

But back then in February, back at the very start, this was a thrill ride. Along for the journey were, at first, Rise Against and old friends Thursday. In Europe in March and April, LostAlone and Funeral For A Friend would tour with them, while in late April and May in the US they would take Muse out on the road as their support act.

That Muse were already set to play two back-to-back headline performances at Wembley Stadium in June 2007 (returning the favour by asking My Chemical Romance to be their support) dem-onstrates just how big, bold and exciting My Chemical Romance were in the US. After all, there weren't many bands who could take out a stadium headline band as a warm-up act.

On the eve of the tour, Frank talked about how much he was looking forward to it – despite the length and intensity of the string of dates.

'It's going to be fun,' he said. 'Maybe we're gluttons for punishment because we love that shit. When people ask us where we live, we say, "In a bus." Our mail might get sent to Jersey but we barely live there. It's one of those things. It's always painful to leave your family and loved ones but it's something we've grown used to, that feeling of leaving home and not being there. But we know that this is what we were made for, this is what we have to do.

'You either have it or you don't. We all got bitten by that bug early on. It's not something you can describe. The feeling you get from writing a song and playing it in front of people, and having them give you such a great feeling back is such an amazing connection. It's like a drug – it's the best high you could ever have. It makes you feel alive on such a crazy level. But if you've never experienced it, it's hard to really put it into words. Once you have that, I don't know how you could ever let it go.'

The band's booking agent Matt Galle, who pieced together much of the US tour, says they had become a different, more resolute band than the one who drank their way through their first tours. 'When they were younger, they were like "Oh shit! Everything's at my fingertips. People are partying everywhere,"' he says. 'Then they grew up – we all did – and figured things out. They realized they had responsibilities, that this was a business and that it was their life and that they couldn't fuck around any more.

'When *The Black Parade* came out, it became a big family on the road. People would exercise during the day – it was the total opposite of any kind of party or anything like that. It was video games, or people going shopping, going to comic book stores. They would go sightseeing and things like that. They liked having some sort of routine.'

Not only did My Chemical Romance want to do the majesty and brilliance of *The Black Parade* justice, the band also realized they owed a debt to their growing numbers of fans. If the band were asking them to come to arena shows, then they had better deliver. It was the cause of some nerves. 'The magnitude of the shows brought up a lot of anxiety,' said Frank. 'Two years ago, we were the first band on the bill who nobody gave a shit about. All of a sudden we're headlining and people are calling our music great. In your head that feels great but at the back of your mind there's that nagging thought that says, "You better be really fucking good then."'

They left very little on the table in terms of their stage production. Galle remembers that they took seven trucks full of stage equipment on the road, and had four buses to cart them and their crew around. He says they 'spent so much money on production' and used 'every bell and whistle' in the grand set-design, lighting and pyrotechnics.

'The theatrical stuff brought so much to it all,' he says. 'You don't see a lot of acts doing that these days. It's one thing to come up with the ideas, but to pull them off is another thing. They could really sell it and people knew it was from the heart, rather than being contrived.'

For Gerard, it was all about making *The Black Parade* everything he imagined it could be. If the band were going to take themselves to the edge of sanity in recording it, they were certainly going to ensure they made it special when they played it live. In order to ensure the show came across as grandly as he imagined it, he found that he was more controlled onstage. Gone were his visceral, spontaneous and undeniably thrilling performances of before and, in their place, was a more honed and precise singer. Where once no one knew what Gerard would do next – least of all him – now came something that was rapier-like in its directness.

'The game plan used to be, "Well, if you like us, you like us. If not, never mind,"' he said. 'I would flail and whatever happened, happened. It's not that I'm calculated about it now, but there's more confidence. We've come to terms with what we are and what we mean to people and that's given us a confidence that makes us grander onstage. There's less thrashing about but it means more. It's like, "Play smart, not hard." I want to have a command over the audience, I want to give them something to believe in or to fight for. I want to give people a sense of hope.'

The first leg of The Black Parade World Tour took them around the United States: nineteen dates in twenty-three days. Midway through it, on 7 March 2007, shortly before the band played, Mikey married his girlfriend Alicia Simmons backstage at the Orleans Theatre in Las Vegas. Gerard was his best man – though only because Mikey wasn't allowed to have the entire band as his 'best men'. The happy couple would be allowed one day together – a rest day – before the tour continued towards its conclusion in Reno, Nevada, on 16 March. By 20 March they were across the Atlantic in Plymouth beginning the European leg. They played seventeen shows in twenty-one days across England, Wales, Scotland, Ireland, Germany, France, Sweden and Denmark, with the UK run culmin-ating in two sold-out shows at Wembley Arena and a private competition-winners' performance at the small Koko theatre in Camden. After that performance in particular, they all looked dead on their feet – admittedly, they had just come offstage – but it was a tour that was exacting a physical toll. Frank had been forced to step down briefly with a stomach complaint and was replaced by his tech Matt Cortez while the guitarist recovered – including for the second Wembley date. 'That kid's moving up in the world – he even got to play Wembley,' said Frank, perhaps a touch enviously.

Four days after the European tour, My Chemical Romance were back in the States with more dates across the country lined up. But it was here that their schedule caught up with them again. Mikey left the band temporarily on 18 April amid fears it was a recurrence of the depression that had struck him down during *The Black Parade*'s recording. Frank, however, was quick to play down the worries. 'No, not at all,' he said. 'Tell everyone not to be worried about him at all. It's a much better thing than that, we should all be very happy for him and should wish him well.'

In fact, Frank said, it was because he wanted to spend time with Alicia. 'He's just taking the chance to be a newly married man. It's exciting. When we suggested it, he jumped at the chance – like any normal guy would. He's just very thrilled at the moment. He's opened a new chapter in his life. He's so young and he's just got married, so this is a great thing for him to do. We're really happy for him. We want him to be able to enjoy those little things in life that sometimes people take for granted. I don't know where they're going on honeymoon yet but then I'm not sure I'd tell you if I did know anyway.'

Inevitably, though, the rumour mill went into overdrive with fans and media speculating that he was leaving for good, or that it marked the first stage of the break-up of the band.

'Both of those are completely untrue,' said Frank. 'Because of the position we're in, we get to do some amazing things. We get to do things that we've dreamed of since we were kids. But, at the same time, we're also denied a lot of things that we've also wanted to do – like being there at certain landmarks in our families, or not being there for the people we love. We don't get to enjoy some of the normal things in life that others take for granted. No one in this band wants any one of us to miss out on that stuff if we can help it. Those things are very important.'

Frank, also newly married to his wife Jamia Nestor, joked that he had an ulterior motive behind agreeing to Mikey's departure: 'I was definitely a big supporter of the idea of Mikey going away just in case I have the urge too! I was like, "Oh yeah, go and do what you want to do. Hey, guys, you remember I'm married too?"'

But the band had a full summer of touring lined up. Though Mikey was replaced by Matt Cortez, his absence meant that they were embarking on their longest run of dates yet without one of their full-time members. 'Oh, we're not worried about that,' said Frank. 'Mikey's missing out on some smelly aeroplanes and crapping in a porta-potty. I'm sure that had nothing to do with why he decided to take off . . .'

There would be other problems just around the corner. On 29 April My Chemical Romance and their support act Muse were both forced to cancel six shows as a result of a salmonella outbreak among the bands and crews. When they looked back on The Black Parade World Tour in years to come, they would point to moments like this as proof that the road was out to get them.

It wasn't just illness either. They found themselves under attack from other musicians too. The singer Marilyn Manson claimed the snide lyrics to his 2007 song 'Mutilation Is the Most Sincere Form of Flattery' were about My Chemical Romance. 'I'm embarrassed to be me because these people are doing a really sad, pitiful, shallow version of what I've done,' he sniffed. 'If they want to identify with me then here's a razor blade. Call me when you're done and we'll talk.'

The band found that, instead of being asked about their music, they were increasingly asked about Manson's comments instead. 'We still haven't found someone that has knocked us down that we need to take seriously,' Gerard said. 'If Elvis Costello said we sucked we would think about it a bit but usually it is comments from someone with a new record to promote so the remarks ring hollow.'

Frank waded in too. 'The funny thing is that he seems to have lashed out at us about the make-up. That's weird to me, because I had heard of Alice Cooper before I heard of Marilyn Manson. I don't know how he could be mad at us. We never came out and said we were going to call ourselves by a girl's name and then a serial killer's name. I'm really sorry if he feels we ripped him off. It would have been nice if he could have said something to our faces but he's been all smiles every time I've seen him. Maybe he's doing it for the press. Some people just like to talk.'

Despite the problems, they also found much to enjoy. Though there were illnesses, absences and injuries, My Chemical Romance were not unwilling or unhappy while on tour – well, not by that point anyway – and to meet them then was to see a band who were soaking up experiences as often as they could.

They had their share of firsts too. They headlined a festival in the UK for the first time – the Download festival at Donington Park, the celebrated home of British metal and for years the site of Europe's biggest metal festival. They were proud, but approached the show with a little trepidation given the treatment Slayer's fans had meted out to them at Reading the previous year.

'Just being asked to play Download was an honour but to head-line it was a dream come true,' said Frank. 'Whenever we get offered a show at a prestigious festival, I always go online and check the past people who have played there. Some of the people who have played the slot we played at Donington are mind-blowing – bands like Black Sabbath, Iron Maiden, Metallica, Guns N' Roses. I got a lump in my throat reading that. I was like, "Wow", especially as we are still a young band. I guess we've been fortunate enough to get a lot of attention but part of me still thinks headline slots like ours should go to bands who have been around a lot longer – bands like Green Day or Red Hot Chili Peppers who have been doing this for years and years. I don't feel like we don't deserve it but it's still a little surprising. Having said that, I'll still take it!'

It was the connection with Iron Maiden, who heavily inspired the band members when they were growing up, that stuck in Gerard's mind the most. Still, there were many there who felt that My Chemical Romance were not metal enough to be headlining the festival. Despite the fact they were arguably the hottest rock band in the world – and had a rabid following in the UK – the festival pro-moter Andy Copping faced criticism for asking them to play. He says it was a gamble that paid off handsomely. 'I think it was an inspired booking, but I'm always going to say that. All the abuse the band took was ridiculous. Our sales in 2007 were really strong, and it ultimately paid off.'

By the time My Chemical Romance were due onstage, there were plenty of whispers around the festival site that sections of the crowd were preparing to bottle them. There were rumours too that My Chemical Romance had arranged for a big net to be put in place at the front of the stage – at the first sign of a bottling, the net would fly up and protect them. In the end a reasonably tame shower of bottles greeted their arrival, something which they ignored almost entirely.

'People asked us if we were worried that we would be bottled after what happened at Reading but we really weren't worried at all,' said Frank. 'Honestly, I've played over three hundred shows in which we've had bottles thrown at us, but I've never talked about any of those gigs as much as I've talked about Reading. I guess that makes that show a big success. So was there a fear of the show being an awesome success? No, not really!'

He did admit to nerves though as he stood onstage and thought about the calibre of bands who had also headlined in the same place. 'Going out on that stage at Download was great,' he said. 'You look out on a sea of people and you can't see where it ends. But it's pretty daunting to get up on a stage that big and in front of that many people. To play a slot that bands like Black Sabbath have played means you have some legendary shoes to fill. All we wanted was to do it justice – to put on the best show we could.'

For the performance, My Chemical Romance ditched the *Black Parade* set-list they had been touring with and, instead, played a proper festival headlining set. The show was littered with hits from *Three Cheers* and swelled by the big hitters from *The Black Parade*. It was an undeniable success – Andy Copping's decision to book them was proved correct, while the band's decision to accept such a slot also proved to them that they were now operating at the level of a festival-headlining band. It was a big step.

'That was absolutely mind-blowing to me,' said Frank afterwards. 'We don't really think of ourselves as being on that level. To me, this still feels like the same little band that started playing in Jersey. We're really not the sort of people who wander around going, "Look at how big we are!"'

They wouldn't have time to, either. They had one day off afterwards, which they spent in London, then they flew straight to Russia. For a feature for *Kerrang!* magazine, I ghost-wrote a tour diary that covered the next few days of their lives. The dates would take them across Russia, to Italy and finally back to London to support Muse on the second of their sold-out Wembley Stadium shows. It meant that, in the course of ten days, they would have played their first ever major festival headline slot, played their first shows in Russia, then played at Wembley Stadium for the first time (albeit as a support act). Speaking to them, it was immediately clear just how exciting a time it was. They would talk about their experiences down crackly Russian phones, or with the background noise of a motorway service station blaring down the line and I would make sense of it for the magazine. First came Frank's view of playing in St Petersburg. It provides an interesting snapshot of that time and of how busy they were.

'We flew into St Petersburg and arrived late, so went straight to bed and slept,' he said. 'The next day, we played our first show here in Russia, which was completely fucking amazing. Unfortunately we had to drive straight to the venue from the hotel the next morning to do a few interviews, so I didn't get a chance to see a lot of the city, which I hate. After the show, we had to rush straight back to the hotel because we're travelling to Moscow really early tomorrow. The worst part was not getting to meet any of the fans. I don't like visiting new countries and not being able to see any of it or meet the kids. So: sorry St Petersburg. I feel awful about it. I promise next time we're here that I'll come out and say hello to as many people as I can.'

He pointed out how odd it was to tour without Mikey – still on sabbatical from the band as they played around Russia and Europe. 'What I'm really noticing, though, is how much I miss Mikey. Fuck, man, I miss the shit out of him. I'm so pissed off he isn't here. I want him to come back as soon as humanly possible. The only good thing is that we get to play with Matt Cortez, who's a really good friend of ours. The ladies seem to like him too – he's not bad on the eyes!

'I email Mikey every day. Actually he told me to stop emailing him the other day because I was sending him so many messages. He's doing very well though, he and his wife bought a puppy and they're hanging out and just being married. He's living the life and having a great time. I wish them well – but not the best, because I don't want him to enjoy himself so much that he doesn't come back.'

By the time the band were in Moscow, it was Ray's turn. They had a little more time there, and he says he enjoyed just being a tourist for a while.

'I really never thought I'd be in Russia, so I'm having a fucking awesome time. There's a public holiday on here now, so there are a lot of festivals. It means that people are out on the streets, drinking, partying and having a good time at all hours, so we've been doing the same. When you're in Russia, you've got to drink vodka and enjoy yourself.

'Tonight, we took a boat cruise. There were hundreds of boats, all travelling in a group. Everywhere you look you can see people dancing and partying on the other boats as you go under all the bridges here. Meanwhile, there'll be other people letting off balloons everywhere. It's pretty fucking amazing.

'I'm much happier when we have a little time to look around. We usually have such a hectic schedule that we don't get any time to do anything. We end up spending all our time backstage and, after a while, every dressing room starts to look the same. You could be anywhere. If you're lucky, you get an hour to go and have a look around. Now we're trying to work it so that we get one or two days off every now and again, so we can actually explore. It's really beautiful here.'

But as much as he enjoyed the chance to sightsee, he was also struggling with the amount that My Chemical Romance were travelling. The following day he was tired and jet-lagged – a feeling that was increasingly familiar. 'We're travelling through so many different time zones in such a short period of time that your body never really has time to adjust,' he said. 'I'm always passing out at odd times of the day and then waking up in the middle of the night. I spent most of my time in the hotel room today. As far as I know, Bob and Gerard did the same. Sometimes you just need to lie in bed all day.'

On days off, when not exploring, he would sit in his room or in the band's bus and work on music – often alone. It was frequently where he was happiest, locked away with just a guitar and his ideas for company. 'Today I added some drums to something I've been working on,' he said. 'It's a pretty fast, punky kind of song that will probably be a My Chemical Romance song one day. I'll wait until it's more formed before I play it to anyone else though. I play some stuff to the other guys, if it's nearly finished, but some of the stuff I record is strictly for me, just little jam sessions with myself. I'm trying to learn more about recording and mixing, so I've been doing a lot of experimenting just to see what happens. I'm really happy killing time doing that.'

The day after the Moscow show, they were in the hotel lobby at 7 a.m. to travel to Italy. 'Being in all these time zones means you never really know what time it is,' said Bob. 'I tend to just sleep when I can and get up when I have to. I'm used to it now. When we landed in Venice, we jumped in some boats to the hotel. Going through Venice on boats is such a stunning experience. Every building here is like a piece of art. I find it weird when I look at the people who live here – I wonder if they know exactly how amazing this place is or whether they take it all for granted. Toro said he feels like he's walking around in a museum.

'I love the culture too. Everyone seems to be sat in little cafes, looking out over the water and drinking coffee. That the easiest way to get somewhere is on a gondola always makes me smile. I could really get into this lifestyle. Actually, if you take away the boats, our lifestyle in My Chem is quite Italian – we sit around drinking coffee and smoking cigarettes all day just like the Italians do.'

My Chemical Romance were billed in the middle of the day at a festival at Parco San Giuliano in Venice. Above them were The Killers, Linkin Park and Pearl Jam but there were reports of a storm that might scupper the festival.

'Literally five minutes before we were due on, it started pouring down,' said Gerard. 'Then it started hailing and then the wind came. It was insane. It was like something out of a movie. Just as we were supposed to go on, the sky darkened and the storm ripped apart the festival. It was actually really scary. We were watching speaker and lighting towers collapse near our road crew and near the kids in the crowd. Afterwards, we heard that only eight fans were hurt. That's awful but thank God it was so few and that nobody got killed. It could have been a lot worse.

'It was a weird day after that. Everyone was really frazzled. We had to stay on site because all our gear was trashed onstage. The police wouldn't let us get it because the stage wasn't safe. It means we have to cancel our show in Switzerland, which is a real shame.'

Gerard filled his time on the road by drawing characters and sketching out ideas for a comic book he was working on called *The Umbrella Academy*. In the hours of travel, he could often be found with a sketchbook and a pen as he drifted off into imaginary worlds. It's how he occupied himself on the long drive out of Italy and into the UK.

After driving through the day and night across Europe, stopping for smoke breaks in service stations and then ploughing back on across the continental motorways, they arrived at Wembley Stadium at 4 a.m. for their support slot with Muse on 17 June. Disorientated, they barely knew where they were when they woke up.

'As soon as I got up, I went to have a look around to get my bearings,' said Gerard. 'I walked around the stadium and it's so impressive, then I had a look at Muse's stage set-up, which was equally impressive. It was incredible.'

He had a moment, as he wandered around the huge empty stadium. He thought back to where the band had begun and where they were now. He thought about how much had changed.

'Whenever we play a club, I like to walk around it to get a sense of the room, so I did the same thing at Wembley. It actually made me very nervous. It was strange; I got the same feeling as I did in the very early days of My Chemical Romance. We had only been a band for three months and we were playing in basements. Then one day we got a phone call saying that Coheed and Cambria had dropped out of a support slot with Jimmy Eat World at the Allentown Fairground in Pennsylvania, and would we like to play? We were such a baby band then and I remember getting up onstage then, thinking, "I'm not prepared for this." That's exactly the feeling I had when I walked out at Wembley. I thought, "Oh my . . ."'

By the time they were due onstage, the adrenalin had kicked in and he was ready to face the crowd.

'Some singers say that big gigs like this go past in a blur but I'm very aware when I'm up there,' he said. 'Ever since I've been sober, I've always been aware of my surroundings onstage; it's pretty rare that I'll get lost in the moment unless it's a completely killer show. Having said that, it takes quite a while to take everything in when you play a stadium, so I was pretty nervous. It was one of the biggest crowds we've played to and, though we're used to playing in front of other people's fans, it's not often that you're playing in front of 70,000 of them. But it was really Muse's day, so I wanted to play as well as we could but leave them to take the glory. This show wasn't about us, it's about them.'

There was one thing that was nagging at him – nagging at all of them as they travelled around the continent. Though fill-in bassist Matt Cortez was performing admirably, and though he was a long-established member of the crew, he was not Mikey.

'None of this has been as fun as it could have been because Mikey isn't here,' said Gerard. 'I really miss him. He's doing really well and it sounds like he's getting exactly what he needs, which is just life and experience. I really miss the kid, though. It's a heavy drag. The first thing I'm going to do is go visit him when this tour is over. We've had a blast on this tour but it would have been so much better if he was here.'

The European leg of the tour finished in Helsinki on 3 July and My Chemical Romance took time off afterwards – though not much. By 25 July they went out on Linkin Park's travelling Projekt Revolution music festival. Matt Galle thought the tour was a risk: either it would pay out and the band would broaden their audience, or it would fall flat when Linkin Park's more mainstream fans dismissed them. He was pleased to see the band flourish. 'They had those meatheads eating out of their hands,' says Galle.

They were the second headliners underneath Linkin Park, and were among old friends in the shape of Taking Back Sunday and The Bled, while also on the bill were Placebo, the Finnish band

HIM, Saosin and others. But it was the headliners of the second stage, Mindless Self Indulgence, that Gerard was most interested in.

While on the Projekt Revolution tour he became close to Mindless Self Indulgence's bassist Lindsey Ballatto – Lyn-Z, when onstage.

There were plenty of similarities between the two. Though born in Scotland, Lindsey grew up in a small town in Connecticut and says she was shy as a girl. 'I was the nerdy art girl in the corner and I was the total fat kid,' she said. 'I was huge.'

Like Gerard, she wanted to be an artist and she too went to New York to try to make it happen. She was accepted into the Pratt Institute art school on the basis of her dark, autobiographical illustrations. Her first exhibition was in the basement of a burned-out building, her artworks taped to the wall. 'It was very punk rock,' she said.

It was at that first show that she met Jimmy Urine (real name Jimmy Euringer), the creative force behind Mindless Self Indulgence. He asked her to audition for the band, though she could barely play the bass, and she gave it a go, though nerves got the better of her. It was only on her last attempt to play one of the band's songs – 'Tornado' – that she convinced them she should join.

'I had put a film canister filled with Bacardi151 in my bra, and I had matchsticks in my pigtails and a strike glued to the back of my bass,' she said. 'So I took the shot, pulled the matches out of my hair, struck the back of the bass and blew fire all over the room – almost setting Jimmy on fire. They were like, "OK, you're hired."'

Mindless Self Indulgence were formed in 1997 by Urine as an over-the-top soundclash of styles between punk, hip-hop, electronica, dance, metal and industrial. Far more musically talented than he is often given credit for, Urine's music has often been overlooked as simply being reactionary for its own sake, which tends to miss its subversive point.

My Chemical Romance played with them shortly before recording *Three Cheers for Sweet Revenge* in New York and in New Jersey in 2003, and it was there that Gerard first met Lindsey – 'we kind of hit it off back then, but I was in a relationship and nothing transpired,' he said. But when they toured together in 2007, things were different.

In fact, Gerard had been in something of a strange space, romantically, before meeting Lindsey. Having ended one relationship during the making of *The Black Parade* and another subsequently, he was single at the start of 2007 and happily so. A meeting with one of his long-time idols, the comic book artist Grant Morrison, had led to a conversation about fame, being a rock star and enjoying life for what it was. It would have a profound effect on Gerard. He came away from it determined to live life more fully.

'He and his wife took me out to lunch,' said Gerard. 'It was one of those meetings where you get complete clarity. First of all, it was like we had been friends for ten years. The way we could talk to each other was amazing. He and his wife were such a unit and they were so free. He looked at me and said, "You're on this crazy fucking trip right now. You're on an adventure but you haven't taken it. You've been living this for the last five years but you haven't enjoyed it."

'He wasn't talking about girls or the stuff that comes from being in a rock band. He was saying that I can go wherever I want, I can see whatever I want, I can do whatever I want – I can meet the weirdest people in the world, they can make me feel alive. He said I needed to take this thing by the balls right now because it's insane. He said that [My Chemical Romance] were saying something about the world that nobody was saying, that we were plugged into something that was coming – a sense of bravado, fuck-you attitude death-rock. He said we need to just enjoy it.'

It was what Gerard needed to hear. Having been so immersed in *The Black Parade* and My Chemical Romance, he had forgotten that there was a life outside the band. It was why he was so intense and introspective. Rather than enjoy the band's success, Gerard would evaluate it and feel uncomfortable with it. Morrison told him that he needed to relax.

'At that time, I don't think he was aware of how much of a rock star he actually was,' says Morrison. 'I was in bands when I was young and aspired to be what he was for a long time. So, seeing someone who was actually living that dream, I thought I should remind him to be aware of it and to enjoy it. When your record's huge and you're in the middle of that, you're barely aware of what's happening around you but that's actually one of the most interesting times in a band. I told him to remember he was a rock star and that he should have fun with it and should play with it.'

It was the start of a firm friendship between the pair. Gerard had grown up reading Morrison's comics and, at first, was thrilled to simply meet someone who was comic book royalty. But the two became friends quickly.

'I'd seen "Helena" and "Welcome to the Black Parade" on TV and I was really impressed by that last video,' says Morrison. 'I loved that song and the video was great: it was like Sgt Pepper in the afterlife and that really appealed to me. When we met up, we really hit it off. We really clicked and became very close friends immediately. It was a complete meeting of minds – or maybe we'd once been Egyptian Pharaohs or something! We spent hours talking and it was very easy and friendly.

'What drew me to him was that we were able to talk about all sorts of things. I recognized that he wasn't just a singer in a band: he's a kid from art school who had big ideas. Once I'd listened to the other albums, I realized that each one was a distinct art project and that appealed to me. He wasn't locked into just one image of his band and he was willing to grow and change.'

By January, Gerard had taken Morrison's advice on board. He said then: 'Grant is living. I need to start fucking living. I look to the future and it's open. The world looks more like a playground than a battlefield now. I can do whatever the fuck I want.'

But though Gerard talked a good game, when faced with reality he was still a little fragile. He tried to enjoy being single but he struggled with it too. 'Well, shit dude, I still get lonely,' Gerard admitted to me in a long phone call. 'Even in clubs when there are like forty women there. I'm always going to be that guy though. That's my lot. That's my character. I can be in a club with 120 people and I'm still the loneliest guy in the room. Maybe there's a part of me that loves living in that eternal Smiths song. Do you know what I mean?

'I've been enjoying being free and not having to make phone calls,' he continued. 'It's a good feeling at first but then you check into a hotel room and realize there's no one you have to call, that there's no one who misses you. Well, there are friends and family that miss me, but there's no one who misses me like a girlfriend does. I'll sit there and stare at the wall and go, "Well, I can do what I want . . . but what exactly do I want to do right now?" When we were on our last European run I would just go out at night and walk around alone. I was thinking, "Well, this is interesting . . ."'

And then he met Lindsey again on Projekt Revolution. 'I was at a point where I was completely OK with being alone for a very long time, free of lousy people,' he said. 'And literally out of nowhere, someone who'd I'd met four years ago when the band was a baby band, opening for her band, comes back into my life. We just picked up where we left off. It's always when you're not looking for it. I was totally fine, and then I get hit over the head! It was like getting hit by a truck.'

By 3 September 2007 he would be married after an intense romance on the road with Lindsey. A member of the touring staff was coincidentally an ordained minister, and he married them backstage at the Coors Amphitheatre in Englewood, Colorado. The next day the happy couple went to the nearest mall to buy rings – 'I think they were a couple of hundred bucks,' said Gerard.

Not that they would have long to enjoy it. For Gerard and Lindsey there would be no time off as Mikey had enjoyed. Though My Chemical Romance had a month off the road, a month to recuperate from just over a year of shows, Gerard would head back out on the promotional trail: this time to launch *The Umbrella Academy* comic book he had been working on while touring.

Created and written by Gerard, and drawn by Gabriel Bá, it was about a disbanded group of superheroes who reunite after the death of their adoptive father. The first limited series was called *The*

Apocalypse Suite. Published by Dark Horse, it ran from September 2007 until February 2008 and had been pieced together almost entirely in hotel rooms, backstages and airport lounges around the world. For Gerard, the fact that he had managed to get a comic book published was a big deal. It was, after all, comics that had been his first love before music – and it's arguable that, had he not become disillusioned with comics in 2001, he would never have formed a band at all.

'I don't really care how big it gets, that's irrelevant to me,' he said. 'That means that I've been able to write it artistically and without thinking about it selling a lot. That's the most important thing – it's how we write music too. Fortunately, the two seem to have gone hand in hand. I'm quite lucky that way.'

It was well received, with critics impressed and surprised that Gerard clearly had a deep love for the form. Many had expected him to be a rock star playing with art, rather than someone who had a long attachment to comic books. As it was, it was another success to continue the triumph of *The Black Parade* and its accompanying world tour. In fact, had My Chemical Romance decided to bring things to a halt in September of 2007, they could have looked back on a wildly successful year in which they had worked hard and reaped deserved rewards.

But they didn't do that. Instead, they went back on the road.

15: DROWNING LESSONS

On 7 October 2007 My Chemical Romance were in Mexico City for the start of another round of touring. The month off in which Gerard had launched *The Umbrella Academy* was behind them and they would have precious little time away from the band for the next eight months. They were joined by Mikey, playing his first shows with the band since he had left them in April, and they were delighted to have him back – especially since the Mexico City performance would be a special one: it was here that they were going to kill *The Black Parade*.

Having toured the record for a year, My Chemical Romance thought it deserved a fitting end. So they brought out the production one last time, sending the show to its grave with a last, dazzling performance as the entire band wore their *Black Parade* uniforms. They commemorated the end of the run by filming the show, later releasing it on DVD and as a live CD in June 2008 as *The Black Parade Is Dead!*

Perhaps it should have been a fitting finale to a triumphant album cycle, but the band would get no such respite. Next came a couple of shows supporting Bon Jovi in New Jersey before November was spent in Europe, and December spent in Australia, New Zealand and Asia. By the end of January 2008, they were back in Asia. February was spent in South America. March brought another European tour, April a US tour and finally the end was in sight with a showcase headline performance at Madison Square Garden. It was the thought of that show that kept them going – it was, after all, at Madison Square Garden that Mikey and Gerard had watched The Smashing Pumpkins all those years ago and decided to form a band.

To play there would make all the travelling and touring worthwhile. But it would take some getting to.

The reason My Chemical Romance went back on the road was because, a year after release, *The Black Parade* was selling as well as it ever had. 'It was maybe a year into the touring that things got really big,' said Frank. 'So we thought, OK, we'll have to keep going. So we stayed out another year. It was crazy, we couldn't say no to anything. I think we were trying to prove something to ourselves – we always thought the album was great and, when other people started to think the same, we felt we owed it to the album to give it everything.'

The Black Parade had become a phenomenon. Certainly Warner Bros were delighted at how well it was faring. 'It was amazing, man,' says A&R man Craig Aaronson. 'That album took them from being a big rock band in America to being a world force. It was a good time for the band and the label. We were so proud of that band at the label. They were so interesting and unique and they were just killing it – that helped our label out a lot too. We benefited a lot from having them and it meant lots of other bands wanted to sign for us too. It was a total win-win situation.'

However, that's not to say that Aaronson believed they should still have been on the road. He thinks they should have packed it in sooner – at the end of 2007 at the latest – taken a break and started to think about a new album at the start of 2008. 'It became a marathon,' he says. 'They did one tour too many – and that happens because people offer you a lot of money.'

Gerard also thought My Chemical Romance should have stopped touring in September 2007. He says they were tired but felt they were being 'baited to go and play this dream show' at Madison Square Garden. Without new songs to play, he was surprised that people still wanted to come out to see the band. 'We were so accessible at that point and we had very little to offer. We weren't really writing anything new. We didn't feel creatively stimulated any more,' he said.

Already prone to injury and illness – Gerard's ankle, Bob's burns,

Frank's immune-system issues, food poisoning, and most seriously, depression – further problems began to mount. Bob was forced to pull out of a number of shows, including the cancelling of a date in Maine, because of issues with his wrists that grew into carpal tunnel syndrome – a condition that numbs the fingers and thumbs.

Bob was replaced for the Bon Jovi shows and the UK tour that followed first by Save the Day's Pete Parada and then by Thursday's Tucker Rule, but he still came along to assist with the stage set and the pyrotechnics. He returned to the kit in January 2008 for the Asian tour. Frank too was briefly forced to pull out of the tour after the first date of the UK leg in Newcastle in November 2007 after learning of a family member's illness. He was replaced by the Drive By frontman Todd Price. But the constant setbacks and frequent stand-ins were beginning to wear them down. My Chemical Romance were exhausted. 'It really felt like we were being run along a cheese-grater,' said Frank of the tour then. 'We were leaving bits of ourselves all over the world. We needed time to regroup, we needed time to remember why we do this,' said Frank.

They wouldn't get it. And as the tour rumbled on, Frank would have something like a crisis. Like Mikey, he would come to look back on the album as a period in which his mental health took a heavy blow. But whereas Mikey's problems happened in the course of making *The Black Parade*, Frank's came while they toured it.

Though he had grown up in a house full of musicians, and though making it in a band had been Frank's lifelong dream, when it all started to happen for him it was almost too big for him to comprehend. Part of it, perhaps, was that he was the band's punk heart – and playing arenas and mega-shows had never been part of his aspirations. He accepted that was the level My Chemical Romance were at – but in doing so, he became victim to nausea and panic attacks each night before going onstage.

'I was going nuts,' he told me. 'You go through this feeling of being under a weird microscope; you feel like people are going to suddenly uncover the fact that you're not supposed to be there. It was surreal and it felt as though we weren't living it somehow. It was like a rented life – it never felt like ours and it never felt comfortable. It was full of pressure.'

And on top of the anxiety was the guilt. He felt he was letting himself and his family down: he was the one musician in the family who had really made it, yet here he was getting overwhelmed by it all. 'I had grown up loving music and wanting to be a musician,' he said. 'I wanted to play huge shows and I wanted to be in magazines when I was growing up. But when it came down to it, I realized I would have been happy if it had been a little smaller than it was. We got to a level where I felt like maybe I didn't belong and that people would uncover that I shouldn't be there.'

The weight of standing in the wings as 8,000 people waited for him to play was almost too much to bear. He was prescribed medication to help him deal with the anxiety, but while the drugs helped, it meant he performed from within a fog of narcotics. 'We were playing shows to more people than I could ever imagine and all those people were there because they really cared and believed in it, but in order for me to get up there and not choke I had to take this medication that made it feel like I wasn't there,' he said. 'You feel like you're crazy and you're wondering what's wrong with you because you're not enjoying it.'

And so, each night before he would walk out onstage, a ritual came about. When all five of the band were on the road together, their pre-show warm-up was the same: Gerard and Ray would perform jumping jacks, Bob would play on his practice pad and stretch, Mikey would high-five everyone and Frank would take his pills.

'There was a running joke for most of those shows,' said Frank. 'I'd take my pill bag out ten minutes before going onstage and be like, "All right, guys, see you tomorrow!" I'd take what I took and would then flash forward to the next day.'

The flights, the shows, the days in between and the nights in anonymous hotels were beginning to blend into one long, miserable experience. Over the course of its gruelling tour, *The Black Parade* had gone from being an ambitious celebration to a tedious slog. By the time they started the final US leg of the tour on 28 March

2008, it was twenty-three months since they had started recording it – nearly two years. They were looking ahead only to the
Madison Square Garden show, after which they knew they could
collapse.

'There were times we didn't know what country we were in, we
didn't know anything,' said Mikey. 'We could have been in the US
or Germany, we didn't know. We'd just get pointed at the stage and
head in that direction.'

'We kept going until the end and we basically made it as hard
as we could for ourselves,' said Gerard. 'We'd look at the options,
then, for some reason, choose the hardest one. It was like, "Can we
make it so we don't go home for four months? Great." "What can we
do to make this more difficult?"'

The tiredness resulted not in arguments but in a lack of communication between the band members. They would wander from
airport lounge to hotel lobby to stage in a trance, iPods on, heads
down, eyes on the floor. Frank would bury himself in a book, Gerard
would pull his headphones on – headphones, tellingly, that he had
started calling his 'shut-the-fuck-ups'.

'We didn't talk much,' said Gerard. 'We were quiet. We didn't
dislike each other and there were no problems, but there was no
talking. Eventually that can lead to problems, but it didn't for us. We
just had our headphones on a lot. Not much fun.'

And in that, they had hit upon what was wrong. They simply
weren't enjoying themselves any more. All the fun of *The Black
Parade* had gone. 'We needed some time to regroup and just be
people,' believed Frank. The band thought they were overexposed.
They thought they had said everything they could possibly say, yet
still there were magazines keen to interview them. No matter that
they had explained themselves, their album and their lives a thousand times to a thousand different journalists, there was always one
more who wanted a piece of them.

'We'd see ourselves in a magazine and it would make us mad,'
said Gerard. 'It was like, "Again?" So if we felt like that, God knows
what it felt like for the average person. Everyone must have been so

sick of us. I remember walking into a bookstore and there were four magazines with our faces on them. I felt like I couldn't escape us wherever I went. You knew not to go near music television, but even on regular television we'd pop up. You'd be in some country and some weird performance you'd forgotten about would appear on air.'

'There was no off switch,' said Mikey. 'People expected you to be the dude onstage for twenty-four hours a day, seven days a week. There was the workload too, flying everywhere, playing everywhere, getting so little sleep. Put all those factors together with the stress of trying to maintain a home life too, and it's hard.

'When you're on that kind of schedule you can begin to feel like a circus act. We were being chugged along and we couldn't get a second to breathe. It makes you forget why you were doing it; we were just so frazzled. There were shows that I emotionally missed out on; I was there but I wasn't there, if you know what I mean.'

During the recording of *The Black Parade*, My Chemical Romance had felt they had to suffer in order to make it great. And here they were, two years later, still touring it, still reliving it, still suffering. Emotionally, physically and mentally, they were drained. And they knew it.

'There was one incident towards the end – it was our sixteenth show in a row without any breaks,' said Gerard. 'We were in Australia and I remember forgetting the words – which is an odd thing after sixteen shows in a row. That had never happened to me before and I tried to work out why and I think it was because I couldn't feel them any more. They were starting to escape me. I felt like I wasn't giving the fans everything I could. That was a clear indication to go home.'

But they didn't. In fact, things got worse.

At the end of March 2008 rioting broke out in the Mexican city of Querétaro north of Mexico City as teenage emo fans were set upon by gangs. Footage filmed on mobile phone cameras and posted online showed large groups screaming, 'Kill the emos!' and violently attacking anyone they considered to be part of the subculture. The attacks spread to Mexico City and were largely blamed on punks and metallers, though *Time* magazine reported that many working-class teenagers and young men were also involved.

'It's getting dangerous for us to go out now,' they quoted sixteen-year-old emo fan Santino Bautista as saying. 'We get shouted at and spat on. We get things thrown at us. There is so much hate out there.'

The chief cause of the problem was supposed to have been the way emo fans dressed. In macho Mexico, the stylized black clothes, dyed long hair and occasional use of make-up by males made emo fans a soft target. 'At the core of this is the homophobic issue. The other arguments are just window dressing for that,' Victor Mendoza, a youth worker in Mexico City, told *Time*. 'This is not a battle between music styles at all. It is the conservative side of Mexican society fighting against something different.'

Gerard found he was asked constantly about the situation and expected to act as the spokesman for an emo movement – something he was unwilling to be. On top of that, the band were asked about the situation in Mexico so often, as if it was somehow their fault, that they started to feel guilty.

'People in Mexico were getting hate-crimed on because they wore black and had moppy hair and so anywhere we went that's what people would talk about – they weren't talking about the music,' said Gerard. 'That upset me. They weren't getting to the matter, they were just talking about mascara and bullshit like that. I started to feel this sick responsibility that I had put kids in danger.'

The Black Parade had taken on a life of its own, a life far removed from what My Chemical Romance had ever intended for it. 'That was the scariest thing,' said Frank. 'People were interpreting it in strange ways. It was like a bastardized version of what we had done. It got weird.' Tired out by the end of the tour, they struggled to deal with how it had been subverted. Gerard had a hard time accepting the fact that it was no longer an album detailing his personal emotions. It was no longer an album that was about his hopes and fears, his own vision of life, death and dying. It had been taken away from him and adopted by fans and critics alike who could interpret it any way they saw fit.

'I think that's what ate me up a lot,' he told me. 'I felt like I could control the reaction to the record, which you can't do. Then I felt that I could control it by explaining myself time and time again. Sometimes I was even apologizing for myself – it was really namby-pamby shit. How did I turn into that guy? How had I become the guy who was apologizing for the work he and his friends had done? Or I was defending myself against some bullshit accusation. When did I turn into that guy?

'I realized that the world is a wild animal and you can't change it or control it. You can't ride it; it's going to ride you. That's what I learned from *Black Parade*.'

In May 2008, the British newspapers the *Daily Mail* and the *Sun* reported on the tragic suicide of the thirteen-year-old schoolgirl Hannah Bond, a fan of My Chemical Romance, who had hanged herself. After Hannah's death, an inquest found that she had started self-harming, something that her father said she considered an 'emo initiation'. Hannah's mother said Hannah 'called emo a fashion and I thought it was normal'.

The *Daily Mail*, after previously angering band and fans in August 2006, claimed a link between the suicide and My Chemical Romance, saying Hannah had hanged herself after becoming obsessed with them. They alleged that My Chemical Romance were a 'suicide cult'. The newspaper followed up the story a week later with another piece claiming that all children were in danger from 'the sinister cult of emo'. My Chemical Romance were understandably upset.

'We have recently learned of the suicide and tragic loss of Hannah Bond,' they said in a statement. 'We'd like to send our condolences to her family during this time of mourning. Our hearts and thoughts are with them.

'My Chemical Romance are and always have been vocally anti-violence and anti-suicide. As a band, we have always made it one of our missions through our actions to provide comfort, support and solace to our fans. The message and theme of our album *The Black Parade* is hope and courage. Our lyrics are about finding the strength to keep living through pain and hard times.

'The last song on our album states: "I am not afraid to keep on living" – a sentiment that embodies the band's position on hardships we all face as human beings. If you or anyone that you know have feelings of depression or suicide, we urge you to find your way and your voice to deal with these feelings positively.'

The band member most stung by the *Daily Mail*'s accusations was Ray. Quiet, unassuming and generally the most optimistic member of the band, the guitarist saw how the music he had written had spiralled out of his grasp and was being held responsible for people's deaths, for bullying and for an emo movement with which he felt little kinship.

'Ray has always been positive, he's uplifting,' said Frank. 'But for him to see something he loved so much and for which he gave so much of himself be used as ammunition for hatred or people getting beat up was rough for him.

'That whole emo thing came to a head. Kids were getting beaten up, there was all that bullshit in the press, and then when that poor girl killed herself, people felt they needed someone or something to put that on – and it just so happened to be our band or our record. It was like, "Shit, man. All we wanted to do was to make something beautiful." We went through hell to make that record, and knowing the kind of dude Ray is, it was very rough for him to see what happened.'

For fans of the band, the *Daily Mail* reaction to Hannah Bond's suicide was the final straw. Still angry at the Sarah Sands article in August 2006, and further infuriated by these new allegations, British fans organized a march on the newspaper's offices on 31 May 2008. Protesters came from all over the country – from Brighton, Oxford, Scotland, Wales, Cornwall and all corners. The *Daily Mail* were so concerned that barricades were erected outside their offices and the police called in. One fan, Tabitha Reed, was quoted in the *Guardian* newspaper.

'The *Daily Mail* are liars and all they want to do is put the youth against the adults; they just hate us and it's really unnecessary, it's just wrong,' she said. 'I've read a couple of the articles and they've actually misquoted lyrics and the research was so badly done, it was unbelievable. I actually thought [the story] was a hoax when I found it on the internet.'

Another fan, Vikki Bourne, joined her daughter Kayleigh on the protest.

'Emos are being portrayed as self-harming and suicidal and miserable and they're not,' she told the *Guardian*. 'Since my daughter met the friends she's got, she's happy, she's got a social life, she's not suicidal, she's got confidence. It's about the music and being friends and having fun. I wanted to come here to say that, as a parent, I support what she does; [the band] are not a cult.'

The *Daily Mail* issued a statement saying their coverage had been 'balanced, restrained and, above all, in the public interest'. They said, 'Genuine concerns were raised at the inquest earlier this month on thirteen-year-old Emo follower Hannah Bond who had been self-harming and then tragically killed herself.

'The coroner found "the Emo overtones concerning death and associating it with glamour very disturbing". Her mother had told the inquest that Hannah had been obsessed with My Chemical Romance whose hit number one [sic] on their last album was called The Black Parade [sic].

'Mrs Bond told the court: "In Emo it is a very glamorous death to hang yourself. The band she was into, the music she was into – the whole thing is based on the black parade which is all about dying. She called Emo a fashion and I thought it was normal. I didn't know about the cuts." Her father said he had seen cuts on her wrists and his daughter had told him they "were an Emo initiation". In common with other newspapers we ran an accurate news story recording the coroner's remarks and the parents' comments.'

They also pointed out that their coverage was actually good for My Chemical Romance, and would help sales of their impending live album *The Black Parade Is Dead!*. 'We note it has been pointed out by others that all this provides wonderful publicity for Warners and their impending release of My Chemical Romance's latest album.'

One of the organizers of the march, Caz Hill, says the anger the coverage generated among My Chemical Romance fans was astonishing. Both she and her daughters had long been fans of the band – and were active in the UK branch of the band's fanclub, known as the MCRmy – and found the insinuation that they were part of a 'suicide cult' deplorable. 'My daughters and I were certainly not emos,' she says, 'nor did we promote self-harm or suicide. Neither did any one of our MCRmy friends.'

Those protesting met at Marble Arch at 10 a.m. and Hill says the atmosphere was fun and friendly, 'lots of hugging and chatter'. By 1 p.m., they were outside the newspaper's offices, having their photos taken with the police and singing – 'a useless suicide cult we were!' says Hill.

'There were chants of "Fuck the *Daily Mail*" when the press and TV crews arrived,' says Hill. 'But everything remained very peaceful throughout the whole day. We told the police we had a petition and a folder of fan letters to deliver to the newspaper. They escorted me and a couple of others to the main entrance and we handed everything to the security man.'

It was a symbol of just how much loyalty My Chemical Romance's fans had for the band. Few other groups could hope to generate such action from their crowd – certainly not outside the context of a show. But this was a group of people who saw the band slighted and who, without any direction from My Chemical Romance, set about putting things right. Whether it changed anything was hardly the point: what mattered was that the fans were sticking up for their band in a loud, dramatic and fiercely dedicated manner. It would come to define how strong the relationship was between band and fans.

But events like this, and the fact the newspaper had written the story at all, fed into Gerard's fears they were no longer in charge of *The Black Parade*'s message. 'I felt super small,' said the singer. 'We had no control.'

By the time of the *Daily Mail* protest, My Chemical Romance had finally come to the end of The Black Parade World Tour. The very last date had shone like a beacon for months for two reasons. First, because they could finally stop. And second, because it was at the legendary Madison Square Garden – a landmark venue whose size symbolized all that they had achieved. They kept their eyes on it constantly, counting down the days.

But when they finally reached the date they had looked forward to for so long, the band were falling apart from exhaustion. 'They looked tired. I knew they were fried,' says Craig Aaronson. John Slimin, a British fan who had seen over forty My Chemical Romance shows and had become close to the band as a result, flew to New York for this landmark performance. He saw that there was an unusual atmosphere around the band on what would be a wet and cold night.

'It was one of the strangest gigs of theirs I've been to. The whole day was just amazingly strange. Normally when I go to gigs, I'll go and hang out with them beforehand – and bearing in mind I'd gone halfway around the world for this one – but it just felt like the communication lines were down.'

The support bands that night were Drive By and old friends Taking Back Sunday, but when My Chemical Romance got to the stage, though they played well, things did not seem right to Slimin. 'There was stuff onstage that was a bit weird,' he says. 'They said "If you never see us again, it's been great" and a few other things like that. I remember thinking, "Hmmm . . ." But it wasn't a poor performance – they were a slick operation at that point. Gerard was on form. He talked about The Smashing Pumpkins and pointed out where he had sat with Mikey.'

One person who remembered very little of the show was Frank.

Though he too held up Madison Square Garden as his number one venue to play, onstage he appeared absent and spent. Firework Frank had long ago checked out and, in his place, was the medicated version. 'I wasn't quite there,' he said. 'It's sad to me that there are certain shows that I can't tell you anything about. If you played me footage of that show, it would feel like the first time I had ever seen it. That's a shame. You should be able to enjoy things like that. But it was so momentous to me, so nerve-wracking and so painful for me to be able to get up there that I had to medicate to get through it. That sucks. I guess you have to be careful what you wish for sometimes. I was scared shitless, so I had to take a bunch of pills and hope for the best.'

Just one incident from the performance sticks in his mind, one moment of humour among the fog of the show. When not being used for concerts, Madison Square Garden plays host to the New York Knicks basketball team and the New York Rangers ice hockey team – rivals to Frank's beloved New Jersey Devils. 'I remember telling the guys in the band that, when we played "Not Okay", instead of saying "trust me" I was going to say "Rangers suck". They said, "Erm, no. Don't do that. Please don't do that." When we played the song, I realized I was never going to get the opportunity again so I did it! I felt like the guy in the movie driving the atom bomb into the mothership! Saying "Fuck you Rangers" to a sold-out Madison Square Garden crowd was something I always wanted to do.'

They closed on 'Helena' that night, the curtain falling on *The Black Parade* as the final notes of the song rang out. Exhausted, elated, triumphant and tired, they went back to their dressing room – initially thrilled. 'It was fucking amazing,' said Gerard. 'That was a lifelong dream and it was the first show I've been genuinely nervous for in a long time. There was so much emotionally riding on it for me.'

But, after Gerard had walked from the stage and as he could feel the adrenalin draining out of his body, he thought about the future. And he didn't see My Chemical Romance as a part of it. 'I was in the bathroom towelling off and Ray came in to talk to me,' said Gerard.

'He said, "Maybe you need a break, maybe you need to go and start a band to work stuff out of your system." I remember saying that night, "If we never do this again, thank you." I wasn't saying that in a threatening way, there was resolve. That is what's scary. It felt like it was accurate.'

Ray was worried. But he felt the same. He felt like Madison Square Garden could be the end. 'Gerard was tired. We were all tired, but he was more tired than anybody,' said Ray. 'He needed a break. Physically it was hard but the mental strain was the worst. As much as everyone in the band takes things on, Gerard takes a lot more on and has a lot more put on him. He's got more pressure and stress. I could see that take its toll after that show was finished. I just thought, "If people don't get a break, this might be the end. This might be the last show this band plays." We had been ground down to the point where, creatively, we felt we had nothing else to give. That was the worst part.'

John Slimin says that backstage, where there should have been an air of celebration, it actually felt like a wake. 'The aftershow was what really felt like the nail in the coffin. That was just weird,' he says. 'They had a massive room set out with a nice bar and a buffet laid on. It was a bit like a wedding reception, to be honest. Frank was bubbly and he had the guys from Pencey Prep there. Mikey had a chat but I didn't see Ray at all. Gerard came in for a millisecond with Lindsey and hardly spoke to anyone. It all felt a bit bleak. It was sad.

'When I got on the plane home a few days later, I thought it was all over. I expected to see an announcement within a month that the tour had half-killed them and they were moving on. It was bleak, there's no two ways about it. Nobody within the inner circle had a shadow of a doubt that that was the lot.'

The band were burned out. Their oldest friends, in the room to enjoy the moment of triumph, looked at the five of them and barely recognized them. Caz Hill, who had organized the *Daily Mail* protest march, was there and says it felt like 'all the pleasure had gone out of things. Ray was trying to gloss over the fact Gerard was going around telling everyone this was their final show. It wasn't the triumphant Madison Square Garden show that it should have been at all.'

Such was the mood backstage afterwards that Frank can't even remember if they said goodbye to each other when they left. Instead, they all went their separate ways and would barely speak again for months.

'When we were on the road we were the only people we knew so we would all hang out and we really enjoyed each other's company,' he said. 'But when we were off, we were off. That was it. We didn't see each other. When that show ended, it felt even more final than normal. I didn't know what to think. I got kind of depressed about it but I never voiced it to anybody because it felt like it might come true if I said it out loud. Nobody said anything though – it was never brought up. There was just silence.'

They all felt it. Even Ray, despite his diplomacy job backstage and generally positive demeanour, had fallen out of love with all the baggage that came with being in the band. 'You end up having to do so much stuff outside the music and it all takes a little piece of you,' he said. 'All we wanted to do was play songs onstage but that slowly stopped being the focus of the day because there was all this other shit to do. So, yeah, we all thought it would be amazing to start a band that no one fucking knew about – because that way you could get onstage and play music without all the other shit.'

Perhaps Mikey summed it up the best. *The Black Parade* was a record that caused him deep mental anguish, sent him out of the band and into the hands of therapists. It was a tour that had drained My Chemical Romance, forced them to defend themselves against tabloid accusations and bottlings at the hands of angry festival crowds. But it was also an album that had delivered them all their dreams: a towering creative achievement that had made them festival headliners, seen them hailed as the most important alternative rock band in a generation and reinforced their own self-belief in their music. It had been a firework display of contrasting emotions. Mikey looked around the dressing room in the aftermath of that bittersweet final show and thought that it was probably the last thing they'd do onstage together.

'That Madison Square Garden show really felt like it was the ending credits. There was an undercurrent that it might have been the end,' he said. Then he thought back over the previous couple of years and let out a sigh. '*Black Parade* was just another planet – we didn't expect any of that.'

16: MY LOVENOTE HAS GONE FLAT

The vacuum that followed The Black Parade World Tour was almost harder than the tour itself. My Chemical Romance went through the same problems they faced at the end of the *Three Cheers for Sweet Revenge* tour – returning home to find that life had moved on without them – only more so.

'It was very, very strange,' said Frank. 'Maybe it's a selfish thing but, when you're away, you think everything else stops. Your world is only what you're witnessing, then you get home and everyone is fucking old! Shit happens when you're gone that you don't understand.'

They all felt the same. 'People's kids are walking, talking and have hair and teeth,' said Mikey. 'Your parents have got older, everything has got older. It freaks you out.'

What made it more difficult this time was that no one in the band was absolutely certain My Chemical Romance had a future. No one was sure that they wanted it to have one either. They fell into an abyss in which what came next was simply one big question mark.

'When something drains you as much as it did after Black Parade, you end up not knowing if you have the want to do it any more,' said Frank. 'You still have the love but maybe not the want. When you go back to your normal life, there's always something in the back of your head asking, "Is this going to happen again? Are we done?"'

Their biggest problem was that they were so jaded from *The Black Parade* experience that, even if they were to carry on, they had no idea where to go. Gerard, for so long the creative hub at the centre of the band, was simply unable to come up with ideas. Ray spoke to him then, asking if he wanted to carry on. He was concerned by Gerard's state of mind. 'His brain is always buzzing with new ideas, he's always wondering what the next thing is,' he said. 'What was scaring him was that, with the band, he didn't know what the next thing was. He couldn't see a future.'

'That's exactly what it was,' agreed Gerard. 'I didn't know what was next.'

Gerard began to think that his career probably didn't lie in music. He switched his focus to comic books, turning away from the band – largely because it took the pressure off him as a personality. There was something very appealing about that.

'The thing about doing comics is that nobody asks you about your personal life,' he said. 'They don't ask you about which drugs you used to take, they don't ask you if you're breaking up, or if you can speak about the break-up. They talk about the work in the same way I wish people would talk about the work in music. In music, people want to know what makes you tick. In comics, people don't care.'

In July 2008, he was awarded the prestigious Eisner Award for *The Umbrella Academy*. The comic book industry's equivalent of the Oscars, it was a genuine honour to be recognized. Gerard and his collaborator Gabriel Bá won the prize for Best Finite Series or Limited Series, putting him in the same company as famous winners Alan Moore, Stan Lee, Frank Miller and his friend Grant Morrison – all comic book royalty. It was another sign to him that he didn't need music any more.

'The Eisners were really big for me,' he said. 'It was scary at the same time, because it was another thing that said to me, "Hey you could go and do this. You won't have a huge career because it's comics and so more modest. But you could make a living doing it." Winning awards for comics was almost quite scary because it proved that I could go and do that. I got wrapped up in that for a while. I was thinking, "I don't have to be a singer any more."'

The next instalment of the comic was *The Umbrella Academy: Dallas*. The six-issue series ran from November until April the following year, and revolved around the Kennedy Assassination. It was full of dark comedy and, of course, death and destruction. 'It's definitely political; it deals with a subject in American history in which people might not obviously see a sense of irony or black humour,' Gerard said. 'I'm not doing irony but there is black humour. It's a very tragic event.'

It was well received – another string to Gerard's bow – and his friend Grant Morrison was particularly complimentary. 'I was especially impressed with the second book, the Kennedy one, that was really great,' he says. It was so impressive, in fact, that by November a deal was signed with Universal Pictures to turn the series into a movie – but though a script has since been written, the project has yet to surface.

Gerard's success threw him into a spin, a searching of the soul to discover where his future lay. 'If I didn't feel safe doing the thing I loved the most, which is music, then what could I possibly do?' he said. 'So I was looking for any other outlook I could.'

Deep down, he probably knew that his musical career wasn't over. But, post *Black Parade*, it felt like things couldn't continue as they were going. He simply wasn't having any fun.

'The touring hadn't killed my desire to make music but I do remember Ray coming into the bathroom at Madison Square Garden and saying, "Maybe you should start another band,"' he said. 'I was afraid of what My Chemical Romance was doing to everybody. In the end, it was Frank who ended up starting another band and I could tell that he was feeling the same thing I was: he still wanted to make music but he didn't want to do it the way we were doing it.'

Frank dealt with his own tailspin by diving headlong back into music. He got home from the Black Parade Tour and met up with some old friends who had been tinkering around with songs back in 2006 and had played Frank some of the music during *The Black Parade* sessions.

'They'd recorded a demo – three songs, no vocals, just skeletons of songs basically – so I got in their car, listened to it and said, "Wow, this is really good." I didn't expect it to be as good as it was.

They had plans to use a friend they had grown up with, a guy called Danny, as singer. I kind of forgot about it, other than to say, "Hey, let me hear it when you get a singer and get some vocals done."

'Time went by and, when I came off tour, I asked them how the band was going. They were saying it probably wasn't going to happen, that Danny hadn't written any lyrics, and that they probably weren't going to do it.'

Frank began to realize that something like this might be the perfect antidote to the *Black Parade* experience. It would be small, under the radar and carry no pressure with it. It could be a vehicle to his innermost thoughts and a release valve, while also taking place outside of the glare of My Chemical Romance. It also felt true to his roots. While committed to his main band and the grand sounds they had unfurled on *The Black Parade*, Frank was undeniably the member of the band most in thrall to hardcore punk – an avenue that was increasingly closed off in My Chemical Romance. This new project, called Leathermouth, might present an opportunity to explore those sounds while getting something visceral out of his system.

'So I asked if they'd mind if I tried out for them,' he told me. 'I said, "Give me a couple of days to write some lyrics to the songs and we'll see how it goes." I wrote lyrics for two of the songs, then we recorded it down in a little practice studio in Jersey and decided, "Fuck it: let's throw it up on the internet." We pretended we were from Spain – we put Live from Spain: Leathermouth – and that was it. All of a sudden, people started to listen to it and dig it, so we thought we should probably write some more songs and play some shows. I just did it because there was no one else who was going to do it. What came out was some pretty heavy stuff.'

The band was originally Andrew Escobar, Vincent Averelli and Steve Oyola, but Frank has since claimed that the three of them found religion and didn't want to work on Leathermouth any more. So alongside his old Pencey Prep pal John 'Hambone' Maguire, My Chemical Romance's touring keyboard player James Dewees (who moved to drums) and guitarists Rob Hughes and Ed Auletta, he started to record songs in various New Jersey basements. Predominantly, it was Frank's project.

'The way we recorded the record really lent itself to a kind of organic writing,' said Frank. 'I'd be off for a week, I'd see my family, and then for a couple of nights of the week I'd go down to the basement, hit record, and see what happened. Some of the lyrics were written out, some were written on the spot and that's why it has such a raw sound: I hit record myself, then ran over to the mic and started to sing.'

He describes the music as 'honest, raw and confrontational' and it is certainly extreme. In writing on the spot, he accessed a lot of pent-up fury and rage. '5th Period Massacre' details a school kid going on a shooting spree while Frank asks why such things are frequently blamed on the music the perpetrators listen to. Following the emo riots in Mexico and the band's treatment at the hands of the *Daily Mail*, it is easy to imagine where part of Frank's inspiration was coming from.

'I'm sick and tired of people blaming it on entertainment, parents and mental illness,' he said. 'We're putting the blame on everybody except the [bullies] who are making these people's lives a living hell every day. No one is asking what made them feel like they had to go in and destroy everybody.'

'Your Friends Are Full of Shit' has Frank screaming that he wants to commit murder. The rest of the album is littered with references to death, knives, lies, theft, anger and vengeance. It is not a light listen. The closing track, 'Leviathan', was written off the cuff – Frank unleashing a stream of consciousness into the microphone. He sings again about murder, about blood and suffocation. It's clear that, post *Black Parade*, the recesses of his mind were not pretty.

'On "Leviathan", there's almost the idea of leaving the microphone on and the spirits of the room are supposed to talk to you through the feedback,' Frank said. 'So I just hit record and just started to ramble about what was on my mind. It's about letting yourself go and being almost a medium for whatever's going on.'

On 'Sunsets Are for Muggings', he was writing more personally.

'That's directly about my experiences with psychologists,' he told me. 'All my appointments tended to be late at night or in the evening. I think there's a huge problem these days in dealing with mental illness. I've dealt with depression issues, anxiety and different kinds of mental breakdowns throughout my entire life, with me and with other people in my family.

'Basically that song is about talking to these people, opening your heart up to them, letting them know your deepest secrets and, the next time you go in, they probably don't know who the fuck you are nor do they even give a shit. It's not about curing people because that's not where the money is. Once they've cured someone, they don't get paid any more. It's sickening to me.'

The record was clearly coming from a dark place. The interview I conducted with him about the project took place on the phone as he was walking with his wife around – of all places – Disney World, shortly before the record's release. The juxtaposition between his theme-park surroundings and what he was talking about was nearly enough to be funny had he not sounded so serious.

'I still have moments where the hate bubbles up inside me and I just can't take it any more,' he said, the sounds of the park's rides jingling in the background. 'As far as Leathermouth goes, it was formed really from a need to play. I needed to do it just to stay sane. Being out there and touring for ten months a year, things start to bubble up inside you.'

The band's first tour was in August 2008, just three months after the end of the Black Parade Tour. For Frank, the best way to get over the experience of being on the road too long was to go back out on the road.

'If I don't play I feel dead inside. So, when I was off from My Chem, to play in this band and to tour was a godsend.'

They supported James Dewees' Reggie and the Full Effect and then, later, Mindless Self Indulgence, who Gerard's wife Lindsey played in. The idea, initially, was to be anonymous. 'Nobody was supposed to know who was in the band,' said Frank. 'But, in order to play shows, that was impossible because I'm not going to hide behind a mask or anything like that because I don't want to hide from the feelings I'm putting across in the lyrics.'

Initially he was concerned that his My Chemical Romance fame would somehow dilute Leathermouth, or that it would mean fans came to see him play simply because of who he was rather than what he was doing. He was sure though, that if fans were only coming to see him because of his day job, then they would leave disappointed by the hardcore punk he was playing.

'When we did our first tour in August with Reggie and the Full Effect, there were a handful of MCR kids here and there,' he said. 'Some liked it a lot and some had the weirdest faces I've ever seen – they were cringing at me! But I don't want people to be thinking, "Oh, Leathermouth are a couple of kids and that faggot from My Chemical Romance." I don't want it to be about that, so I was kind of getting into a character. We put on bright, white uniforms so we are almost the anti-My Chemical Romance. We got away from the black, and away from everything that people expected from us. Hopefully that means people can think this is just Leathermouth, rather than thinking it's the band of that guy in My Chemical Romance.'

Importantly, though, the process worked. Frank found that he could empty himself into the microphone as he played each night, unloading the tension he had built up in My Chemical Romance. 'I didn't feel mad or angry any more,' he said. 'After three or four weeks I had gotten everything out and I was good again. This is like medicine – it's the pill that I was looking for.'

The album itself was released through Epitaph in January 2009. It was initially intended to be released through Skeleton Crew, the record and clothing label that Frank ran with his wife, but he decided it might be too much of a drain on his time and energy to be responsible for all the aspects of the album. It was greeted by a cautious reaction from critics. '"5th Period Massacre" sounds like a man vomiting razor blades over an antisocial buzzsaw dirge,' wrote *Rolling Stone*, who decided the album was abrasive and confrontational but not without flaws. *Alternative Press* commented on its 'sheer brutality and shock value', saying it was the 'complete anti-My Chem experience', and though most reviews were positive, few predicted Leathermouth would outstrip Frank's day job. But then that was hardly the point.

Slowly and surely, though, My Chemical Romance's focus was returning to their own music. Gerard had been playing around with some new ideas, having bought himself a red Fender Jaguar guitar and an armful of guitar pedals. Plans for new music might have been vague but they were gaining momentum. At the end of August, he posted a message on the band's website.

'We're living, decompressing – *The Black Parade* took over two years to tour and six months to make so that's a lot of existing in a fictional world, and we're just extremely happy to live in a real one for a while. One thing I can let you know is that we're excited. Genuinely more excited than we have ever been to be in this band, make some new music. And we have ALL been writing new material in our own separate worlds.'

The problem was that, as he pointed out, their worlds were very separate. Bob was recovering from wrist surgery following the problems he suffered on The Black Parade World Tour, Mikey was in New Jersey with his wife Alicia, Frank was playing in Leathermouth and Gerard had moved to Los Angeles with his wife Lindsey. Ray, for his part, was on honeymoon, having married Christa in the summer of 2008. As far as Frank can recall, Ray's wedding was the first time that all five of My Chemical Romance had been in the same room since they played Madison Square Garden.

'[The wedding] was beautiful,' wrote Gerard in his post on the band's website. 'I'm not sure where the happy couple is right now but I am sure wherever they are, they are really enjoying it. I have never seen him happier in my life. So we made plans to get together soon and make some demos, see where our heads are at, take it slow. If explosions happen in our heads right away who knows how soon we could have a record out; we aren't in any rush but we get just as anxious as you to find out what the next "thing" is going to be.'

By October 2008, My Chemical Romance were in the studio – but not to work on music of their own. They went into New York's Electric Lady studios – originally built by Jimi Hendrix and used by the likes of Bob Dylan, John Lennon and AC/DC – to lay down a spitting, Sex Pistols-esque cover of Dylan's 'Desolation Row' for the soundtrack to the *Watchmen* film. As an adaption of Alan Moore and Dave Gibbons' graphic novel, the film appealed to the band's love of the original comic books. The experience of recording again would be the ice-breaker My Chemical Romance needed after *Black Parade* and it was proof to all of them that not only did the band have a future, but they could still work together extremely well.

'That was a lot of fun,' said Frank. 'I really felt the band was over after *Black Parade* and being asked to do that, especially given that we were all fans of the comic, was amazing. Getting to record at Electric Ladyland was like "Holy shit!" That was one of my favourite things we ever did as a band – I love the way it came out. Everyone did a killer job on that song. The stars aligned. And we had never gotten to record in New York City before either, and that's the shit you read about growing up.'

Frank may have been a fan of the comic book – but he was not half as much of a fan as Gerard. 'The first thing that came into my mind when I heard we were going to be on the soundtrack was, "Holy shit, Gerard must be shitting himself!"'

'I think you'd be hard pushed to find anyone that didn't rate *Watchmen* as the greatest, most important graphic novel ever created,' Gerard told *Kerrang!*'s Paul Brannigan. '*Watchmen* was as important to me as any band. It was totally plugged into me going to punk clubs at the time and seeing bands. I didn't see any difference between reading *Watchmen* and listening to *My War* by Black Flag.'

But they were understandably nervous. Covering someone as influential and revered as Bob Dylan was intimidating in itself, and the fact the original song is eleven minutes long brought further issues.

'There are certain things you don't fuck with,' said Frank. 'You don't fuck with The Beatles, you don't fuck with the Stones and it's very hard to fuck with Dylan. But as far as I know, he has heard us cover the song and does approve, which definitely eases some of the anxiety about it. Maybe someone was just telling us that to make us feel better, but until Bob Dylan comes up to me and says, "You fucking butchered my song," I'm gonna believe he liked it.'

Gerard explored the lyrics, then set about editing them down to shorten the track. 'I chose the verses with lyrics that were most pertinent to *Watchmen* and arranged it down to three minutes. We wanted to go for a Sex Pistols type approach but I actually played one of the mixes to Steve [Righ?, guitarist for Mindless Self Indulgence] and he said, "I think it kinda sounds like Slade!"'

The song closed the film without obviously angering Dylan fans, or upsetting My Chemical Romance fans. More importantly, the act of getting back into a studio together had whetted band appetites. They felt the scars of *The Black Parade* healing, the exhaustion dissipating and inspiration returning. 'The energy and excitement was definitely back,' Gerard said, adding, 'I literally could have started work on the next album right then. We all [had] songs and I could have hit record right then. So we've used the momentum of that session to get us into the mood for making the next record.'

Following the recording, Ray flew out to LA to talk to Gerard about new music. Bob, who was in town too, joined them, and the three of them jammed some new ideas. 'I was on bass, Ray was on guitar and Bob was on drums and then we'd switch instruments,' said Gerard. Following that session, there was another get-together in December after the band filmed the video to 'Desolation Row'. 'Before we knew it, we had three or four songs. It was very natural,' said Gerard.

'There's always the fear when you get back together that no one will have anything and no one will be feeling inspired, but that changed within the first hour,' said Frank. 'There's no awkwardness, it's just fun.'

At the time, they weren't sure where the music was heading.

They were only sure of one thing: that they didn't want to repeat the intensity of *The Black Parade* process in any way. Gerard, in particular, wanted to fire a record out as quickly and spontaneously as possible. 'We feel we have momentum, which will end up leading to us doing something very visceral and very quick,' he said. 'We don't want a *Black Parade* experience where it feels drawn out and we're generally unhappy when we're making it.'

It was still very early days but the ideas they were beginning to develop were the exact opposite of what had come before. Unlike *Black Parade* and, to an extent, *Three Cheers for Sweet Revenge*, this was to be a straight-ahead rock 'n' roll record, without a concept, without characters and without personal demons – largely because, as Frank said, '*Black Parade* was such an undertaking that, had I been Gerard, I would never have wanted to write another fucking story again.'

It wouldn't take months and wouldn't come wrapped in trauma, self-destruction and mental problems. It would be a party. It would be a record for people to dance to and have fun with. It would make touring the thing a much more enjoyable process.

It was an understandable reaction, given what had happened when recording and touring *The Black Parade*. But it was a terrible decision.

17: SAVE YOURSELF

In June 2009, My Chemical Romance started work with the producer Brendan O'Brien on their fourth record. Extremely experienced and successful, O'Brien was someone the band had considered recording with on *The Black Parade*.

He had worked under the legendary producer Rick Rubin at Geffen Records, and in the nineties engineered and mixed Red Hot Chili Peppers' *Blood Sugar Sex Magik* and mixed Sound garden's *Superunknown*. He also produced Pearl Jam's *Vs.*, three Stone Temple Pilots' albums, Rage Against The Machines' *The Battle of Los Angeles* and Korn's *Issues*, among others.

In the noughties, before working with My Chemical Romance he produced Bruce Springsteen, Mastodon, Audioslave and AC/DC. As CVs go, his was exceptional. If My Chemical Romance were wary of creating an album with the same emotional and personal intensity as *The Black Parade*, then O'Brien was clearly a high-quality replacement for Rob Cavallo.

Writing began in earnest in February 2009. The experience of recording 'Desolation Row' and of jamming at the end of 2008 was enough to convince Gerard and the band that it was time to return to the day job. 'I think it hit a point where I missed creating so much,' said Gerard. 'I was doing comics but I knew what I really missed. We hit a point where we just had to start because we wanted to make music. I knew I wanted to make music. Was it the right time? Who knows?'

The band talked about what they wanted the record to sound like, what they wanted it to feel like. Rock music was at an interesting crossroads at that time. Some of the biggest records of the late noughties, aside from *The Black Parade*, were the likes of Green Day's rock opera-esque *American Idiot* or Muse's flamboyant *Black Holes and Revelations*. Alongside *The Black Parade*, those records shared something grand, theatrical and artistic.

Green Day and Muse would both try to repeat the formula with, respectively, *21st Century Breakdown* and *The Resistance*. Neither album would go on to fare as well as its predecessor. My Chemical Romance knew that they must not try to do the same again – both for creative and personal reasons.

'Maybe people right now just simply want to have a good time, you know?' Gerard said. 'Maybe they just want to feel free. Maybe they don't wanna rebel. I just don't think people wanna throw Molotov cocktails any more. I think people just wanna fucking rock.'

'There's no better way to say that. It's one of the least intelligent things to ever come out of my mouth but that's kind of the point, you know?' he continued. 'People just wanna fucking rock! Let's go out and escape! Let's go out and go on an adventure! I don't know that people want to make statements right now. I can't comment on anybody else's record, but I certainly feel something in the air, like, people just want the truth and they don't need a big story . . . they just want to let go and cut loose.'

This time, they would make a rock record, pure and simple. 'It felt that the right thing was to strip everything back,' said Ray. 'We had fun writing the songs too – a lot of them were very raw, very driving and full of energy.'

Gerard was very vocal about what the record would not be. First and foremost, it would not be *The Black Parade*. Secondly, it would not tear them apart. 'We had twenty rules,' he said. 'Even on the first day of pre-production, even during the writing process, I spewed out a bunch of them: there's going to be no concept was the first. There would be no interesting song titles was another – although I think I said pretentious rather than interesting. Anything we'd done in the past, I was starting to damn. There were going to be no costumes, no pageantry, none of that. I think perhaps I was worried I was going to have to face dark shit again in order to make great art.'

They knew exactly what they didn't want the record to be. The problem was that they didn't know exactly what they did want it to be.

'I don't think we had a clear picture for a while,' said Frank, a year later. 'We knew we were inspired to create with each other but I don't know if we knew what we wanted to create. We decided what the record wasn't going to be before we actually wrote it. It was not going to be *The Black Parade*: no concept, no costumes, no exuberant layering. It had to be stripped down to its barest form. We wanted to more literally reference our influences as kids, as opposed to taking those influences and evolving them. I think we were rebelling against what had gone before and who we were. We wanted to fuck our world up. But in doing that, I don't think we achieved our potential.'

So it was that everything was pared back. 'We wanted to bring it back to how it was when we used to rehearse in a warehouse in New Jersey,' said Mikey. In doing so, they rattled through the tracks. 'It wasn't a breeze writing those songs, but it wasn't as though we had writers' block,' said Frank, and Mikey claims they wrote at least thirty songs. But though they were writing relatively quickly and well, the rules they had written for themselves were becoming a strait jacket.

For Gerard, there was a major distraction when the band started recording at A&M studios in Hollywood. He and his wife Lindsey had welcomed their daughter Bandit Lee Way into the world in late May, just weeks before the sessions started. Gerard threw himself into fatherhood, though he was very protective over his daughter – something he says was a result of looking after Mikey most of his life ('Lindsey calls me the safety inspector,' he said of his cautious outlook with Bandit).

Inevitably there was still a large part of his mind on his daughter as he set about working on *The Black Parade*'s follow-up. He was neither able nor wanted to devote his entire attention to the record. Instead, he wanted it done quickly.

'I had been a dad for two weeks and then we went into the studio,' said Gerard. 'I more or less went straight from hospital to the studio. It almost felt like, "Right, let's get this next album over with. Let's pop it out real quick."'

But he was finding it hard to get an angle on the album. Without a concept, without characters and without all the things that had previously made My Chemical Romance what they were, he was struggling for direction.

'Oh, absolutely. I lost my voice and my confidence,' he said later. 'I didn't know what I was trying to say any more.'

'I definitely remember conversations with Gerard where he'd say, "I don't know what to write any more, I don't know what to say,"' said Ray. 'He was finding it a chore to write lyrics to songs.'

'It was a chore,' agreed Gerard. 'I felt like I was sitting there doing a job every day. I was like, "OK, cool, I've got another one in the can, let's go sing it." Maybe lots of people do that.'

So despite starting the process by wanting to record songs without the same emotional toll as before, Gerard found that the results did not resonate with him in the same way that songs on *The Black Parade*, *Three Cheers* or *Bullets* had. He began to question what they were doing, and while he enjoyed some songs, he felt increasingly uneasy about the general direction they were taking. Others in the band, however, did not feel the same.

Ray would later say that they had been working on songs that he 'really loved'. While Frank in particular felt that, though the songs they were making with O'Brien lacked *The Black Parade*'s emotional intensity, they were still very good songs. 'I know Gerard was having a rough time with things and he was struggling with what to say but I definitely saw Ray and Mikey blossom,' said Frank. 'As a band, we were still searching for something but the things we did find were extremely fun, invigorating and creatively fuelled. There was a purity and fun-ness to it.

'There are songs in those sessions that I really feel were among our greatest songs. I was excited about some of the way those songs sounded too – there was a lot of work on tape, which was something I had always wanted to do. That was very fulfilling for me.'

Frank and Gerard had differed before on the sacrifices that needed to be made in order to make music. Even during *The Black Parade* sessions, Frank had said to Gerard, 'Hey, you know that you can just write a song. You don't have to kill yourself,' only to get the feeling that was not how his singer worked. But he felt Gerard had taken that way of thinking on board when the sessions began with O'Brien. The whole point, after all, was to write a record that did not involve a long, dark creative process. But whether that was the original intention or not, something about it stopped working for Gerard.

'Brendan's approach to producing was a lot different to Rob's,' said Frank. 'I don't know if maybe G just needed someone like Rob at that point. Or if he needed someone to push him in a different way. Or if he just needed some time. But he definitely was not happy. But at some point, we had set out to make a record that wasn't as in depth as what we did on *Black Parade* – and we did that. And then, when it was done, a lot of people were like, "Maybe this wasn't the best idea."'

The record was due to be titled *Save Yourself, I'll Hold Them Back* – though *Conventional Weapons Were No Match for Them* was, according to Frank, a close second. It fizzed from the proto-punk of tracks like 'Death before Disco' (later reworked as 'Party Poison' on *Danger Days*) to the straight ahead Ramones-esque 'Black Dragon Fighting Society' – a ninety-second blast of chaotic riffs under a bubblegum punk vocal that resurfaced on the *Danger Days* box set. Alongside such garage-rock eruptions, were more adult rock songs such as 'Save Yourself', 'The Only Hope for Me Is You' (both of which were included on *Danger Days*, the latter becoming 'Save Yourself, I'll Hold Them Back') and the sentimental 'The Light Behind Your Eyes'.

Gerard had even returned to the idea of telling stories, on a song called 'Trans Am', one that would later morph into 'Bulletproof Heart' on the *Danger Days* album. It was a story about a boy in a Judas Priest T-shirt called Johnny and a girl called Jenny – and suggested that Gerard wasn't entirely convinced by his own ploy of simply delivering straight-ahead rock 'n' roll songs without a plotline.

'It's a fictional, metaphorical song really, but one about leaving home and running away – about doing whatever you can to run away,' said Gerard. 'Because that's the point of starting a band – you get in the van to run away.'

But once tracking had finished, the problems started. My Chemical Romance began to mix the record with Rich Costey, the producer who had mixed parts of *Three Cheers for Sweet Revenge* and whose work with Foo Fighters, Muse, Mars Volta and many others had made him a hugely respected name. It wasn't that Costey couldn't find the right mix; it was that Gerard had lost confidence in the songs they had recorded.

'When we started mixing, Gerard was very vocal about the fact it just didn't feel right,' said Ray, who had been forced at the time to fly home to deal with some family problems.

'I kept calling him, saying, "Something's off here,"' said Gerard. 'I couldn't do a track order. Every day I'd pick four different songs I liked, and then I wouldn't like the rest. It was the absolute opposite on previous albums – on those records we hit a point where we had too many songs and we couldn't fit them all on the album.

'It was impossible to get eight songs that I loved. Sometimes I'd get to six; sometimes I'd only get to two. Rich Costey was mixing it and it was like there was an elephant in the room. He was trying to get sounds out of it that he just couldn't get; we couldn't make it sound ambitious no matter what we threw at it. We started doing additional tracking, we were piling on more vocals and we started playing with keyboards. That was the first experimentation that happened during the entire process and we had already recorded the album! The only experimentation happened during the mixing and that's pretty scary.'

They pushed and pulled at it, trying to force the album into shape but they felt that something wasn't quite right. 'We just weren't getting that feeling,' said Mikey. 'It felt like we were going sideways instead of jumping ahead.'

'They weren't bad songs,' added Frank. 'They just didn't have that greatness.'

Gerard felt the songs did not hold together as an album. And he did not feel as close an association with them as he had with *The Black Parade*-era songs, partly as a result of how they were created. For Frank, though, that was less of a problem.

'I could have made a tracklisting out of it that I would have been excited about,' he said. 'But I don't feel like it was a cohesive, well-thought-out record with a beginning and an end. I think that's where Gerard and I differ – some of my favourite records are just a collection of songs.'

What made it harder was that those outside the band who had heard the songs told the band they were good. 'It was very strange,' said Mikey 'We were wondering if we were crazy. It was like getting married to someone who everyone thinks is great but you're thinking, "Yeah, but you don't know her . . ."'

Still, though, the process rumbled on. The band played two secret shows on 31 July and 1 August, 2009 at the Roxy Theater on LA's Sunset Strip and slipped new songs 'Party Poison', 'Kiss the Ring' and 'The Drugs' into their encore. They must have been further confused when the songs met with an enthusiastic response. Months later, in January 2010, with the mixing supposedly complete, Gerard appeared on the cover of the *NME* to talk about the record. The accompanying photo shoot – with Gerard dressed in raincoat, white shirt and tie – suggested a new, more mature, adult rock star, while the photos themselves were so chic they might have been for a men's style magazine. Everything, it seemed, was primed: a more mature sound, a more mature look and a more mature record.

'We had singles picked, people were pumped about it,' remembered Mikey. 'We'd done some interviews and some covers and we were ready to go.'

'And then we said, "This isn't good enough,"' said Frank.

★

The niggle in the back of their minds during recording and mixing had grown into a major concern and then, finally, a full stop. For Ray, the songs simply needed something else – he just wasn't sure what. Part of the problem was that they realized that channelling MC5 and delivering raw, down-and-dirty rock 'n' roll simply wasn't enough. 'The soul just wasn't there,' said Ray. 'We realized that we [hadn't been] doing the things that we're really great at. We were trying to do something different and that meant we weren't letting the songs be what they wanted. We had all these restrictions on everything.'

For Craig Aaronson, the problems stemmed in part from the relationship with Brendan O'Brien. 'Unfortunately, Brendan was the wrong producer for them, I think,' he says. 'I don't think there was much inspiration once they got into the studio and it ended up being a flat experience.' It's unlikely that this was O'Brien or the band's fault. In a high pressure creative environment there are inevitably times when things simply do not work out. No blame should attached to either side.

Gerard's issues went beyond the music. He looked at the cover of the *NME*, the grown-up Gerard with neat hair and slick, designer clothes and was wary of what he saw. The music the band had made had turned him into the sort of respectable rock star easily absorbed by the mainstream. He no longer felt like an outsider and he didn't like it.

'I was getting offers to be on covers by myself,' he said. 'I had my hair cut, I was on the cover of the *NME* wearing a tie and a raincoat. I was looking at that image going, "Is this what I'm going to look like from now on?" We were trying to mix this record having cut our hair, having hit the gym and all that stuff. And we had all these offers coming in that we would never have got on *Black Parade* or *Revenge* because we were so crazy-looking then. They were offers to be on the covers of certain men's magazines and things like that. At first it was flattering. I thought, "Oh cool, I guess that means I'm growing up." And then you realize that it's the biggest trap of all, it's the giant bear trap that's going to stop you from running.'

Gerard was thinking hard. He was thinking about what he had become, he was thinking about where his life was. 'For a bunch of guys who got into it not for [money], we had found ourselves living comfortably,' he said. 'We weren't living extravagantly but it was nice to be maintaining a mortgage, especially with a baby.'

A part of him wondered if he could be satisfied by that. It was, after all, the sort of life a lot of people would dream of: financial stability, a nice house, car, family and some respectability. And then he looked at the music My Chemical Romance were making: mainstream punk and anthemic rock, but without the same depth of emotion, thought and feeling as before. He decided that, somewhere, his band had taken a wrong turn.

'I think I was confused,' he said. 'I thought that rejecting everything we had done before would help us move forward. But we stripped layer after layer after layer and it took the recording of an entire record for me to realize, "Oh wow, there's nothing left." Everything I love about My Chemical Romance – making the art, dreaming up these personas, the costumes, videos and visuals – was all gone. There was nothing for me to do in the band any more. I was really terrified. I thought, "Is this it? Is this the one that we put out and people go, 'They've lost it. They've lost their ambition. They're resigned to clocking in and paying the mortgage.'" That, to me, is what that album sounds like.'

Conventional Weapons – as the collection of songs would become known – needed a rethink.

18: DANGER DAYS, HERE WE COME AGAIN

When Rob Cavallo, by then the head of creative at Warner Bros, heard *Conventional Weapons* in late 2009, he was worried.

'Warner Bros came to me and said, "Can you fix this album?"' he says. 'I was like, "I can't fix this." They asked if I could just mix it or something, but I couldn't. I didn't know what to do; I didn't know how to get the energy out of it. It sounded to me like the performances were broken. It didn't make any sense to me. I'm sure Brendan O'Brien could have made sense of it because he had recorded it, but I couldn't figure it out. I didn't see how I could work it. It wasn't there in the tracks for me and I couldn't do anything.'

My Chemical Romance had turned to Cavallo in an attempt to rescue *Conventional Weapons*. He found it tough to see them so confused as to their direction, saying they were 'like a band who had been in a car accident'.

The band wanted Cavallo to produce some more songs for the album in the hope that some new tracks might help complete the record. They went to his home studio and surrounded themselves with synths and keyboards, looking to head in new directions. Cavallo sat them down, talked to them, and tried to work out what was going wrong.

'I asked them what they were trying to do, and they told me that they wanted to make a down-and-dirty rock record,' he says. 'They wanted to make a rock record where they were just rocking because they were a rock band. I've seen that happen to rock bands before. They have a really big record, and they put in a seminal performance on an album, and then they retreat from that. To their credit, Gerard and the band knew that they had retreated from aiming high and from aiming towards the truth of what they needed to do.'

Cavallo thought that a raw, party record was not the sort of record My Chemical Romance should be making, nor could make convincingly. But with the band off balance and fraught, he knew he had to build them up rather than knock them down.

'They found themselves in a situation where they had spent a good portion of money and had ended up with a record that they couldn't find a way to mix or finish,' says Cavallo. 'They were like, "What happened?" I had to tell them, "This happens sometimes and it's not your fault." I mean, it was partially their fault but I had to get them to believe that it wasn't.

'They wanted to make a down-and-dirty rock record but really they didn't want to do that. It was probably more that they didn't want to suffer the same kind of pain that [they went through on *Black Parade*]. It's a scary thing to go through that pain – like I've said before, you die a little every time you make a great record. *Black Parade* was so emotional that the idea of going through that process again seemed very daunting.

'So when I got to them, I think they had paid the price of not going through the full process. They had tried to do something quick and easy and it turned into something that became long and expensive. They were left holding a bag that they didn't want to be holding.'

The band were not only impressed by what he had to say, they were touched by how much he cared for them. 'He told us what a shame it was to see a band who were just stagnant and worrying about putting out an album they weren't proud of,' said Ray. 'He was upset to the point of tears and we had never really seen someone care about the band as much as, if not more than, us. He is the biggest champion of the band you could find.'

First Cavallo convinced them that *Conventional Weapons'* problems were not their fault, thereby freeing them, he hoped, to work out who and what they were supposed to be. Then he set about reinvigorating them. 'I recharged them with the spirit of rock 'n' roll. I told them how great they were. I said, "Fuck the last record – you can't look back at it and you can't wallow in it. The only thing you can do is decide, defiantly, what it is you want to do – and then go do it." I told them that, if they wanted to be big and bold, then they had to be big and bold. I told them to push the envelope, regardless of what kind of price they would have to pay to get there. It only took two days. After speeches like that, they were like, "Let's rock!"'

Gerard had been getting inspiration from a different source. In January 2010, he took a brief holiday from Los Angeles with Lindsey and Bandit for some thinking time. Out in the California Desert, somewhere near Joshua Tree in a rented bungalow, he had what he calls 'an epiphany'. Lindsey was instrumental in the process: Gerard says it was a chat with her that finally gave him the courage to give full vent to his creativity again.

'I was out there with my wife and it was the first time that someone said to me: you are an artist,' said Gerard. 'She said, "There are a lot of things you like to do and a lot of things you're good at, but you're an artist. You're not just a musician, look at what you did on *Parade*." She could see better than me how I was connecting the dots. But she said I needed to own that. She gave me permission to be an artist.'

Two years previously, Gerard had been talking to one of Frank's old Pencey Prep bandmates, Shaun Simon, about a comic book idea Simon had had. Simon had called it 'The Killjoys' but Gerard had translated that in his head to be 'The True Lives of the Fabulous Killjoys'. 'Really, we were doing a lot of commentary on the kids we were, the world today and the adults we've become. We were talking about corporate clean-up versus filth.'

Gerard, Simon and the artist Becky Cloonan had toyed with the idea of a masked post-apocalyptic gang – the Killjoys – who battled a megacorps with laser guns and radical ideas. In the singer's head, the outlaws would drive a dusty, beaten-up muscle car and so he had set about making a model of one.

'It all started with this image of a spider with a lightning bolt and a muscle car. It was basically a Batmobile. So I got this model from a hobby shop without any idea of what I was going to do with it and I spent three days painting this thing. I put all the battle damage on it and it was actually a very pretty and accurate little model. Then I threw this upside-down American flag on the side fender and put a load of graffiti on it. Then it just sat there as I started working on this comic.'

The comic book was just an idea that had been rumbling along in the background before and during the *Conventional Weapons* process. But there was something about heading out to the desert with Lindsey and Bandit that helped Gerard realize that, not only was it a great comic book idea, it could be the birth of a great concept for an album. Suddenly, the characters and concepts he had stripped away for the previous record began to reappear before him again in the shape of the Killjoys. And with them, he rediscovered what he loved about My Chemical Romance: stories, plots, characters and personae.

It recharged him as he reached for a guitar. He started playing an old riff the band had never managed to make move correctly. It would eventually become a song called 'Na Na Na'. Which was when things really started to come together.

'I had a vision,' said Gerard. 'I had always imagined this record took place in the desert but it didn't sound like it for some reason. I wrote a song called "Na Na Na" and I realized that's what I wanted. I was writing all these crazy lyrics out and they were fearless and fucking reckless. I had this vision in my head – and everything I had been working on in the comic, the masks, the laser guns, the cars, everything, started to swirl around in my head.

'I was almost writing the song as the trailer for a film that didn't exist. I was thinking about guys doing donuts and shooting laser guns into the air, hyper violence, video-game violence.'

The song itself – eventually christened on the album 'Na Na Na (Na Na Na Na Na Na Na Na Na)' – was precisely the sort of punk burst they had been aiming for on *Conventional Weapons* but had been unable to deliver. It was loud, proud rock 'n' roll, complete with a sparklingly immediate chorus and the fizzing guitars of the down-and-dirty record they wanted to make. But it would also come to have the finger-clicking camp that was part of the old sound – Gerard demands to see jazz -hands at one stage – blended with the futuristic synths they had been playing with. Most of all, though, it was simply exciting: a riot of colour and adventure – something not born from misery or pain, but from thrills. As well as teaching Gerard to re-access his creativity, Lindsey encouraged him to put any worries about how the world would react to this change of direction to one side.

'She gave me permission to be an artist,' he said. 'Then she also said the words, "The aftermath is secondary." That's something every artist should believe. It's actually a cool phrase because it means the aftermath is still semi-important – but it's not as important as doing it. It's a very loaded phrase. And that became the corporate slogan of the imaginary company I had made up [as part of the album concept].'

And with that, things began to flow. Gerard returned to LA and My Chemical Romance crammed themselves into Cavallo's tight little studio – Ray said it was so small 'you would hit someone if you stuck your arm out.' It took a couple of days, and then Gerard mentioned that he had a new song.

'G said, "Hey, I've got this song,"' said Ray. 'So we tried it out in the studio. For the first time in a year, you could feel us going ahead on all cylinders. The creative juices and the energy was back. As soon as "Na Na Na" was done, then things definitely changed. That proved what we were capable of. It changed the game. We had to reassess everything at that point and start afresh.'

My Chemical Romance were back on track – or at least they would be, just as soon as they dealt with a difficult decision.

At the beginning of February 2010, My Chemical Romance sat down with Bob Bryar and asked him to leave the band. Frank said it was not a hasty decision but one they had been considering for some time. A month later, in March 2010, they announced his departure.

'Recently it seems as though every time we write to you guys we have bad news, and we apologize for that, but we've learned in life you can't have the sweet without the sour,' wrote Frank in a statement on the band's website. 'As a band we have been very fortunate over the years that our sweet times have greatly outweighed the sour ones, and a great deal of that is owed to you, the fans. Which is why we wanted this news to come from us and not some bullshit gossip site. As of four weeks ago, My Chemical Romance and Bob Bryar parted ways. This was a painful decision for all of us to make and was not taken lightly. We wish him the best of luck in his future endeavours and expect you all to do the same.'

They were awkward when speaking about it afterwards. Each member of the band was vague, preferring to keep the reasons for Bob's departure between the five of them. Bob has never subsequently discussed his exit. 'It was ultimately best for us and him,' said Ray. 'I think the parting of ways was best for all involved, whether some of us know that or not right now.'

Frank was the most explicit and said it was an upsetting decision to lose the drummer, but revealed their relationship had been falling apart for some time.

'There's no way we could have done this record the way we were,' he said. 'That's really the only way I can put it. It breaks my heart that it had to be this way but I understand why it did. In order for the band to move forward and survive, it needed to be the four of us.

'It didn't come from out of the blue. It wasn't anything hasty. I don't think those things can be. When you're a part of something and then you're not, no matter what the reason is, it hurts. And when you're hurt, things don't make much sense. I wish him the best of luck. It wasn't working and it was slowly deteriorating and it wasn't fair to us, to him or to fans to put something out and force it. It doesn't work that way, eventually it just withers and dies.

'The band wouldn't have progressed. The band would have ended if Bob hadn't left. It was a culmination of a lot of things and it just wasn't working any more. It was upsetting. It was upsetting to everybody. But it was the only decision to make other than to just call it quits.'

Still, it wasn't an easy decision. Mikey, certainly, was nervous about Bob's departure. He had spent an entire album cycle gelling with him in a way that he had never managed with Matt 'Otter' Pelissier.

'It was scary for me,' Mikey admitted. 'Thinking back on the Black Parade Tour, I knew every hit he was going to make. We were locked in super-tight. When [his departure] happened, it was a sad thing. He was a close friend. I didn't know what was going to happen. Would I gel with the next guy? I never really gelled with Otter. It was certainly a problem for me.'

Rob Cavallo has come closest to pinpointing the reasons for Bob's exit, and suggests that it was the old story of creative differences. 'It wasn't easy because they realized Bob Bryar was a person who didn't agree with what they were doing artistically,' he says. 'It was very tough. It was right while they were doing "Na Na Na" that they realized they couldn't have Bob be their drummer.'

It was the producer who suggested his replacement. 'He was all, like, "I've got the guy!"' said Mikey. And that guy was John Miceli, the then near-fifty-year-old long-time drummer for Meat Loaf, who Cavallo had worked with in 2009 on the classic rock artist's *Hang Cool Teddy Bear* album. 'John flew in and was sweet, cool and accommodating,' said Mikey. 'No attitude. Our music wasn't something he listened to, but he was as excited as we were making the record. He was totally in the trenches with us.'

With the difficulty behind them, My Chemical Romance began to focus. Cavallo waited for the band to get themselves sorted, then asked them again where they were going.

'We started having real conversations about what the record was going to be like and what the truth of what we were feeling was. From there, the wheels started turning,' he says. 'I said to them, "Guys, the only way that we're going to get out of this is if you go towards the truth of what you want to do. That's when the art will flow. But the thing is: you have to be fearless about it. You can't say that it'll be too much work." I told them to go to the studio and to play what they felt.'

Whether he realized it or not, Cavallo had tapped into exactly the same mantra that Lindsey had given Gerard in the desert. In telling the band to be fearless, in telling them to head towards the truth, he was also telling them that the aftermath was secondary. It was what Gerard needed to hear.

My Chemical Romance told people that they were still working on *Conventional Weapons*, but deep down they knew they were working on a new record. 'Verbally, we never said we were going back to the drawing board,' said Mikey. 'But that's what we did.' But because it was never something they acknowledged out loud, it meant they could write without the constraints of *Conventional Weapons*.

'We didn't think we were writing a new record so we didn't ever say, "That's too crazy" or "We can't put that on a record," There were no rules this time,' said Frank. 'We were just writing songs however they hit us and then eventually realized that it was becoming a record.'

And as they began to access new sounds, to play with synths and augment them with guitars, to experiment with dance rhythms and incorporate them into rock music, they realized that the list of regulations they had drawn up for their previous album was gone.

'We realized the rule book was in cinders on the ground,' said Mikey. 'We threw it away and it was like a dream. It was like being chained and then getting free – we found a whole new world that we didn't know was there.'

Aside from Cavallo, his engineer Doug McKean and other band insiders, they barely told a soul what they were doing. 'We were just talking amongst ourselves,' said Frank. 'The feeling that we wanted to do more was a secret at that point, we didn't really let anyone else know that. It was just between us.'

But whether the band thought they were making a new record or not, to Cavallo it was a necessity that they did. Cavallo says they were not allowed to work on the songs O'Brien had previously recorded. For Cavallo, the band had only three choices: scrap the O'Brien songs, re-record them or simply release them. My Chemical Romance were certain they didn't want to release them and so the decision was clear: they must rewrite and re-record them, or they must ditch them. 'We didn't have a choice,' says Cavallo. 'We had to make a new record.'

It was no bad thing anyway. Craig Aaronson believes My Chemical Romance had moved on from most of the O'Brien songs by then anyway and that they weren't particularly interested in patching up the songs, irrespective of the clause.

'I think, really, the band were just over that record and wanted to do something else,' Aaronson says. 'They had made two albums in a row that were very creative. And the one with Brendan just wasn't going in that direction. They had worked with Rob on *The Black Parade* and they were inspired to create magic with him again. By the time we talked about re-cutting tracks with Brendan they were into a new sound.'

Brendan O'Brien was approached for comment on his period with My Chemical Romance and replied that, though he wishes the band all the best, he would prefer not to be interviewed.

In many ways, Cavallo believes, the clause in O'Brien's contract was a good thing. Rather than try to patch things up, Cavallo says it meant the band had a blank page from which to start again.

'I think it was a hundred per cent necessary that they started from scratch,' he says. 'When they came to me, they were very confused about things. But what they were absolutely sure about was that the record they had made was not something they could get behind. It made them really sad. They didn't know what to do and they didn't know how to fix it. It was unfixable. So it probably helped that there was an all-or-nothing clause in the contract. It made it easier for them, because they went, "Well, we can't hold on to any of this shit so we're starting over."'

Aside from the four songs that survived the *Conventional Weapons* sessions – songs that would be re-recorded as 'The Only Hope for Me Is You', 'Party Poison', 'Save Yourself, I'll Hold Them Back' and 'Bulletproof Heart' – they scrapped them all. It was not easy, but they believed it was necessary.

'That was hard,' said Ray. 'It was really hard for me because we had put a lot of time and effort into those songs. There are some I really love but you can't ignore that energy. You have to be able to change and adjust. Music is like a flowing river – you can't swim against it. If you do, you're fucked. You have to go with it, you have to let it take you where it's going to go. The easy thing to do would have been to release it. There's no denying that it's hard to work on something for a year and then just throw it away. But it was our choice.'

'It was the best thing for the band to go in and do something else – and it wasn't cheap,' says Aaronson. 'But they had to follow their vision because they were over the Brendan experience. And, like it always does with Gerard, once they had started on a creative path he just started coming up with ideas – and you don't want to get in the way of that.'

Once the decision was made to officially scrap *Conventional Weapons*, it felt like a weight off all of their shoulders. Gerard said the band were on such a creative rush after piecing 'Na Na Na' together that they simply rode the momentum rather than anguishing over the decision they had made.

'There was no tension,' said Gerard. 'It happened right after "Na Na Na" and we were all in it together. When you get something great you just have to grab it and hold on. Everyone in the band is such an artist that they know that.

'We stepped into the new thing right then; we stepped into that new sound that we had hoped for. And we literally just walked into it. And it was loud, noisy and we knew we better hold on to it. We knew there were no rules any more – we just had to go do it. We couldn't be the sort of people who said, "Yep, we've made a record, it's good enough, who cares, let's go tour on it." We don't fucking do that.'

'Once we put the past in a box and looked at the future, then it got fun,' said Mikey. 'We opened a new door, we opened a door into a whole new world. That doesn't happen a lot and you've got to grab it when that happens. That was when we realized what was going on, that's when we decided, "Those other songs? Forget about them."'

'I think, in order to move on with *Danger Days*, we felt we had to cut those sessions dead. Maybe it's us, but we've always felt the need to burn down the past before we move on,' Frank said, looking back at this period in 2013. 'But even as we were doing that, I had a weird feeling about it. I know for a fact that not everyone feels like this – but when we were recording *Conventional* it was one of my favourite times in the band.'

There was, of course, the small matter of telling Warner Bros that the follow-up record to *The Black Parade* it had been so anticipating had been shelved. And that all the money they had spent in the studio would need to be spent again. And that they would have to wait a lot longer for the band's fourth album . . . It could have been a very tricky conversation – but as it turns out, it was easy.

'[Warners] had a great relationship with this band,' says Aaronson. 'It never got to the point where we were at odds and we didn't disagree with [the band] over their choice. [Warners] had made a lot of money from them and the general sense was, "OK, if that's what you want to do, then we'll support you guys." So we talked about some stuff we could work on in their deal, and there was no huge drama. There was really no drama.'

Cavallo, then a senior hand at the record company, agrees that Warners were remarkably calm about it. 'The business part of it was just the business part of it,' he says. 'All the band did was rack up some more debt; there was an adjustment to the deal which I can't really speak about because I wasn't a part of it. But the important thing at Warners was that, when you're dealing with an important band like them who had sold a lot of records, you support them and allow their growth to continue. Warners said, "So you're making a new record? OK. Go make it.'"

So they did. My Chemical Romance worked at full throttle, riding the energy they found after 'Na Na Na' lest it disappear.

'Anything we thought was daring on *Black Parade* was now old hat,' said Gerard of the process. 'We were going to go much crazier and much further than that. And we were going to do it with conviction because we knew what it was like to be in that artistic prison. Every song was a victory over that. We just fucking exploded that whole thing.'

They continued to record in Cavallo's back yard studio – though perhaps that description doesn't do the place justice. 'It's a garage that's been converted into a studio,' says Aaronson. 'It's got a big-screen TV above the board and a drum room off to the side. The band would sit on a nice long couch behind the board and they would have an amplifier in the room. It was state of the art, and had a vibe like a nice-sized, comfortable living room. I lived two miles up the road, so I would go over there and go for walks with Rob and we'd talk shit through and we'd talk about how to bring out the best from the band.'

Though Gerard was enthused about the new sound, he admitted to some trepidation about starting again, given the difficult gestation of *The Black Parade* and the problems it had caused Mikey in particular. 'When we realized we were going to re-record the album, I turned to Mikey and said, "Danger days, here we come again."'

But this time, it was different. For the first time in their recording history, My Chemical Romance and their singer didn't have to go to that dark place at all. They found Day-Glo colours, desert landscapes, high sun and bright skies in the new music they made. Gerard did not have to suffer to make music.

'It wasn't about singing about fucked-up shit, it was about

digging deep and working hard,' said Gerard. 'The beauty of this record was that it was fun. This record was fun to make.'

The album would be called *Danger Days: The True Lives of the Fabulous Killjoys* and it would be recorded in a flash of inspiration. '"Vampire Money" was the second track we recorded,' said Ray of the thrash-punk closer to *Danger Days*. 'It's a full live take and that's, I think, the third time we did it – and you can hear that energy in it.

'From then on, there were no restrictions. There was no limit on what sort of songs we could write, what sort of sounds we could get in the studio; it was the best collaborative experience you could ever hope for.'

It was clear the band were all-in, determined to push forwards. They would switch instruments, each of them playing some guitars; Ray and Frank playing occasional bass; all of them experimenting with synthesizers. 'Planetary (GO!)' was an example of the roll they were on, and also evidence of the fact they felt able to push boundaries again. It was the sort of song that My Chemical Romance had been hoping to write for years – a dance-punk song. One night, it just popped out.

'That was really fucking crazy for us,' said Ray. 'It was late at night and Gerard heard the hook. I wanted a four-on-the-floor kick and we wanted to do a dance thing, but we wanted it to fucking shred and we wanted to make it ours. That song is the epitome of not having any rules. That's one of those songs where you think "Fuck it, who cares?" And as long as you make it great, and it comes from the right place, then it's going to be awesome. That was the song where we thought, "Let's really go for it, fuck it. Let's use keyboards because they're really aggressive." They can be louder than guitars could imagine being.'

And when it was done, they were stunned.

'We were like, "Wow! We made a fucking dance song. But it's a dance song with a vendetta,"' said Gerard. 'We'd never heard a dance song like that. The way everyone was playing so hard, and the way the lyrics had such a vendetta, we'd never heard anything like that. Nobody could do that song but us.'

Pulling it off gave them even more confidence to experiment. Next came 'Sing', bursting with new sounds and triumph as Gerard delivers a giant, fist-in-the-air chorus. It would go on to be the album's biggest hit.

'"Planetary (GO!)" was the song that opened us up to the keyboards and electronic side of the record,' said Ray. 'It's kind of undeniable and that energy really carried us into the next song, which was "Sing". I think the top of the record is almost the order they were all written [excluding 'Vampire Money']. Those first three songs were all really key in showing us we could do anything we wanted to.'

The sessions were marked by two moods: hard work and creative flashes. They would be in the studio, grafting on tracks and then – bang! – out of nowhere, a new song would hit them.

'The studio was interesting,' said Ray. 'We could go two or three days without anything happening, then someone would get up at dinner and say, "I've got a fucking idea, let's go," and you'd end up with the basis of a great song at the end of the night. That's what creation and art is about. It's about that hit of inspiration. This record was written entirely in the studio; it wasn't done over three or four months in pre-production, which meant that we weren't done on the songs by the time we recorded them. There was such a flood of ideas, it was beautiful.'

'Everything was so immediate because we wanted to get everything into the world as quickly as possible,' said Gerard. 'That's fucking awesome. It's most pure when it's immediate.'

Gerard, for his part, was reinterpreting the ideas he and Shaun Simon had been thinking about for *The Killjoys* comic book and fitting them into the format of the band. The concept was probably the most convoluted yet, but it was one that was deliberately bright, bold and aggressive. Set in 2019 in the California desert town of Battery City, the record creates a vision of a post-apocalyptic future in which people's emotions can be controlled by pills made by Better Living Industries. Outside the city live a gang called the Killjoys – Party Poison (Gerard), Fun Ghoul (Frank), Jet Star (Ray) and Kobra Kid (Mikey) – who are fighting that corporation. They work with a radio host, Dr Death Defying (who would be voiced by Mindless Self Indulgence's Steve Righ? on the record), who also opens the album with a stylized monologue in which he repeats Gerard's mantra that 'the aftermath is secondary'. Seeking to track the Killjoys down are Better Living Industries' hit squad, the Scarecrow Unit led by the character Korse and his Draculoids.

How much the concept informed the actual songwriting itself is vague. 'It was a useful tool, but it wasn't really present,' says Cavallo of the theme. But perhaps more important was the fact it gave Gerard something to fall back on and something with which to inspire himself when the going got tricky.

And as much as the concept came to the fore after the record's release, during its creation Gerard was intent on making a statement on consumerism and fame. But he was doing something else too: killing off the band's *Black Parade* image as spectacularly as he could. *Danger Days* is the polar opposite of *The Black Parade* in that it is not overtly about the band and their emotions. Nor is it a record about death – instead it is about rebellion, life and escape into fantasy; it is about subversion, commercialism and infiltration. As was so important to My Chemical Romance, it was also about defiance – because what could be more defiant than a rebel gang undermining the authorities?

'There's a lot of rebellion in there,' said Frank. 'It's rebelling against the rules people have for cleaning up for the greater good. Something like "Na Na Na" is dealing with people's perceptions: you can't have a T-shirt with a pill on it but you can have one with an Uzi on it? What are we doing? Are we cleaning things up or are we dumbing things down? Are we pretending things don't exist? It's a record about an alternate future where there are no rules. *Black Parade* had a big concept but, at the same time, it was very personal. It was about life and death. This record is more universal.'

Gerard was attacking fame too – both his and that of the people he saw around him in Los Angeles. He was taking aim at celebrity culture, at its empty importance, at the slew of reality-TV stars and at the fact that it took very little to become well known. He later said that one of the favourite lyrics he'd ever written was in 'Planetary (GO!)': 'I really like "Fame is now injectable" because it sums up how I feel.'

Gerard was also taking a swipe (largely on 'Vampire Money') at the vampires and blood that so littered *Three Cheers*. He attacks the fact that vampires had become mainstream through TV shows where once they had been the preserve of horror fans and readers of comic books, outsiders both. In doing so, he was dismantling all that My Chemical Romance had been in order to start again. It's why he envisaged technicolour biker clothes and ray guns for the band in their videos as a contrast to the monochrome military-marching uniforms of before. He was killing what My Chemical Romance were and reinventing them. But he was doing it in a way that only he and his band could.

'We do something that nobody else does, so let's embrace that,' he said. 'Let's not hide from it. Is it a concept record? No, but does it have a high concept? Absolutely. Is it a transmission from 2019? Sure, why the fuck not? Is there a DJ called Doctor Death Defying? Sure. Do we have crazy motocross outfits? Sure. We have a muscle car with a spider on it. We've got fucking laser guns!

'At the moment, life is either imitating art or dictating it and I like to see this thing as a giant pop-art experiment. We want to take ownership of pop, and of using pop art as a weapon. I only came to that because of friends like Grant Morrison. He sat me down and said, "Art is not a dirty word – why are you trying to run from it. It's what you do, you make pop art – and now you can make it bigger than anybody. The world has given you the opportunity to use colour as something new. There's such a lack of it everywhere else, so embrace it."'

And it was in that pop-art colour, in that technicolour explosion, that My Chemical Romance found their way again with *Danger Days*. When they emerged from Cavallo's studio in August 2010 – a year and a month after they had first gone into the studio with Brendan O'Brien – they did so with smiles on their faces.

Those smiles, though, were papering over some hairline cracks. Bob's departure, the scrapping of *Conventional Weapons* and the amount of time they had spent in the studio suggested that their creative instincts may not have been fully aligned. But, in the euphoria of completing *Danger Days*, it was easy to overlook such issues and celebrate the completion of their fourth album. Gerard, certainly, was looking ahead with optimism.

'The future's bulletproof,' Gerard said on the eve of *Danger Days'* release. 'It's bright as hell, it's bold, colourful and very fast.'

19: LOOK ALIVE, SUNSHINE

It was in late September 2010 that My Chemical Romance began to talk about *Danger Days* to the press. The album was set for release in November, and there was something in the atmosphere around the band then that suggested a kind of happy mania had taken hold. It was as if the paint had dried just moments before the doors to the party were opened.

'It's quite scary,' said Frank at the time. 'We're flying by the seat of our pants here. We're driving into the sun and hoping we stay afloat. But as long as we're having fun, fuck it.'

Frank and his wife Jamia had become parents to twins just six weeks earlier, and he had a dazed look on his face as he conducted interviews alongside the band at the Sunset Marquis hotel in Los Angeles. 'It's a dream come true and they're the most beautiful human beings I've ever met. I'm sure I have to say that but it's true,' he said of his daughters. 'They don't come with any instructions and that's really fucking strange. You're scared shitless but you know that it's going to work out. There's nothing like it. It's only been six weeks and I can't remember my life without them.'

Then he thought for a moment and smiled. 'Two at the same time was a little hard to deal with, though,' he added.

But frazzled though he might have been, he also seemed happy – as did all of My Chemical Romance. Gerard, slimmed down to stick-like proportions, had dyed his hair a vivid red. Mikey's hair was blond and all of the band had ditched the blacks, greys and blood reds of old to dress in vibrant colours. Underneath bright blue California skies and in the Sunset Marquis's lush, luxurious gardens, they dazzled.

There was a buzz. But it was different to the one that had defined them as they launched *The Black Parade*. Back then they were driven by intensity. This time, they seemed driven by exhilaration. They had released a teaser trailer for *Danger Days* and it had gone viral on the internet. It featured them as their new colourful characters in a shoot-out in the desert, firing ray guns and skidding a muscle car around dusty desert highways. The trailer featured the slogan 'The aftermath is secondary', and carried with it an air of not giving a damn about anything.

The themes that the promo clip introduced – the characters, the desert, the car and the central concept of the album – were Gerard's constructions and one of My Chemical Romance's points of difference: put simply, no other band in the world was making music with such a 360-degree vision. No other rock band was drawing on art, drama and storylines in such a way. It was why Gerard was determined that everything should be right – including the specifics of the marketing campaign.

To ensure that happened, he had walked into the Warner Bros office with a flipchart under his arm and a presentation in his head. He had called a meeting with all the people who would be working on the record, from A&R to the press, art, radio, TV and marketing departments. He explained in detail the *Danger Days* concept, the colours, the plot and the songs. He left them stunned.

'When he really told it, it was pretty great,' says Rob Cavallo. 'It took him about twenty minutes. He captivated the audience of all the marketing people. It was a pretty great thing. He had a storyboard and the whole thing.'

'It was typical Gerard vision,' says Craig Aaronson. 'It was tight as all hell – he totally knew what he wanted. I love it when artists can see the whole picture and see artwork, videos, everything. It makes everybody's life so much easier. You want that to come from them, you don't want it to come from some marketing guy at a record company. Everyone was fascinated and then we were off to the races.'

So to meet My Chemical Romance shortly afterwards was to meet a band who appeared relaxed and confident in what they had made. They had only just finished with the album, and they still existed within the bubble of excitement they'd created when they recorded it.

'Well, wait for the world to punch us in the face a little,' laughed Gerard. 'Check back in five months . . . No, we are positive. This is what we love to do, but it took us a while to realize that because of over-touring.'

There were some similarities to *The Black Parade* days though. Once again, Gerard had a vision that he was keen to get across irrespective of the questions he was asked. Sometimes, when interviewing him, it's best to simply let him talk. We started by discussing the end of *The Black Parade* and how the band felt they had lost control of the album, given how it was misinterpreted and manipulated. Within the space of a few short sentences, Gerard had summed up how *Danger Days* was a reaction to that, dismissed *Conventional Weapons* and delivered about ten headline-worthy quotes. All anyone interviewing him then had to do was keep their mouth shut and let him speak.

'We felt super small. We had no control,' he said about the end of The Black Parade World Tour before going on to explain how things had changed. 'I learned to really fucking embrace that lack of control. I have no control any more – and, by admitting that, it means nobody has any control over us. We're all fucking wild. That's what *Danger Days* is. It's saying there are no rules, there's no control. No one's in charge, this is pure chaos.

'This album started as a love letter to rock 'n' roll and it's turned into a nail bomb. It's a cruise missile pointed at rock 'n' roll now because the love letter [*Conventional Weapons*] was the most boring thing we had ever done. *Danger Days* is a warhead. It's going to destroy you so you can live forever. Rock has been so good to me that the best thing I could do to it is to fuck it up majorly so it can live again and have a life. Bands are getting killed by pop radio, bands are bickering amongst each other because they're no longer having the impact they once had. What are we doing? Let's go after the big boys and girls.'

Unlike with *The Black Parade*, he said that he couldn't have cared less what people thought of *Danger Days*. He said he wasn't going to read the reviews, nor was he going to look at online opinions. He said it was an album that was made with a spirit of skewering consequences so why should he start caring about them now? Of course, it was hard to believe him – as Cavallo says, 'Gerard is an artist who cares deeply about the aftermath' – but it sounded good.

'I talked a big game about not caring about reviews when *Black Parade* came out,' said Gerard, 'but I didn't stay true to that. I cared. That was my biggest problem. It was hard too because it went past just being in music magazines, it became a cultural thing. There were cultural accusations thrown at us which made it harder to ignore. Now, though, I say: bring that shit on. I'm plainly saying what I mean on this record. I can't imagine people are going to ask me too much about the lyrics because I'm not hiding behind anything. It's really blunt.

'We have real belief, but it's belief coupled alongside zero appreciation for how it's received. That's very different from *Parade.*'

The fact that *Danger Days* was nothing like as personal as *The Black Parade,* looking outward and addressing consumerism and globalization rather than Gerard's intimate feelings, made it easier for him to take this stance. Furthermore, by insisting he did not care about the record's reaction, he was protecting himself from any attacks he might sustain from critics or the likes of the *Daily Mail.* He teamed up with Colleen Atwood, the designer who had worked on the *Black Parade* uniforms, and came up with a costume that would make him deliberately noticeable. To go with his vivid red hair was an electric blue leather jacket and a bright yellow mask that he'd wear onstage. He was making himself a target and, in so doing, telling people he was tough enough to take what they threw at him.

'When you look at that guy in that yellow mask and bright red hair, then you could spot him a mile away if you needed to take him out,' he said. 'Doing this is like turning the volume up on that and saying, "I'm right here! Look at me! Check me out!"'

The rest of the band were no less noticeable. Mikey wore a bright red leather jacket and yellow tiger-print T-shirt. Frank sported bright yellows and Ray black leather with a scarlet patch. They looked every inch the dusty post-apocalyptic gang the Killjoys were supposed to be.

There was a reason for the bold costumes beyond the concept. *The Black Parade* became a depressing experience, something which wasn't helped by its imagery being so starkly monotone. As *Danger Days* shredded the musical legacy of its predecessor, so the band's new image was destroying the black and whites of old. Black, Gerard reasoned, had once been the colour of the underground and of outcasts. But, having seen the commercialization of emo on the back of their success, and the fact that 'emo-chic' had become fashionable, he was now utterly repelled by it. With *Danger Days*, he was hoping to distance his band from it. And, while they were at it, they were going to do away with the vampire iconography they had once been beholden to but which was now part of mainstream popular culture.

'We're living in a different world now,' said Gerard. 'Black is no longer dangerous. Vampires have become accepted in culture, they're mainstream as hell. You can get vampire stuff at Target [the mass-market US store]. So what's dangerous now? It's colour. Colour is super dangerous. That's the thing that's going to get a reaction.

'We were almost tailor-made for that vampire, gothic movement. That was our band! So that's why we completely turned our back on it and had no involvement in the films or TV shows. We wanted to go forward past that. People would lose interest very quickly if we were to do that again.'

Frank agreed: 'One of the main goals is to bring the colour back. Black's great but you have to let go of that ball and chain at some point. And we're not fucking teenagers any more, man, and nor are the kids who grew up listening to our band. They need a new outlook and so do we. What they need out of life, we need out of life and that's why I think this record is going to be so good for them.'

'We've learned to smile more, we try not to take things so seriously,' said Mikey. 'It's not the end of the world all the time. Things are pretty OK, let's just fucking smile. That's what I tell myself; just enjoy life. I'm a different dude. Life's awesome now. I'm more relaxed, I'm happier and more comfortable in my own skin. I feel like I did when I was sixteen or seventeen. I get excited about shit, I get happy about it.'

For the photo shoot to accompany the *Kerrang!* article I was writing, Warners had commandeered a large, blank-walled room in the hotel. Against the stark whites of the room, the colours of the band's clothes exploded. Gerard's red hair was like a beacon, the band's post-apocalyptic uniforms shining behind him. They leaned in close as photographer Paul Harries captured it all, then rushed around to look at the screen of his camera between set-ups.

'Look at all the colours!' marvelled Gerard. 'That's exactly what we wanted!'

Alongside this optimism were also some nerves. As much as the band pretended not to care about the reaction to *Danger Days*, they had certainly thought about it.

'Well, of course you get scared every time you put out a new record,' said Frank. 'It's frightening. You're putting yourself out there and you're so vulnerable. These are audio versions of your hopes and dreams. You're showing everyone what's inside you. We've worked on this for so goddamn long. Then you put it out into the world and people either accept it, love it, hate it or they rag on it. They bastardize it, they interpret it the wrong way. That's a scary thought, man.'

And they were aware that writing a new record in which they determinedly set about killing off everything from the last one – their hit – was, at best, risky. Then again, they reasoned, who ever made great music without taking risks?

'I hope at first that people are scared,' said Frank. 'For me, those are the records that end up being my favourite. I want people to feel uneasy about it. It is a transition and it is something new. Once you see the world we've created, though, I think people will have a lot of fun with it. There's a lot of room here for people to join in and make it their own.'

But mostly the mood was of confidence. They appeared to surge with self-belief – and with that, the old My Chemical Romance defiance returned. As well as everything *Danger Days* was – a thrilling, post-apocalyptic, futuristic rock album – the record was also a swipe at their critics and those who had called them a suicide cult. It was a protest flag for My Chemical Romance to wave.

'If people are accusing us of fucking people up, of destroying youth culture, then let's be that dangerous, let's be really fucking dangerous,' said Gerard. 'If you wear a mask and have bright red hair you're not a vampire, you're not emo, you're not a wrist-cutter like they call you. You know what? If people want to be afraid of us, then let's really make them afraid. We're going to express ourselves in really bold, fucking awesome ways. That's scary to people.

'What were people really afraid of anyway? That we're a death cult? Or that they couldn't relate to the band their children were listening to? They couldn't imagine being a teenager because they couldn't remember it. They couldn't imagine that being a teenager can be fucked up and dark at times. They all forgot this.'

As My Chemical Romance prepared to go out on the road again to tour the album, they would have been forgiven for barely recognizing their band. The musical and conceptual reinvention they had gone through after *The Black Parade* was coupled with business changes too. They had parted ways with their manager Brian Schechter the previous year – as was their way, they never publicly offered reasons why – and were now looked after by Lauren Valencia at 3D Management, the company which was home to bands such as Coldplay. Elsewhere, the chairman and CEO of Warner Brothers, Tom Whalley, had been replaced by a team comprising Rob Cavallo and two other executives – though at least having Rob Cavallo as chairman gave My Chemical Romance a powerful ally at the head of the company. Inside the band there were personnel issues too: as far as playing live was concerned, My Chemical Romance needed another new drummer. It had been a busy summer of reorganization in the run-up to *Danger Days'* release.

'That was an insane time, there was a lot going on,' Frank said. 'We didn't even know who was going to be playing drums: we were thinking, "Shit! What are we doing?" There were changes at the label too. It felt like nobody had any idea what was happening.'

The drummer they chose was Mike Pedicone, who became a touring, rather than full-time, member of the band. They had toured with him when he was in the metalcore band The Bled back in 2003 and then again subsequently on the Warped Tour, so he was an old friend. After leaving The Bled, he had gone on to play for Helmet, the Bush singer Gavin Rossdale and had toured with the punk band The Bronx in their sideproject Mariachi El Bronx. Mikey phoned him in early July and asked if he wanted to audition. He did. And six rehearsals later, he was part of the touring line-up.

'There's definitely a different energy,' said Ray of Pedicone's arrival. 'He picked up our vibe right off the bat. We'd be jamming for half an hour in between songs and he'd be finding accents that weren't there before. That was really exciting. We're definitely tighter. With Pedicone playing the drums there's a different intensity to it. It's tighter but a little more unwieldy at the same time.'

'He makes us sound like animals,' said Gerard. 'He really pounds the drums – I feel like I've got to do less work now, he makes us look tough.'

Pedicone's first show would be the first stop of the *Danger Days* tour – to be called The World Contamination Tour – at London's Hammersmith Apollo, a big venue in which to earn your spurs. But for the drummer and the band, it felt like a natural fit.

'The first night we played in London felt like it was just us playing in a garage,' said Pedicone. 'Forget that there were five thousand people jumping around – it had a really small feel to it. I can legitimately say that I haven't felt as close with every member of a band as I do with these guys.'

In the run-up to that first show of the tour, the band had been flat out. They made two videos – one for 'Na Na Na' and the other for second single 'Sing'. Both would bring to life all of Gerard's comic book dreams. For the first one, co-directed by Gerard and Robert Schober (known as Roboshobo), My Chemical Romance introduced the Killjoys, the post-apocalyptic desert gang that all four of the band made up. In it, they are pursued by Korse (played by comic book artist Grant Morrison) and his gang of henchmen, the Draculoids (including the Mindless Self Indulgence singer Jimmy Urine), who are out to capture a young girl called Missile Kid (played by Grace Jeanette) who the Killjoys are looking after. Throughout, everyone involved in the shoot appears to be having the time of their life and understandably so – largely, after all, the video is them running around the desert shooting ray guns. 'It was like playing games when you're a kid,' said Gerard. 'You create an imaginary world where anything is possible – but this time it was real.'

The video is crammed full of bespoke items, many made by Gerard, that introduce the world of Battery City and Better Living Industries, the post-apocalyptic town and sinister mega-corps that were central to the *Danger Days* concept. The attention to detail in creating the props included in the video is impressive as the band hack vending machines for laser guns and drive their car through the desert before a shoot-out finale after Missile Kid is kidnapped.

'A lot of thought went into the way that was dressed: if you look at a patch, it's a made-up company, if you look at the sticker on the side of the car, that's a made-up company,' said Gerard. 'Thought went into all that, but the plot was just whatever. That was us being able to do a load of crazy shit and then making that happen. We built a world and we can do anything in it.'

Grant Morrison had a whale of a time being involved. He had become a close friend of the band and was delighted to be asked to be a part of the video – even more so when he found out he was to be the baddie Korse.

'Getting to do shoot-outs was the most ridiculous fun – the minute Gerard asked me, I jumped at it,' he says. 'Gerard had some ideas of what he wanted to do but even at the time, no one knew what Korse – the character – was going to look like. I said I wanted to look like Doc Holliday the way Val Kilmer played him in *Tombstone*. I wanted to be a raging consumptive and to wear some Western clothes.

'The filming for the car chases on the first day took so long that there ended up being an awful lot of improvisation on the second day. I got caught in a burning car, which becomes a lot more fun when you realize that nobody gives a fuck! They just kept filming! That band is constantly setting people on fire in their video shoots.'

The video was compared to *Terminator 2*, to *Blade Runner* and most potently to the *Mad Max* films. Tellingly, given the band's desire to kill off *The Black Parade*, there was also a scene in which a skeleton dressed in one of that album's military jackets is seen half buried in the desert.

For 'Sing', the second single, they had more fun again. In the video, the Killjoys attack Better Living Industries' headquarters – the band still revelling in the elaborate comic book world they created around the album – as they attempt to rescue Missile Kid after she was kidnapped in the 'Na Na Na' video. They blast their way into a corporate office block with laser guns, before they are attacked by Korse and his Draculoids and an unholy shoot-out ensues. Korse kills Gerard ('which made me an enemy to teenage girls everywhere,' laughs Morrison) before the rest of the band are shot – but not before Missile Kid escapes. Again, filming the video was a riot.

'We were running around this huge corporate office shooting guns,' thrilled Gerard. 'We're four grown-up men, running round an office shooting cops for hours! It was like being a kid!'

'Imagine how much fun that is,' said Ray. 'I couldn't even believe what we were doing. That's the theme for this record: having fun. I thought "Na Na Na" was incredible but "Sing" was amazing too. I couldn't believe it was us doing it. It was a magical two days of shooting.'

On its release on 22 November 2010, *Danger Days* was met with almost uniformly positive reviews. In *Rolling Stone*, Melissa Maerz wrote that Gerard was 'pissed at everyone: junkies, party girls, Hollywood and most of all himself, for getting so damn famous'. She noted the abundance of synths and said it rejected 'bloated celebrity rock' and praised its 'simple loud-fast defiance'. *Alternative Press*'s Jonah Bayer said the record is 'literally the sonic equivalent of a comic book.' He added, 'How they were able to construct an entire multi-layered universe (sonically, lyrically and with narration!) for listeners to get lost in – while writing some of the strongest and catchiest songs of their career – is anyone's guess.' In the *NME*, the respected rock writer John Doran called the record 'utterly fantastic'. 'Never mind that punk bollocks, here are MCR the pop group,' he wrote. 'And they're amazing.' Dave Simpson, one of the *Guardian*'s long-standing music critics, cottoned on to the crossover appeal of the album: 'Darkness remains in songs that seem to party their way to some impending Armageddon but the album should delight their fanbase while appealing to people who previously wouldn't be seen dead listening to MCR.'

In *Kerrang!*, I wrote: 'It's hard to think of another band currently operating on so many levels as My Chemical Romance. More than just an aural experience, *Danger Days* . . . inhabits its own imaginative environment. Some bands are content to make music, here My Chemical Romance have created their own universe of characters, companies, mysterious DJs and science-fiction news reports. On its own, *Danger Days* is a sensational record; as the centre-piece to a grander vision it's glorious.'

For a band who had not released a record for four years, it was a very strong set of reviews. But then the trouble began. While the critics believed the record was good, *Danger Days'* sales performance was less impressive. Though it went into the Top Ten of the Billboard albums charts and to Number 1 on the Billboard rock chart, it didn't stick around long. In the UK it only went to Number 14 on the album chart. In fact, it didn't earn a Number 1 slot on any major album chart anywhere in the world. Warners were disappointed.

'When the album came out, and its first week sales in the US were, like, 100,000 to 110,000 I was like, "Oh fuck",' says Craig Aaronson. 'I was so bummed out. That band deserved more than that. It just goes to show how important that time frame and the fact they had been away for four years was. Four-year break? Huge decline.'

But then again, the same had happened with *The Black Parade*. When that record first came out, it did not explode. Instead, it grew and grew as the band toured it ferociously. The problem this time, though, was that My Chemical Romance were in no mood to repeat the relentless *Black Parade* touring experience. *Danger Days* would not receive the same kind of boost.

The World Contamination Tour began in London on 23 October 2010. Like the album it accompanied and the band at its heart, it was a very different animal from The Black Parade World Tour. There would be no grand set, for starters. It would be performed on stark stages decorated solely by an iconic Stars and Stripes flag on which was daubed the *Danger Days* spider logo. My Chemical Romance would not be marching back into the arenas of old; this would all be a lower key affair.

'We were sensitive and cautious with their touring because we knew there wasn't a huge crossover radio song,' says their booking agent Matt Galle. 'So we kept them in rooms we knew they would sell out. We went into three to five thousand capacity theatres and ballrooms and we did multiple nights there instead of doing seven to ten thousand capacity rooms. It worked great and it meant they sold out ninety-five per cent of the rooms they were in.'

He says there were a number of reasons behind the fact the band did not bring the sort of elaborate production seen on The Black Parade World Tour. Part of it was a financial decision, but the greater part was that they simply wanted to get up onstage and play without the pageantry getting in the way.

'With Black Parade, they used every bell and whistle and they spent so much money on production,' says Galle. 'Then they looked at what they came home with at the end and they were like, "Jeez". They wanted to make the show grandiose and great but they didn't realize it was going to hurt that much. They had like seven trucks and four buses. They had a huge castle onstage that opened up.

'After that, they wanted to go back to their roots and to be a band again. They didn't want to be about costumes and bells and whistles any more. They wanted more energy from their punk roots on that album, which is why they wanted to play it bare. They wanted it to feel up close and personal.'

'What we did on *Parade* was to intentionally do a really big, theatrical show,' said Gerard at the time. 'Now we want to do something different. Because *Parade* was so focused on alternate identities and theatrics, I think it's now more exciting to strip those away and just play well – it's been a long time since people have seen that, so that's why we're not bringing a big, elaborate stage production. We're not stripping down in a "keeping it real" way, we're doing it to show a different side of us.'

'I think the stage show relates to how the band feels,' said Frank. 'There was a time that we wanted fire because it was cool to see fire. But after doing this record, we just want to fucking play. We want it to be about us and the audience at the moment. Down the line, we might decide we want to have lasers so, if that happens, we'll get some lasers.'

They were very different offstage too. Before *Danger Days*, My Chemical Romance were a solitary and quiet bunch while they were on the road. They would huddle around laptops, playing *World of Warcraft*, keeping to themselves. Gerard once said: 'Crazy shit just doesn't happen on tour. Do you really want to know what happens on our tours? Xbox. That's what happens. And you know what? If all that crazy stuff did happen, I'm not going to tell people, "Hey, you know what? I took a shit in a hairdryer!"'

But on the *Danger Days* tour, they were determined to enjoy themselves – though perhaps not with hairdryers. They wanted to sightsee, to relax, to have experiences.

'I really just want us to have an adventure with the record,' said Gerard. 'On a lot of tours [previously], I literally never left the hotel. I would put that Do Not Disturb sign on the door and wouldn't even let housekeeping in to clean up. I holed up. This time, I just went out for hours. If I wasn't going out for dinner, I was walking around. I have to get out of the hotel now – otherwise you're just looking at hotel rooms all day.'

And he was as good as his word. Two days before the Hammersmith Apollo show that opened The World Contamination Tour, you would have found Gerard in a luxury London department store buying everything in sight. 'I fucking shopped my ass off,' he told me enthusiastically. 'I found this store called Selfridges. I had never been there. Dude, I lost my goddamn mind in there.'

I asked him how much he spent, and he began to look sheepish. The rest of the band fell about laughing.

'I would say . . .' started Gerard, then began counting up purchases on his fingers. 'Well, I got this jacket, I got that thing, I got that . . . I actually can't fucking say. It would be embarrassing! People would think I'm a dick. They'd go, "This guy's a fucking sell out." That's how much I spent.'

Through near hysterical laughter, Ray managed to choke out: 'He was the champion shopper. He was wandering around going, "What were you *thinking* bringing me here?"'

So relaxed was Gerard that he had started to drink again prior to *Danger Days'* release – nothing serious, just the odd glass of wine. It pointed to the fact that he was easing up, that he was reluctant for life to become as intense as it had been in the past. He even started to dismiss his sobriety as relatively unimportant.

'It became such a thing,' he said. 'It was so goddamn important to everyone but me. You start to feel like the two guys in The Smiths who wanted to eat cheeseburgers but had to pretend not to. I understand that kids look up to me, that some people might have gotten sober because of me. But it's not an important thing for me any more.'

Initially, it was a happy tour. Offstage, My Chemical Romance were determined not to take life so seriously. Onstage, they had songs that they enjoyed playing simply because they enjoyed them and not because they were part of a grand idea or about their deepest emotions. In rehearsals for the tour, they would jam endlessly. Rather than bring a song like 'The Kids from Yesterday' to an end, they kept on playing – extending it out to what felt like fifteen or twenty minutes, pounding away on its outro for the pure joy of it.

'Translating the *Black Parade* songs to live was terrifying,' said Gerard. 'This stuff is the complete opposite. Even the stuff that has digital elements, the samples and things, are liberating in a way because they sound great.'

At first the tour was completed in short bursts. That was just as they wanted it: 'Touring, in some ways, is a young person's game,' said Gerard. 'If I was twenty-four, then being banged around like a ping-pong ball would suit me really well. In fact, it did suit me when I was that age. Now, though, it's a lot harder.'

From late October until early November 2010 they toured the UK and Europe and then stayed off the road until early December when they played key cities around the US. At Christmas they took more time off and it meant that, by January, when I travelled out to watch them rehearse for the second UK tour of the campaign, they were relaxed and refreshed.

In a nondescript warehouse in Los Angeles, they had set up as if onstage – the spider-adorned Stars and Stripes that was the *Danger Days* emblem was the backdrop behind them and their crew buzzed around them. They had been working on acoustic tracks for a radio show, and were fine-tuning the set-list for the next leg of the tour – the longest stretch yet, from late January to late March in Japan, the UK and Europe. It would be followed by an American tour through April and May. There was a slight sense of dread that they would be on the road for so long, but it was only a niggle.

'As much as I'm looking forward to playing the shows, I wish it was a bit more broken up so that we could go home for a few days,' said Frank, thinking of his young children. 'To be completely honest, as excited as I am, my heart is also having palpitations. Things are scheduled better than they have been in the past though.'

Yet they were excited about it too. While there were regrets about being away from home, they were enjoying playing the new material live. And it was that surge that kept them buoyant.

'There's such a great energy and vibe up there now,' said Ray. 'It feels as though everybody's playing to each other, there's a great sense of camaraderie. And playing the new songs is always exciting – we're still learning them as we go, getting the feel of them, but playing new things for people is always one of the most exciting things. "Vampire Money" is in the set now and that's good fun, because it's nothing but pure energy.'

And so they were looking to the positives too. Where once Gerard might have been upset by long periods away from home, he was now looking at ways to use the time. Partly, he would spend his free hours working on *The Killjoys* comic book.

'I'm just about to start it, actually,' he said back then. 'This tour coming up is going to involve lots of downtime where we'll be sitting in airports and hotels. That's how I wrote *Umbrella Academy*, so that's how I'm planning on writing this one. I want it to come out this year and we're aiming for the autumn. It's been plotted for a while and it's going to have a looser, more experimental, Japanese energy than *Umbrella Academy*.'

He had also got his head around not being at home with his wife and daughter, largely by compartmentalizing his life. When he was on the road, he was Gerard the singer. When he was at home, he wasn't. Clearly he had come a long way from the days where he saw little distinction between being onstage and off – the days when he had been drinking destructively in the wake of finishing *Three Cheers for Sweet Revenge*. So, when My Chemical Romance toured *Danger Days*, he treated it like work – but in a good way.

'In some ways I feel like I'm at the office now, it feels like I'm doing a job,' he said. 'And that's a good way to think about it for me, because it makes me more focused and less bitchy about it. And I know that when it comes to the end of the day I get to go home and be with my family. I'm here for a set defined time and that's good to know. So when I'm here, I miss the shit out of them and I'm always thinking about them but that makes me focus on the work because I can lose myself in it. If I were to do that at home, it would be a bad thing. So I'm here to work, but I'm also here to have a great time.'

Their new attitude, coupled with the fact they were playing songs that were less intense than of old, was working.

'It was more enjoyable, it really was,' said Frank, looking back on the tour in late 2013. 'It was fun to play the songs and we had a lot of songs to choose from at that point. I didn't feel this huge looming pressure; I felt we were just there to play our best. I thought it was going to be a lot harder to work in a new drummer but it was surprisingly easy to make that transition. We played some really great shows.'

Something that helped was the crowd response. Though they may have been playing smaller venues than at the end of The Black Parade World Tour, if anything it tended to concentrate the reaction. The people in the crowds at these shows were the hardcore and they didn't disappoint. Frequently, they would line up around the block in advance and, almost to a person, they would be wearing costumes inspired by My Chemical Romance's *Danger Days* personae. The band had encouraged fans – or Killjoys as they would become known on this album – to invent their own names, design their own outfits and buy into the concept. It was a lofty aim, and one My Chemical Romance weren't certain would work.

'The kids better be dressed up really fucked-up,' said Gerard before the first night of The World Contamination Tour in London. He was joking and mock challenging the fans, but there was a part of him that was serious. 'I hope I'm not disappointed. If they aren't, I'm gonna be like, "I dunno if I want to do this any more." There better be masks or I'm going to be pissed. What's the fucking point if they're not going to dress up? If they don't come up to me and tell me their Killjoy name, I'm going to be bummed.'

But as they rolled into each town they saw swathes of fans dressed in dazzling colours, with eye-patches and wild hair, and wielding laser guns. It's hard to think of another band who could inspire such wholehearted commitment to what was essentially a grand art project. It's hard to think of any other fans who would run with it in such imaginative ways either.

'Seeing everyone dressed up in their Killjoys outfits was awesome,' said Ray. 'We would watch them through the windows when we arrived. There was such a great vibe.'

The relationship between band and fans had always been strong, and would become stronger still in the wake of the earthquake and tsunami that hit Japan in March 2011. Shocked by the events, Ray in particular felt the band needed to help in whatever way they could. He noticed a hashtag on Twitter – #SINGItForJapan – and set about reworking the band's song 'Sing' in order to re-release it as a charity single with proceeds going to Red Cross Japan. He enlisted musicians and studio engineers, encouraging them to donate their time, redrawing the song so that it floated on strings and delicate piano rather than juddering on throbbing synths. The band's fans then sent in thousands upon thousands of video clips of themselves holding up messages of support for the people of Japan. Around the world, people held fundraisers on the back of it – with the UK wing of the MCRmy raising £4,000.

'It was really exciting; it was a really collaborative thing,' Ray told MTV. 'Anybody we [asked] to be part of it wanted to give their time – all the orchestra players, they were looking for a way to help and we got in contact with them and they said, "Absolutely." And then having kids submit video footage and drawings and pictures, it was overwhelming.'

Not everyone was so enthused. In April, the controversial right-wing US broadcaster Glenn Beck attacked 'Sing' after it was used in the TV series *Glee*. He accused the band – who he misnamed Chemical Romance – of peddling propaganda. Reading out the song's lyrics, he urged parents to be vigilant against bands such as My Chemical Romance. 'Pay attention to the lyrics,' Beck said. 'It's an anthem saying "Join us." How can you and I possibly win against that?' He added, 'Our whole culture right now is set up for you and the values you grew up on to lose. You don't have to live by the standards that society has set.'

Unfortunately, Beck himself hadn't been paying attention to the lyrics, mistaking the word 'webways' that Gerard uses in the song for 'railways'. The singer delightedly corrected him in a blog on the band's website.

'I think the word Glenn Beck was looking for was "subversion" not "propaganda", because I don't know what it would be considered propaganda for – Truth? Sentiment? And I can't tell what he's angrier about – the fact that it's how I feel about the persistent sterilization of our culture or the fact that it's on network television for everyone to hear. And railways? Is it 1863? Seen any children living on these lately instead of the internet?

'I'm actually shocked that no fact-checking was done on the lyrics,' Gerard continued. 'I mean Fox is a major news channel, covering factual topics in an unbiased and intelligent – oh wait – to quote the man himself – "You don't have to live by the standards that society has set." I couldn't agree more.'

Consider Beck's criticisms slapped down.

In August 2011, having spent much of the summer playing festivals and arenas across Europe, My Chemical Romance played perhaps the most high-profile show of their career: they would be headlining the world-renowned Reading and Leeds Festival. Previous headliners have included the biggest rock bands in the world and a clutch of My Chemical Romance heroes: Nirvana, Pixies, Metallica, Rage Against The Machine, Oasis, Pulp, Blur, Foo Fighters, Radiohead and The Smashing Pumpkins.

But there was something more personal about My Chemical Romance's return to Reading. It was there in 2006 that they had been bottled, and it was there while leaving the site that Gerard had vowed never to return unless he was headlining the place. Five years later, his band had earned their chance. They were aware of what a big deal it was.

'Every time anyone mentions headlining Reading, we get nauseous,' said Ray beforehand. 'I'm fucking scared. I'm scared as hell. It's a huge fucking deal and we've really got to do justice to it. It's a real honour to be given this show, so we've got to do it right. I think the best way to do that is to try and treat it like a normal show – that's the only way not to be overawed by it. So we'll do what we normally do: we'll have a hug before we go on, then we'll go out and enjoy it.'

They wanted to do something special to mark the occasion and tossed around a few ideas as to how they could make it momentous. Someone had the idea of asking the Queen guitarist Brian May – Ray's idol – if he would play.

'I mean, no one had his number or anything but our lawyer Stacy or someone at our label reached out to him,' said Frank. 'He said yes, but had to do something else with Lady Gaga the next day [when My Chemical Romance would headline Leeds]. We were like, "Fuck, really?"'

'He is one of the nicest guys I have ever met; he has such a beautiful spirit. He was so nice to us and he had no reason to be. If anybody in the world has earned the right to be a fucking dickhead, it's that dude. But you can't work out how it's possible for him to be so nice. He's so talented and so amazing. That was definitely a life highlight.'

May himself was equally delighted to have been asked. Chatting at the *Kerrang!* Awards a few years later, he talked about how thrilled he had been to be playing with a band who rated him so highly. 'It was great, I enjoyed that so much,' he said. 'It's wonderful to play with people who grew up on us. That night was amazing and they're a wonderful bunch of people.'

Frank, who in the past had often been mentally absent during the band's biggest shows thanks to the medication he took to control his nerves, remembers Reading in sharp focus. Because Reading was a different thing entirely.

'That was one of the big shows I do remember. It was very surreal,' he said. 'Leading up to it, we had gone to Brian May's house to practise with him. That was crazy, it was nuts! Holy fuck, that show! We said that the credits should have rolled after Madison Square Garden but in the build-up to Reading we were saying, "Fuck, we get another one of those shows!"'

The set was a triumph. Opening with fireworks, smoke and 'Na Na Na' they then launched into 'I'm Not Okay (I Promise)', before delivering a bombastic set – one full of anthems, from 'Famous Last Words' to 'The Kids from Yesterday' and the live debut of 'S/C/A/R/E/C/R/O/W'. Brian May arrived for a cover of Queen's 'We Will Rock You', before joining them on their closer, 'Welcome to the Black Parade', as confetti cannons erupted all round.

'We have truly never seen any band give so much to any performance ever,' wrote Dan Martin in his *NME* review. 'And that counts.'

It counted for My Chemical Romance too. For so long during *The Black Parade* years, they had felt diminished by the big shows as they felt like microdots under the glare of arena and stadium lights. They felt the music had overtaken them, that they were being tossed around in its wake. Headlining Reading, in front of a potential onsite audience of 87,000 and a live TV and radio audience of many hundreds of thousands more, they at last felt that they belonged.

'To me, Reading told us that we could keep doing it,' Frank said. 'It felt bigger than any one of us – but in a good way this time. On *Black Parade*, the band felt bigger than us in a negative way. At Reading, it felt like a big entity but one we could live up to. It felt great, really good. We were at the top of our game and we played really well. Everything was good – and we got to play with our hero. It was insane, I will never forget that.'

They left Reading on a high. But within a week, they would be brought sharply back down to earth.

20: DISENCHANTED

On 3 September 2011, just a week after the Reading headline appearance, My Chemical Romance issued a statement to say that they were sacking their touring drummer Mike Pedicone. They were in North America touring with Blink 182 and claimed they had evidence that he was stealing from them.

'Some shit happened last night and before the blogosphere gets all crazy with false statements and ridiculous opinions we want the true story to come from us,' wrote Frank on the band's website. 'But please listen close because this is the only time we are ever going to talk about this. The relationship between My Chemical Romance and Michael Pedicone is over. He was caught red-handed stealing from the band and confessed to police after our show last night in Auburn, Washington. We are heartbroken and sick to our stomachs over this entire situation. The band has no intention of pressing charges or taking this matter any further than we have to. We just want him out of our lives. The people who play in this band are a family, and family should not take advantage of each other like he did. We are currently moving forward, and hope to have a new drummer in place for our show in Salt Lake City, Utah. The show must go on.'

Pedicone admitted he had made a mistake, but said in his defence that his intention had been to set up a member of My Chemical Romance's crew who, he claimed, had it in for him, rather than benefit financially from what he had done.

'Almost as soon as I began touring with MCR I ran into problems with a member of the band's crew who I'll not name,' he said in a statement. 'The problems were many, big and small, but some of them were large enough that they began to greatly impact on me and, by extension, my family. I'd reached my wits' end, and I made what was certainly the poorest decision of my life. Rather than address the issues that I had with the crew member in an open and honest manner, I tried to make them look irresponsible. My intention was to make this person look incompetent. I had no intention of profiting whatsoever. Again, I cannot overstate how poor my judgment was in this situation; it was a tremendous mistake, and it's one I'll regret for years to come.

'I would have liked an opportunity to share my side of the story with MCR, an opportunity to express my remorse. I was never given one. I'd like to thank MCR's members, crew and supporters for giving me some of the best musical experiences of my life in the past several months. However brief our partnership, it was an honour and a dream come true to play with such a talented bunch of individuals. I wish MCR the best of luck in the future, and I'm looking forward to my next endeavour.'

My Chemical Romance were stunned and baffled by his actions, largely because they felt he had fitted into their ranks so smoothly.

'That was fucked,' Frank told me in late 2013. 'When it came to my attention, just the idea that it could be happening, made me think, "No, I can't imagine it." Then there was more and more evidence to suggest it was happening. We had known each other for a long time, we had done Warped Tours together and I have pictures of us from years prior hanging out. I loved that dude, he was fucking awesome. He was super funny and an amazing player. We were having a great time. As a band, I felt like we were on fire. It was ferocious. The only other time I felt like that was on Projekt Revolution, which was another fierce tour. We were just fucking gnashing. I felt invigorated. To the day I die, I won't understand it.'

Pedicone was swiftly replaced with the former The Suicide File and Death By Stereo drummer Jarrod Alexander, and My Chemical Romance continued to tour. But they did so with a nasty taste in their mouth.

By the tail end of 2011, there was a growing feeling that things weren't going quite as well as they should have been. For a start, they spent autumn as the support act to Blink 182, who had recently re-formed to much delight, having been the leading lights in the pop-punk genre in the wake of Green Day at the turn of the century. However, they were an odd fit with My Chemical Romance. Blink 182's knockabout punk and onstage comedy routines jarred with My Chemical Romance's material, while it could be argued that the venues Blink 182 were playing were rooms My Chemical Romance might once have headlined in their own right.

The fact that *Danger Days* was not selling in the same quantities as *The Black Parade* after nearly a year of touring was a disappointment to some within Warner Bros who, according to reports in September 2011, were reconsidering their rock roster. By 2014, *Danger Days* had sold nearly 700,000 albums worldwide. *The Black Parade*, though, had sold 3.13 million albums around the world by the same date. Even *Three Cheers for Sweet Revenge* (which sold 2.57 million world-wide) outsold it many times over. Those sales figures, however, were not something that the band said they cared about.

'That doesn't matter to us at all,' Gerard said. 'But it does matter to other people, which sucks. The slogan of the record was "The aftermath is secondary". We were saying that we don't give a fuck – but certain people do seem to give a fuck. That's a tough spot to be in because people try to put that stress onto you.'

'I know that, sales-wise, there's no way it could live up to the expectation the powers that be had for it,' said Frank. 'They had a number in their heads that they wanted it to hit. But it's not like that any more. Records don't sell that much any more.'

Mikey put it even more sharply: 'People who want *Danger Days* to immediately sell more than *Black Parade* forget that it took two and a half years of touring to get it to that point. And it nearly killed us. To do that again would be foolish.'

Craig Aaronson left Warner Bros and stopped working as the band's A&R man shortly after *Danger Days* was released. But, as an informed observer and someone who was intimately involved in putting out the record, it was clear to him what the problems were.

Though some fans were upset with the band's new colourful image and brighter music, Aaronson believes there was no issue with the look or content of the album. For him, the problem was the length of time that it had taken to make it.

'In the world we're in now, if you don't put a record out for four years then your fans are going to move on,' he says. 'You can't spend that long between albums, it has to be a constant churn – especially in this day and age. People have such short attention spans. Did the four-year break affect things? Yes it did.'

He also feels that not enough work was put in before the release to build up anticipation, suggesting that there was not enough time to excite the band's fanbase. He argued with Warner Bros too, believing that the lead single for the record should not have been 'Na Na Na' but 'Bulletproof Heart'.

'A lot of people disagreed with me so I lost that battle and Rob was now the president of the company, so there was a different structure,' he says. 'I was outvoted. I thought ['Bulletproof Heart'] spoke more than any other song to the band's fanbase and that was more important to me than radio.

'I never went along with the decision to release "Na Na Na". Me and Xavier [Ramos] who did all the marketing thought it had to be "Bulletproof Heart". What happened was that the radio plugger in the UK got a really good response on "Na Na Na" from Radio 1 and that may have influenced things. And Rob liked "Na Na Na" and the band certainly liked it, but this was one of the times I disagreed with them.'

Rob Cavallo, still the chairman of Warner Bros, is well placed to see the big industry picture. He defends the performance of *Danger Days* and says that if it's compared to what My Chemical Romance's contemporaries were doing at the time, then it fared very well. Set against the rock bands who became big at a similar time – Fall Out Boy, Panic! At The Disco, The Used and others, bands who had either split or were treading commercial water – *Danger Days* was a success. Set against *The Black Parade*, though, it wasn't. Cavallo still believes it was an achievement.

'If you go back and look at all the bands who started around the same sort of time as My Chemical Romance and look where they are in the charts, then what you find is that they have all gone away,' he says. 'They all had albums that didn't work. That genre was closing up at that time. So if you look at the performance of *Danger Days*, you realize it had a Top 5 Hot Adult Contemporary record, a couple of Number 1 modern rock records, and 'Sing' was a true, honest-to-God hit. We sold literally ten times [more] than just about everybody else at that time from that genre.'

More importantly, Cavallo thinks that while *Danger Days* did not perform as well as *The Black Parade*, it did successfully reposition the band. He thinks *Danger Days* was a crossover album for My Chemical Romance that moved them from the limits of the emo genre and into a broader rock category.

'For me, we had jumped from one side of the river and onto the alligator's back, and then successfully jumped to the other side of the river – which most bands weren't able to do,' he says. 'Even though it was very difficult and they went through a lot, they stayed successful and had a very successful tour afterwards.

'That emo scene basically died. To look at the accomplishment of My Chemical Romance: they were really the only band that bridged that gap and continued to have hits and sell large amounts of records. They tried as hard as they could, they came back from the dead, and they still had a big album. That's pretty good.'

Cavallo also points to the changing nature of the record industry, the effects of downloading and the declining popularity of rock music as compared to pop and dance music.

'The business had changed overall for every modern rock band,' he says. 'Once, if you got a Number 1 Modern Rock song, it would have meant you would have sold a million to a million and a half units depending on the size of the song. But that had completely changed – a Number 1 Modern Rock song was only selling 150,000 units. It just didn't mean anything any more. It was the death of modern rock – which was really sad to me because I love that sound, time and style, and it is no longer.'

For Cavallo, *Danger Days* was a victim of both circumstance and the fact that the band were attempting to chart new territory. He feels convinced that, had they weathered the storm, they would have come back with a hit record again. It wasn't to be because, as it turned out, My Chemical Romance had more fundamental problems.

Though *Danger Days* was written in a surge of excitement following 'Na Na Na', Frank feels differently about those months now. Looking back with the benefit of hindsight in 2013, he believes the post-*Conventional Weapons* period was actually an uncertain time. The band may not have realized it then, but he now thinks there was an undercurrent of doubt that they were doing their best to ignore.

'I think we were in a weird state mentally. We had scrapped a record and gone into another thing. I think we were wondering what was good. We had so much going on and we had been in two different studios for a long time and there was internal turmoil with Bob being asked to leave. My wife was pregnant and giving birth. It was nuts and I didn't know if we were ever going to get out of the studio.'

It's why Frank, in particular, is not as enamoured with *Danger Days* as the band's united front after its release might have suggested. Certainly for him, the songs that they reworked from the *Conventional Weapons* sessions – 'The Only Hope for Me Is You', 'Party Poison', 'Save Yourself, I'll Hold Them Back' and 'Bulletproof Heart' – were not as good as they might have first seemed.

'There are some songs I am beyond excited about. I'm really glad we went back into the studio to do stuff again because those songs came out of it,' he told me. 'But there are certain songs on that record – and they're mostly the songs that we redid – where I think, "Oh no, that wasn't a good idea." So I have mixed feelings about the record now. I don't know if it's because of how those songs came out the second time around, or if it's because those songs weren't meant to be that way.

'I hear too much of a journey from where they started out to enjoy where they ended up. I'm very much a proponent of the original intent on most things. I wish we had just scrapped it all.'

For both Cavallo and Frank the main problem with *Danger Days*, though, was time. With the record company and band aware of the four-year gap since *The Black Parade*, there was pressure to get it finished and released. On top of which, the band had spent a lot of money in making *Conventional Weapons* and then *Danger Days*. It could be argued that they didn't have enough time to fully realize the concept that Gerard envisioned or to allow the songs to develop. Not that they necessarily knew this when they were in the midst of recording.

'When we went in to do *Conventional*, we had a plan and then we got jolted. And when that happened, I don't know if we really knew what to think,' said Frank. 'Then all of a sudden, we had a plan and then we ran with it. At the end of the *Danger Days* sessions, if we had had a little more time, then we could have honed that plan further. But we had been in the studio for so long, that we needed to get out and go do it. 'I don't know if we knew what we wanted to do right before *Danger Days*.'

Cavallo agrees. He thinks the record was as good as they could do in the circumstances but believes that, with a little more time, it could have been better. 'I think we got it to a place where it was about as clear as we could get it. It was a snapshot of where the band were at the time – and it was the best we could do, because we were under duress having spent all that money. At that time, we were like, "Let's just put our heads down and be as thoughtful and careful but as impassioned as we can." What came out is what came out.

'You can take an artistic view of an album, and you can always say it could be better. I'm sure that even The Beatles thought they had left a few things on the table when they finished *Sgt Pepper*. But if you look at it in terms of the time and money we had and ask "Did we do the best we could do at that point?" then I think you can say we did. I don't think the band left very much on the table. I think they did bare their souls and do the job a band is supposed to do.

'If the question is whether we tried as hard as we could, then my answer is that we absolutely did. We did a monumental job if you look at where they were coming from and where we started on this record.

'They started off below ground in a place of fear and confusion, in a place where they were questioning their ability to even make a rock album. It was rough for them because of the monumental failure of the prior album. To get back on course and do something that led to a Top Five Hot AC single when every other band who had started at their time had fallen off the charts completely was remarkable.'

But it wasn't enough for My Chemical Romance. Something had worked its way into the band that could not be fixed.

21: DEAD!

With the final notes of 'Helena' ringing in their ears, My Chemical Romance stepped offstage at New Jersey's Asbury Park on 19 May 2012 for the last time as a band. They weren't to know that this would be their final set, though the closing lines of their last song were fitting – 'So long and good night'. They were the last lyrics Gerard would sing onstage as My Chemical Romance's frontman.

The singer knew the show was not quite right. He said that My Chemical Romance had played well enough, but that something inside him that day, some strange feeling, had told him their time was up. In a lengthy internet post much later, he wrote about that performance in Asbury Park and said that it was then that he knew they were doomed.

'I am backstage in Asbury Park, New Jersey,' he wrote. 'I am pacing behind a massive black curtain that leads to the stage. I feel the breeze from the ocean find its way around me and I look down at my arms, which are covered in fresh gauze due to a losing battle with a heat rash, which had been a mysterious problem in recent months. I am normally not nervous before a show but I am certainly filled with angry butterflies most of the time. This is different – a strange anxiety jetting through me that I can only imagine is the sixth sense one feels before their last moments alive. My pupils have zeroed-out and I have ceased blinking. My body temperature is icy. We get the cue to hit the stage.

'The show is . . . good. Not great, not bad, just good. The first thing I notice to take me by surprise is not the enormous amount of people in front of us but off to my left – the shore and the vastness of the ocean. Much more blue than I remembered as a boy. The sky is just as vibrant. I perform, semi-automatically, and something is wrong.

'I am acting. I never act onstage, even when it appears that I am, even when I'm hamming it up or delivering a soliloquy. Suddenly, I have become highly self-aware, almost as if waking from a dream. I began to move faster, more frantic, reckless – trying to shake it off – but all it began to create was silence. The amps, the cheers, all began to fade.

'All that [was] left was the voice inside, and I could hear it clearly. It didn't have to yell – it whispered, and said to me briefly, plainly, and kindly – what it had to say.

'What it said is between me and the voice.'

The voice, it would seem, had told him that it was over.

In the months leading up to that one-off show in Asbury Park – in which My Chemical Romance had stepped in for Blink 182 – the band had completed the *Danger Days* album cycle with a final tour of Australia before reconvening in Los Angeles in the early months of 2012. The plan was that they would make the city their base – despite the fact Frank was still living on the other side of the country in New Jersey – and set about making new music, which Warners were still keen to release despite *Danger Days'* struggles.

They rented a big space with the idea of turning it into a compound in which to work. Wary of the difficulties they had faced with *Conventional Weapons* and the pressure of writing with time constraints as on *Danger Days*, they figured they would go back to working as they had done in the very early days. Essentially, they were building the same sort of rehearsal space in which they had played when they first formed – though this one would be bigger, grander and complete with recording equipment.

They hoped that having access to a permanent place in which to create would mean that they could write whenever they felt right, rather than being forced to come up with new material whenever the next deadline drew near. Though it was too early for a full-time producer, Rob Cavallo's engineer Doug McKean would help to bring in any recording equipment they might need and man the desks if they decided to lay anything down. Having worked with Cavallo for years, and helped record both *The Black Parade* and *Danger Days*, McKean knew exactly how My Chemical Romance worked and what buttons to push to make them work better.

'He's an awesome engineer,' Ray said. 'He knows everything. He's a genius. He definitely helps shape the sound of songs. He does funny stuff like play back stuff in a different way or change arrangements and trick our ears and we'll be like "That was awesome! Look at what we did!"'

'I was excited. Ever since I was a kid, I had wanted my own studio where we could go 24/7 and make stuff,' said Frank. 'I liked the idea so much that I said, since everyone else is in LA, then build it there and I'll come out a lot – as much as I didn't want to be in LA.'

Frank has never been much of a fan of Los Angeles, but saw the sense of the band having their own place to work in the city where the majority of them lived. He committed so much to the idea that, in April, he and his wife Jamia had their third child, Miles, in the city. 'I packed everything up, including my family. I had my son out there,' he says. 'And it didn't work out.'

Things seemed positive at first. The band spent a long time putting their studio together and were starting to put it to good use, using Frank's Pro-Tools rig. Though they had never really been a band that jammed in the traditional sense, preferring to focus intently on writing songs, in Los Angeles they relaxed and improvised.

'We started out playing this weird Fugazi kind of stuff, which was pretty rad but was never going to be the record,' said Frank. 'We just wanted to make noise. There are probably hundreds of hours of us just jamming on stuff.'

And alongside the noise that My Chemical Romance were making, Frank was making his own sounds. He had been asked to contribute to the compilation album *Frankenweenie Unleashed*, which accompanied the soundtrack album to the remake of Tim Burton's first film, *Frankenweenie*. Frank's effort was impressive, sounding like a mash-up between the film composer Danny Elfman and the grand punk of *The Black Parade*, and was the first track recorded in My Chemical Romance's new studio. Next, the band worked with the rapper and producer RZA on the soundtrack to *The Man with the Iron Fists* film he was directing. But, though music was recorded, it was not subsequently included in the film.

Really, though, My Chemical Romance were more concerned about their own songs. They decided that they wanted to involve their touring keyboard player James Dewees in the writing process for what would have been their fifth album. They had long used keyboards, yet they had never included a full-time player in their ranks.

'That was a big change for us,' said Frank. 'With that, came the ability to be super dark and have these ominous things going on that really filled us out. Having James around was really cool because he's an absolute genius. I've never met anybody as musically skilled and creative as him.'

Jarrod Alexander, the drummer who had replaced Mike Pedicone, had also settled well and had been lined up to play on whatever the band did next. And with the personnel organized, things appeared to be settling into position. All My Chemical Romance had to do next was write some music.

But though everything appeared to have been lined up – the band, the studio, the engineer – there were problems. Big ones as it turned out.

Gerard was in a bad way during the spring and summer of 2012, physically and mentally. Stuck in the same sort of creative paralysis that had afflicted him midway through the making of *Conventional Weapons*, he had again lost sight of where he wanted My Chemical Romance's music to go. 'I was in a dreamlike state,' he said. 'I had grown in weight – I finally broke two hundred pounds. It was a really dark period. It felt like a dream – it really did.'

In a lengthy internet post later, Gerard wrote, 'The following months were full of suffering for me – I hollowed out, stopped listening to music, never picked up a pencil, started slipping into old habits. All of the vibrancy I used to see became desaturated. Lost. I used to see art or magic in everything, especially the mundane – the ability was buried under wreckage.'

He tried to pull himself together. He looked at his life, at the fact he had a successful band and a studio at his disposal and counted the positives. He told himself, 'I'm really fucking lucky, I wake up every day and make art.'

But though he did emerge from what he called 'the haze', it would bring him only darkness once more. It was at that point that he and the band were supposed to be working in their studio. But though Gerard had been sketching out a concept for a My Chemical Romance record, it would be bleaker than anything he had ever written. The ideas he was working on were concerned, once again, with death – though this time it was the aftermath of it.

'After climbing out of [the haze], it got worse because I became even more paralysed and depressed,' he said. 'I started to work on a record that was a concept record about a group of parents in a support group because they had all lost their children in a horrible way. That was supposed to be the last record. And that's not a story I wanted to tell – and the songs reflected that, you could hear it. All the joy was just gone.'

Gerard confided in his close friends. Grant Morrison says that the singer was conflicted at the time, and believes the fact that *Danger Days* had not thrived commercially had knocked Gerard off balance. 'I think that sent him into a bit of a spin, as it does to so many artists,' says Morrison. 'Suddenly, he was torn between where his creativity wanted to go and where commerce wanted to take him. As a band, you want to be successful and get as many people to listen as possible – but that sometimes clashes with where your head wants to go.'

The music My Chemical Romance were subsequently creating in their studio was sparse and bleak. Morrison says it did not sound like the band at all. 'The material I heard was super-dark,' he says. 'It was very strange and wasn't like anything else they had ever done. They were almost going in a Radiohead direction at that point. It probably wouldn't have worked for them and I think Gerard knew that all along. The last year was a dark time and the music coming out of it was very gothic, I would say.'

Gerard was struggling for direction, creatively unsatisfied and unable to find that spark that so drove his passion. Frank said the music that the band were coming up with reflected the black cloud that had settled. 'It was bleak, man. It was fucking real bleak. I get the Radiohead vibe but I think that's only because none of it was done. There was a weird sparseness to it. We had over an hour's worth of music framed but very little of it was by any means finished.'

The atmosphere in the My Chemical Romance camp was not encouraging. In late 2013, I spoke to Frank at his home in New Jersey. I asked about the mood in the summer of 2012 and whether any positives could be drawn from that time. He laughed a hollow laugh. Then he sighed deeply.

'No, Tom, it didn't feel good,' he said firmly. 'If it had felt good, we would probably have finished the record and we would still be here.'

Later, he emailed me to say: 'In the past the band was able to come to agreements that worked from record to record and song to song. It can't ever be selfish, it's always about what's best for the song. The problems arise when you can't agree on what "that" is any more. So you fight for the art because you think you're doing the right thing, and maybe you are . . . maybe you're all doing the right thing, it's just not right together any more. That's when the paths start to split off.'

Though the piano-led, almost AOR-ish stomp of 'Fake Your Death' was released on the band's Greatest Hits album *May Death Never Stop You* (and suggested a slightly more positive vibe than the bleakness the band say existed then), the music from the sessions was so unfinished that Frank has suggested the rest is unlikely to ever see the light of day. 'It's so far from being done that I don't know how [much of] it could come out,' he said. 'There were a couple of things here and there that might have been finished but I don't think it would feel right to go in and finish the other stuff later. Whether there are versions of things that could be agreed upon that could be considered finished, I don't know. Time will tell.'

Whatever that music sounded like, it was not right.

Following their summer of discontent, My Chemical Romance came to a strange decision in autumn 2012. They decided to release *Conventional Weapons*, the record they had scrapped before *Danger Days*.

It seemed an odd thing to do. This was a band who had spent the last few years publicly stating that they didn't much rate those songs. They had said that they didn't have 'greatness' and dismissed them as unfulfilling. So why put them out there at all?

One reason was that there was a demand from the fans to hear the material. Ever since My Chemical Romance announced that the record would be scrapped, there was a clamour on the internet and across social media for the songs to be heard. In part, My Chemical Romance thought that perhaps their fans deserved to hear what they had created.

Another reason was that some members of the band did not agree that the music should have been scrapped in the first place. For Frank, the songs on *Conventional Weapons* were too good to be buried for ever; he called them 'time capsules', as they took him back to the period in which they were recorded. At a meeting, the band listened back to the tracks, and agreed that there was no reason to bury them. They decided to release two songs a month for five months from October 2012 and through into February 2013 – neither the band nor producer Brendan O'Brien wanting them to be seen as a complete album.

But the band's booking agent Matt Galle points to another reason that *Conventional Weapons* was released. He says My Chemical Romance had already made a decision to take an extended break in autumn 2012. And so, Galle says, the release of the piecemeal *Conventional Weapons* had another, ulterior motive.

'They knew they were going to go away for a little while but they weren't going to announce anything,' says Galle. 'They wanted [the songs] to come out in that way, every couple of weeks, as a way to keep them visible when they weren't doing anything. It was so their name didn't go away.'

The first to be released was the frantic punk of 'Boy Division', recalling earlier *Three Cheers for Sweet Revenge* material in its whirl and release, before the echo chamber guitars and drums of 'Tomorrow's Money' delivered more raw rock 'n' roll – though without, perhaps, the hooks of old. 'Ambulance' was a more considered, adult rock song built on a classic My Chemical Romance chug, though 'Gun' was sparser and hinted at where they would go to with *Danger Days*. It was with 'The World Is Ugly' and 'The Light Behind Your Eyes' that they veered into anthemic, stadium-rock territory – each song reaching for lighters-in-the-air moments.

Just as the first three batches of songs differed from one another, the next release veered from the path again as 'Kiss the Ring' and 'Make Room' presented Hives-esque garage punk that sounded a lot of fun to play but again did not include the hooks they had delivered in the past.

Finally, the last batch from the *Conventional Weapons* session – 'Surrender the Night' and 'Burn Bright' – discover the band on probably their best form. Both are triumphant, anthemic and vast-sounding and might easily have become serious hits. The problem, if there is one, is that they seem to lack some of My Chemical Romance's personality. Since they were originally intended to follow a record as charismatic as *The Black Parade*, this could well have been the issue.

The songs released under the *Conventional Weapons* banner are good but, taken as a whole, do not make up a cohesive album – just as Gerard feared. They do add up to something more significant though: the last collection of new songs to bear the band's name. Because just over a month after the final *Conventional Weapons* release, My Chemical Romance would no longer exist.

*

On 22 March 2013, a short, simple statement was posted on My Chemical Romance's website. Brief and to the point, it announced that they had broken up.

'Being in this band for the past twelve years has been a true blessing. We've gotten to go places we never knew we would. We've been able to see and experience things we never imagined possible. We've shared the stage with people we admire, people we look up to, and best of all, our friends. And now, like all great things, it has come time for it to end. Thanks for all of your support, and for being part of the adventure.'

And with that, it was over. For a band of such grandeur, who delivered such incredible sweeping statements in their time, it was a remarkably perfunctory way to go.

Three days later, Gerard wrote the long entry on Twitlonger in which he recalled the final show in Asbury Park before going on to talk about the end of the band. He began his post with a long story about a bird that had been trapped in his house and which he and his family finally coaxed back outside. 'It is often my nature to be abstract,' he added, though the metaphor seemed clear. Next, he wrote about the band.

'We were spectacular,' he wrote. 'Every show I knew this, every show I felt it with or without external confirmation. There were some clunkers, sometimes our second-hand gear broke, sometimes I had no voice – we were still great. It is this belief that made us who we were, but also many other things, all of them vital. And all of the things that made us great were the very things that were going to end us – Fiction. Friction. Creation. Destruction. Opposition. Aggression. Ambition. Heart. Hate. Courage. Spite. Beauty. Desperation. LOVE. Fear. Glamour. Weakness. Hope. Fatalism.'

He said the band had always had within it a 'fail-safe' or a 'Doomsday device' that would force them to quit when the time was right. Rather than the final bang he was expecting, though, he said that the demise of My Chemical Romance was more of a slow death rattle. He wrote that there had been no tension in their split.

'I can assure you there was no divorce, argument, failure,

accident, villain, or knife in the back that caused this, again this was no one's fault, and it had been quietly in the works, whether we knew it or not, long before any sensationalism, scandal, or rumour. There wasn't even a blaze of glory in a hail of bullets . . .'

Instead, he says the voice that spoke to him onstage in Asbury Park slowly grew louder and louder until, as he wrote, 'I no longer ignored it – because it was my own.'

He wrote about the future, about making more music and about doors opening as others closed. He thanked every fan, and every person who ever played in the band, and then he wrote: 'My Chemical Romance is done. But it can never die. It is alive in me, in the guys, and it is alive inside all of you. I always knew that, and I think you did too. Because it is not a band – it is an idea.'

And with that, My Chemical Romance ceased to be.

The news of the split was dramatic and spread quickly around the world. It made headlines not just in the music press like *Rolling Stone, NME, Kerrang!* and others but on the BBC, on Sky News, and across American, South American, Asian and Australian networks.

Within minutes of the announcement, fans had set up a petition to beg for one last tour. It grew at the rate of two signatures each second and reached well over 20,000 signatures within a few days. The band's break-up post on their website was tweeted over 10,000 times and shared on Facebook over 29,000 times. It was major news.

The outpouring of grief from fans was overwhelming. People of all ages were horrified, aghast that the band would not be departing with a farewell tour or with a new album. Instead, in a flash, My Chemical Romance were just gone.

Speaking to Frank seven months later, he was still upset at how things had come to an end. He warned me that he would find it hard to talk about the split and might not be able to speak about the decision to call it a day at all.

'It's a shame,' he said of the break-up, his voice both anxious and cautious. 'I wish it wasn't a shame. It was such a large part of my life – of all of our lives – but things happen.'

I asked what had happened and he found it hard to get the words out, a long sigh coming down the phoneline.

'I think it was different for everybody,' he said. 'I think if you asked all four guys, you'd get four different answers. I'm not ready to talk about a lot of things. It just didn't work.'

Frank had given up a lot – moving his family out to Los Angeles so that he could be near the studio they had built. Had he felt that he had made big sacrifices only for the rug to be pulled from under him when the band ended? There was a long pause – a very long pause – and then Frank said, '. . . erm, you know, we all had a lot on the line. We're getting into territory that I'm not too comfortable with.'

However, Frank did say one more thing – and it points to the fact that the manner of the split was not something they all agreed upon.

'It is what it is,' he said. 'I can't go into all the details of it. I think, in retrospect, things probably had to end up the way they ended up. The writing had always been on the wall. But the way it all came to an end, I feel, was unnecessary – and that's all I have to say on that.'

For Rob Cavallo, one of the very few outsiders to have ever been admitted into My Chemical Romance's inner circle, the first splinters in the relationship appeared in the studio during the making of *Danger Days*. He says that he hadn't really noticed that anything was amiss at the time, but in retrospect he thinks that was when the split began.

'Even though we got through the record and made something we were proud of, I think what was really happening was something else,' he told me at the end of 2013. 'Gerard and I have recently looked back at that time and we started to pinpoint the cracks of where the eventual break-up had started to form. That's really what was happening. It was still an all-for-one and one-for-all kind of a setting in the studio but it was clear that something was starting to rear its ugly little head. It was starting to get a little bit funky.

'But you couldn't necessarily tell when you were in it – it was hard to see it because everyone was under duress and we were trying to make this album and get it out – but clearly at that time it wasn't right. It was too early for a break-up and we weren't even consciously aware of it but all the personalities were beginning to bump into the same things over and over again. It was starting.'

Again, it points to the fact that not all of the band were on the same page when *Danger Days* was being made. 'I think there was a fundamental disagreement,' says Cavallo. 'The way they were relating to each other was starting to be uncomfortable. And I don't think Frank really agreed a hundred per cent with where they were going. I think he loved [*Danger Days*], but it just seemed uncomfortable. I think he was searching for parts to play on the music.

'There was a little bit of stuff between Frank and Ray during *Danger Days*, I will tell you that,' he says. 'It was about certain kinds of guitar playing. About whether it would be super hi-def guitar playing or whether it would be more down-and-dirty, punk-rock garage guitar playing. I always thought that the great thing about the band was that they had both. That was one of the great things! But between them, there started to be things that manifested as certain kinds of resentment. That eventually turned into the "You don't get me, man" type of thing.'

Of course, hindsight can lend importance to moments that did not seem unusual or significant at the time. Frank agreed that conversations took place but does not remember them as being heated. 'To be completely honest, [there was] nothing particularly memorable for me on *Danger Days*. That has always been the relationship between Ray's playing and my playing though. They are constantly at odds yet working together; it was one of the elements of the band that made it so special in my opinion. As far as arguments, though, that doesn't sound like us, we never really argued until the very end, which in retrospect maybe is one of the reasons the band had to die.'

Cavallo was always conscious of Frank's huge contribution. 'He's such an important part to the ethos of My Chemical Romance; he's such an important thing to what they are. He played lots of important guitar parts. To me, he was the punk rocker in the band. It's like when Paul McCartney sang "It's getting better all the time", he would have been the guy to sing, "It can't get no worse". And you desperately need that.

'I would talk to Billie Joe Armstrong about them and he would say, "I love that band, they're my favourite band. And that guy Frank is the guy that brings it home for me." It was because of that punk-rock anti-hero sort of thing that's inside of him. He's the yin to the yang.

'If you're going to be the guy who plays the adversary, the black to the white – and it is a super important role – then deep down inside everyone really does have to be pulling in the same direction. Everyone does have to share a common vision. And if you don't, or if that relationship starts to fray and crack because people are moving on, then that can potentially be the first relationship to end.'

Cavallo believes that after touring *The Black Parade*, My Chemical Romance were not the united front they had once been. 'On *Black Parade*, the main thing was that everyone was going "Yeah! We're doing this!" You could feel the commitment stylistically,' he says. 'On *Danger Days*, what you started to see was the break-up of that style, where different members were pushing for different things. Also, I think the personalities were beginning to become a little bit more raw. The personalities started to jibe together less. We had a great time. But I could tell someone still wasn't right. We got it right enough to get that record out but there was something still lurking in their relationship.'

He says they had moved apart musically, and he thinks that was at the heart of the split. 'Oh, sure,' he says. 'They're the nicest people and they never want to hurt a fly but there was a growth in musical direction that they couldn't come to grips with. It was just different opinions and guys moving in a different direction. Sometimes that happens – I mean, it happened to The Beatles.'

Cavallo was deeply disappointed that it came to that, though, having forged an intense relationship with My Chemical Romance both as musicians and people. While he describes their decision to end the band as 'bold – I'm amazed at the strength of character it's taken for them to do what they've done', he has misgivings over the fact they did it. I asked him if he thought the band could have weathered their problems and their declining record sales. He was convinced they could have done so and returned stronger.

'Gerard and Ray as writers would have held it together,' he says, his voice tinged with regret. 'They would have written better and better songs and the legend of what they are would have got bigger and bigger. Absolutely. They were a really good band.'

It wasn't to be.

The future would hold different things for each of them. Frank turned to a variety of projects, making vicious, angry hardcore electro-punk with his new band Death Spells, another solo project (including one song with his twin daughters) and a collaboration with James Dewees on his Reggie and the Full Effect record. Ray released one teaser track online called 'Isn't That Something', then played guitar on three tracks of the Cuban-American cabaret artist Voltaire's album *Raised By Bats*. A solo album, *Minimization Procedure*, is set to be released in 2014. Mikey guest-starred in a Gerard-directed TV show called *The Aquabats! Super Show!*, before beginning his own Killers-esque electro music project alongside the Sleep Station frontman David Debiak, called Electric Century – 'I was scratching an itch that I've always had,' he told me.

Gerard released the comic book series *The True Lives of the Fabulous Killjoys* alongside its co-creator Shaun Simon and the artist Becky Cloonan, and announced plans to write more in *The Umbrella Academy* series. He also started work on a solo record, airing a new song called 'Millions' while speaking at the Sydney art festival Graphic, then finishing the album with a short recording session in Wales in February 2014. Gerard's new material, according to his friend Grant Morrison, recalls both the grunge of The Smashing Pumpkins and the Britpop the singer listened to while growing up.

'He's drawn out a lot of the different influences he had in the nineties,' says Morrison. 'There is a little Pulp, a little grunge, and some Pumpkins in there – but it's also very much his own thing. There's a completely new lyrical direction in there as well.'

A final collection of My Chemical Romance songs, a Greatest Hits called *May Death Never Stop You*, finally wrapped up the band's career in March 2014. Including early demos and the unreleased song – 'Fake Your Death' – from their final, aborted sessions in Los Angeles, it features a cover designed by Gerard on which he references the band's history. At the centre of the sleeve is a gravestone, featuring a half-destroyed bust wearing a Black Parade marching uniform. The bust's face includes features from each of the band's members. Lyrics are written onto the gravestone, photos are scattered by its base, and the sleeve represents a memorial to the band. It would bring a closure of sorts. But to the band's fans, it still feels as if My Chemical Romance's split came too soon.

My Chemical Romance's departure leaves a hole. Where are the other bands daring to create whole worlds in their music? Who else can inspire legions of fans to adopt the alter egos of comic book fantasies as on *Danger Days*? What other bands can get the *Daily Mail* into such a lather that the newspaper brands them a suicide cult? Who else created music that was so visual? The world without My Chemical Romance is a far less thrilling place to be.

My Chemical Romance were inspirational, original and stunningly creative. They were stars too, though behaved humbly whenever I worked with them. Put them onstage or in a studio, and they became magical.

Their departure caught many by surprise. But despite appearing abrupt, theirs was the perfect way to go. They did not slither dismally from sight, nor did their songs slip in quality as their act became more pretence than passion. Instead, they pulled the plug while still on a creative high. And so the legacy they leave is one of brilliance and panache: a band who aimed for the stars and who saved lives as they reached them.

Frank feels the same. 'Gerard will tell you this too, but I always felt like our band was an important band. The way I felt about My Chem was like the way I felt about the greats. I know this is so clichéd but I feel like I can say it because I wasn't in the band when it started. I still feel like a fan. I feel like we had the potential to do some great things.'

Though proud of the band's legacy and his part in it, Frank remains distraught that they did not survive. When he thinks about the end, he tries as hard as he can to be sanguine about it. It's just that he wishes he didn't have to be. He still wishes things could be different.

'You know, even The Beatles broke up,' he sighs. 'I don't think it was ever on the cards for us to do it for ever.'

However, he then says one last thing.

'But that doesn't mean I don't wish we could have.'

Acknowledgements

―――――

Though this is not an authorized biography, the members of My Chemical Romance deserve an enormous thank-you for how often they endured my questions over the years, and for not running away each time they saw me walk into a room brandishing a dictaphone. Both Gerard and Mikey Way offered blessings behind the scenes, while Frank Iero bravely agreed to face that dictaphone twice more during the writing of this book. Ray Toro and Bob Bryar were also always far nicer to me than I deserved. I'm grateful to all of them for the generosity they have always shown me and, more than that, for the incredible music they made.

I'm enormously fortunate that so many people agreed to be interviewed about the band – and owe a particular debt to Rob Cavallo, Alex Saavedra and Craig Aaronson for the insights, memories and time they offered me.

I'm also extremely appreciative of all those record company folk who made it easier for me to invade My Chemical Romance's space over the years – Phoebe Sinclair, Andy Prevezer, Hayley Connelly, Suzanne Murray and Dan Lloyd-Jones in the UK and to Mike Sachs in the US. I owe Susan F. Leon several drinks at the Sunset Marquis for all her help both with this book and in the past, while Michelle Rogel and Cheryl Jenets should also feel free to stop in for a few.

Two friends and fans of My Chemical Romance in particular – Caz Hill and John Slimin – provided support, advice and, in one case, an extended loan of something valuable. Thanks are also due – either for help with this book or for help over the years – to Lauren Valencia, Stacy Fass, Geoff Rickly, Grant and Kristan Morrison, John Naclerio, Matt Galle, Brian Schechter, Joe Boyle, Howard

Benson, Rae Alexandra, Cassie Whitt, Emma Van Duyts, Paul Travers, and all at *Kerrang!* magazine.

This book would definitely not exist without the trust and direction shown by Ingrid Connell at Macmillan and the work put in by Kesia Lupo and Tania Wilde. Nor would it be here without the efforts of my agent Matthew Hamilton at Aitken Alexander Associates, a man who never stopped believing. Ben Schafer at Da Capo deserves much credit, while thanks also go to my US agent, Matthew Elblonk at De Fiore and Company in New York, for his indefatigable efforts.

I'm indebted (probably literally now) to Angela Elkins for eagle-eyed advice and to my parents for love, support and for raising me in a house full of books and words.

Extra special thanks is due to 'Metallica' (it's a long story), Paul Brannigan and Ian Winwood for showing me it could be done, Paul Harries for encouragement and stunning images and Caroline Fish for her artistry and talent, not least in her eye for pictures and the stunning cover design. Thanks also to Ashley Maile, who never knew about this but would have been thrilled.

My deepest thanks and love go to my wife Jo and my son Oscar who were endlessly patient, always loving and were even able to turn a deaf ear to me shouting a lot. More essential than all of that, they constantly reminded me what was important.

Tom Bryant

Sources

All quotations are taken from the author's interviews, except as noted below.

page **Chapter 1**

1 'Our parents were kind of scared to let us out of the house . . .'
   Leslie Simon, 'Art Intimidates Life', *Alternative Press*, December 2004

2 'From when I was a kid, my dad said to me, "You can be whatever
   you want," . . .' Imran Ahmed, 'In Their Own Words', *NME*,
   October 2006

3 'What I had to do – and my brother had to do . . .' *Life on the
   Murder Scene* DVD

4 'That was a big mistake, I probably shouldn't have started . . .'
   Kevin Smith Smodcast, My Chemical Bromance, December 2013

4 'I used to be fat . . .' Imran Ahmed, 'In Their Own Words', *NME*,
   October 2006

5 'I just opened my mouth and I was able to sing . . .' *Life on the
   Murder Scene* DVD

6 'He would consistently play something that would blow my mind
   . . .' Kevin Smith Smodcast, My Chemical Bromance, December
   2013

8 '*Man Without Fear* was out at the time . . .' Kevin Smith Smodcast,
   My Chemical Bromance, December 2013

11 'They thought I was on heroin, or something . . .' Kevin Smith
   Smodcast, My Chemical Bromance, December 2013

page **Chapter 2**

22 'There were four hundred people and me . . .' Daniel Lukes, 'The Misfits', *Kerrang!*, 2004

24 'There was definitely a funny collection of people . . .' Leslie Simon, 'Art Intimidates Life', *Alternative Press*, December 2004

page **Chapter 5**

72 'They just slowly started winning new fans and selling more merch . . .' *Life on the Murder Scene* DVD

page **Chapter 6**

91 'I think we had about half a record . . .' Michael Montes, *Florida Entertainment Scene*, 2005

95 'When you're kissing a guy with a beard . . .' J Bennett, 'Monday, Bloody, Monday', *Rocksound*, October 2004

95 'Sometimes it feels like jail . . .' Leslie Simon, 'Art Intimidates Life', *Alternative Press*, December 2004

page **Chapter 7**

106 'The funniest thing about *Three Cheers* . . .' *Life on the Murder Scene* DVD

107 'It was sold out . . .' *Life on the Murder Scene* DVD

110 'While I was tour managing The Used . . .' *Life on the Murder Scene* DVD

page **Chapter 8**

112 'When he hit rock bottom . . .' *Life on the Murder Scene* DVD

113 'I was like, "This isn't even us . . .' *Life on the Murder Scene* DVD

115 'When that decision was made . . .' *Life on the Murder Scene* DVD *Alternative Press*, December 2004

115 'It was like the moment that you break up . . .' Leslie Simon, 'Art Intimidates Life', *Alternative Press*, December 2004

117 '[I] told him to grow up . . .' Leslie Simon, 'Art Intimidates Life', *Alternative Press*, December 2004

page **Chapter 11**

159 'It started out as anger towards Mikey . . .' Andy Greenwald, 'Kings of Pain', *Blender*, December 2006

162 'Right away I felt like I was singing about the thing I was most afraid of . . .' Andy Greenwald, 'Kings of Pain', *Blender*, December 2006

page **Chapter 14**

204 'I'm embarrassed to be me because these people . . .' *The London Paper*, 5 June 2007

204 'We still haven't found someone that has knocked us down that we need to take seriously . . .' *Rocksound*, June 2007

205 'I think it was an inspired booking . . .' 'Andy Copping's Download Memories: 2007 – My Chemical Romance Step Up to the Big Leagues', *Rocksound*, June 2012

212 'I was the nerdy art girl in the corner . . .' Katie Parsons, 'Get Over It', *Kerrang!*, May 2008

212 'I had put a film canister filled with Bacardi151 . . .' Katie Parsons, 'Get Over It', *Kerrang!*, May 2008

page **Chapter 16**

241 'The first thing that came into my mind . . .' Paul Brannigan, 'New Day Rising', *Kerrang!*, 7 February 2009

241 'I think you'd be hard pushed to find anyone . . .' Paul Brannigan, 'New Day Rising', *Kerrang!*, 7 February 2009

242 'There are certain things you don't fuck with . . .' Paul Brannigan, 'New Day Rising', *Kerrang!*, 7 February 2009

242   'I chose the verses with lyrics that were most pertinent . . .'
       Paul Brannigan, 'New Day Rising', *Kerrang!*, 7 February 2009

242   'I was on bass, Ray was on guitar and Bob was on drums . . .'
       Paul Brannigan, 'New Day Rising', *Kerrang!*, 7 February 2009

242   'There's always the fear when you get back together that . . .'
       Paul Brannigan, 'New Day Rising', *Kerrang!* 7 February 2009

243   'We feel we have momentum . . .' Paul Brannigan, 'New Day
       Rising', *Kerrang!*, 7 February 2009

page   **Chapter 17**

245   'Maybe people right now . . .' Dan Martin, 'If I Had the Chance To
       Make *The Black Parade Again*, I'd Make It More Real. This Record Is
       Definitely Real,' *NME*, January 2010

246   'Lindsey calls me the safety inspector,' Josh Eels, 'My Chemical
       Romance Bounce Back from the Brink', *Spin*, December 2010

249   'It's a fictional, metaphorical song really . . .' Dan Martin, 'If I Had
       the Chance To Make *The Black Parade* Again, I'd Make It More Real.
       This Record Is Definitely Real', *NME*, January 2010

page   **Chapter 18**

259   'It was scary for me . . .' Jason Pettigrew, 'The Kids Are Ka-
       Kaw-Lright', *Alternative Press*, March 2011

259   'He was all, like, "I've got the guy! . . .' Jason Pettigrew, 'The Kids
       Are Ka-Kaw-Lright', *Alternative Press*, March 2011

259   'John flew in and was sweet . . .' Jason Pettigrew, 'The Kids Are
       Ka-Kaw-Lright', *Alternative Press*, March 2011

page   **Chapter 19**

277   'The first night we played in London . . .' Jason Pettigrew, 'The
       Kids Are Ka-Kaw-Lright', *Alternative Press*, March 2011

283   'It became such a thing . . .' Josh Eels, 'My Chemical Romance
       Bounce Back from the Brink', *Spin*, December 2010

page **Chapter 21**

299   'I am backstage in Asbury Park, New Jersey . . .' Gerard Way, 'A Vigil on Birds and Glass', March 2013

301   'He's an awesome engineer . . .' Andrew Tijs, *Noise11.com*, February 2012

302   'The following months were full of suffering for me . . .' Gerard Way, 'A Vigil on Birds and Glass', March 2013

302   'I was in a dreamlike state . . .' Gerard Way, Sydney GRAPHIC festival, October 2013

303   'After climbing out of . . .' Gerard Way, Sydney GRAPHIC festival, October 2013

Picture Acknowledgements

The following images are © Paul Harries: p. 1, p. 7, p. 10 (top and bottom left), p. 12, p. 14 (all), p. 15 (all), p. 16 (all).

The following images are © Justin Borucki: p. 2 (all), p. 3 (all), p. 4 (all), p. 5 (all), p. 6 (all), p. 8 (top), p. 9 (all), p. 13 (all).

The following images are © Scarlet Page: p. 8 (bottom), p. 10 (bottom left), p. 11 (top and bottom right).

The following image is © Ashley Maile: p. 11 (bottom left).